Anonymous

Revised Ordinances of the City of Fort Worth, Texas, 1873-1884

Anonymous

Revised Ordinances of the City of Fort Worth, Texas, 1873-1884

ISBN/EAN: 9783337272289

Printed in Europe, USA, Canada, Australia, Japan

Cover: Foto ©ninafisch / pixelio.de

More available books at **www.hansebooks.com**

REVISED ORDINANCES

OF THE CITY OF

FORT WORTH, TEXAS,

1873-1884.

CODIFIED BY HARRIS & WEAR, ATTORNEYS AT LAW, NO. 103 MAIN STREET, FORT WORTH, TEXAS, AND ADOPTED BY THE CITY COUNCIL SEPTEMBER 7TH, 1884, AS SHOWN BY ORDINANCE NO. 160 HEREIN.

1885:
WILLIAMS & STEWART, PRINTERS,
FORT WORTH, TEXAS.

		PAGE.			PAGE.
1.	Official Register	9 to 13	24.	Fire Limits	63 to 64
2.	Alleys	13	25.	Fire Arms	64 to 65
3.	Assistant Assessor and Collector	14	26.	Food and Drink	65 to 66
4.	Bonds, Official	16 to 17	27.	Fourth St. R. W. Company	67 to 68
5.	Bonds, City	17 to 24	28.	Ft. Worth & Denver City R.W.Co	68
6.	Buildings	24 to 25	29.	Ft. Worth St. R. W. Company	69 to 75
7.	Calaboose, talking with prison'rs in	26	30.	Funds	75
8.	Cattle. etc.	26 to 28	31.	Gambling	75 to 77
9.	Cemetery	28 to 32	32.	Gas Works	77 to 82
10.	Chimney, etc.	32 to 35	33.	Grade, city	82 to 83
11.	Combustible mat'r	35 to 37	34.	Gulf, Col. & S F. R. W. Co	83 to 84
12.	Cotton yards	37	35.	Hacks	84 to 86
13.	Council	37 to 39	36.	Hawkers	86
14.	Dead animals	39 to 41	37.	Health	86 to 88
15.	Diseased animals	41 to 42	38.	Houses, Ill Fame, etc.	88 to 91
16.	Dogs	42 to 45	39.	Indecency	91 to 92
17.	Drummers	45 to 46	40.	Limitation	92
18.	Elections	46 to 48	41.	Market places	92 to 93
19.	Engineer	48 to 51	42.	Marshal	93 to 96
20.	Fast riding. etc.	51 to 53	43.	Misdemeanors	96 to 98
21.	Fees, Salaries, etc	53 to 55			
22.	Fences, etc.	55 to 56			
23.	Fire Department	56 to 63			

44. Mobs - - 98 to 99	64. Shade Trees - 146 to 147
45. M. K. & T. R. W. Company - - 99	65. Shooting Gal'ries 148
46. Nuisances - - 100 to 103	66. Sidewalks - 149 to 158
47. Opium Smoking 104	67. Slaughter Pens - 158
48. Pigeons - - 104 to 105	68. Stairways - - 159
49. Police - - 105 to 108	69. Stationery - - 159
50. Pound and Pound Keeper - 108 to 111	70. Streets - - 160 to 173
51. Poor and Dead 111	71. Survey - - 163 to 164
52. Prostitutes - 112 to 113	72. Sunday - - 173
53. Public Place - 113 to 115	73. Taxation - - 174 to 182
54. Quarantine - 115 to 117	74. Theatres, etc. - 182 to 186
55. Recorder's Court 117 to 120	75. Trains - - 187 to 188
56. Rosedale St. R W Company - 120 to 125	76. T. & P. R.W.Co. 188
57. Rubbish - 125 to 126	77. Trespass - - 189
58. Saloons - - 126 to 127	78. Telegraph, etc. - 189 to 192
59. Scavenger - 127 to 128	79. Trinity river, etc. 192
60. Schools, city - 129 to 137	80. Vagrancy - - 193
61. Scrip, city - - 137 to 139	81. Vehicles passing, etc. - - 194
62. Secretary, city - 140	82. Wards, city - - 195
63. Sewers - - 141 to 146	83. Water Works - 195 to 206
	84. Weapons - - 206 to 207
	86. Appendix - - 209

ORDINANCE ADOPTING THE CHARTER.

BE IT remembered that at a regular meeting of the city council of the city of Fort Worth, begun and held at the council room of said council, on Tuesday the 26th day of September, 1876. Present, the Hon. G. H. Day, Mayor, presiding, and W. A. Huffman, P. J. Bowdry, D. M. C. Pendery and C. B. Daggett, Jr., aldermen of said city. A motion was made by W. A. Huffman and duly seconded by P. J. Bowdry, to adopt an act of the legislature of the State of Texas, entitled An Act regulating the incorporation of cities of one thousand inhabitants or over, and to provide for the substitution and repeal of all acts heretofore passed incorporating said cities which may be in force by virtue of any existing charter of said city, approved March 15, 1875, as the charter of said city, and it appearing and being known to said council that there are more than one thousand inhabitants in said city, and said motion being put to vote, was carried by more than two-thirds majority of said council. The following members, to-wit: W. A. Huffman, P. J. Bowdry, D. W. C. Pendery and C. B. Daggett, Jr., voting in the affirmative. It is, therefore, ordered by the city council of the city of Fort Worth that the above recited act, and the provisions thereof, be accepted and adopted as the Charter of the City of Fort Worth, in Tarrant county, Texas, in lieu of the existing charter of said city, and that this order be entered upon the journals of the proceedings of this council, and that a copy of the same; signed by the mayor, and attested by the city secretary, under the seal (corporate) of said city be filed and recorded in the office of the clerk of the county court of Tarrant county, Texas. G. H. DAY,
Mayor City Fort Worth.

C. McDOUGALL, City Secretary.
[L.S.] Filed for record September 28. 1876.
Recorded October 2, 1876, at 9 A. M.
J. P. WOODS, County Clerk.

OFFICIAL REGISTER.

FROM THE INCORPORATION OF THE CITY IN 1873 TO 1884, INCLUSIVE.

Elected April 3, 1873.

CITY OFFICERS.

W. P. Burts, Mayor.
W. T. Ferguson, Treasurer.
Edmund S. Terrell, City Marshal.
N. M. Maben, Assessor.
Frank W. Ball, City Attorney.
John F. Swayne, City Secretary.

ALDERMEN.

M. B. Loyd,   M. D. McCall,   A. Blakeney,   Wm. J. Boaz,
                  J. P. Alexander.

1874.

CITY OFFICERS.

*W. P. Burts, Mayor.
John S. Loving, Treasurer.
T. M. Ewing, Marshal.
G. F. Parman, Assessor and Collector.
J. S. Chapman, City Attorney.
Theodore Hitchcock, Secretary.

*G. H. Day elected Mayor on the 9th day of November A. D., 1874, vice W. P. Burts, resigned October 19, 1874.

C. C. Fitzgerald elected City Marshal December 15, 1874, to fill the unexpired term of T. M. Ewing, resigned.

ALDERMEN.

R. H. King,   A. B. Fraser,   W. H. Overton,   W. H. Williams,
                  Joseph Kane.

1875.

CITY OFFICERS.

G. H. Day, Mayor.
John S. Loving, City Treasurer.
H. P. Shiel, City Marshal.
J. C. Scott, City Attorney.
C. McDougall, City Secretary.
G. F. Parman, City Assessor and Collector.

T. P. Redding elected Marshal, to fill unexpired term, October 25. 1875.

James M. Townsend elected City Assessor and Collector, to fill unexpired term, October 25, 1875.

John Stoker appointed City Marshal by the Mayor and Aldermen February 8, 1876, in the place of T. P. Redding, suspended.

ALDERMEN.

J. J. Jarvis,	P. J. Bowdry,	W T. Maddox,	I. Dahlman,
		D. R. Crawford.	

1876.

CITY OFFICERS.

G. H. Day, Mayor.
John S. Loving, Treasurer.
T. I. Courtright, City Marshal.
R. E. Maddox, City Assessor and Collector.
Henry Feild, City Attorney.

ALDERMEN.

D. W. C. Pendery,	W. A. Huffman,	C. B. Daggett, Jr ,	P. J. Bowdry,
		John Nichols.	

1877.

CITY OFFICERS.

G. H. Day, Mayor.
Henry Feild, City Attorney.
Zane Cetti, City Engineer.
R. E. Maddox, City Assessor and Collector.
John S. Loving, City Treasurer.
C. McDougall, City Secretary.
T. I. Courtright, City Marshal.

ALDERMEN.

John Nichols,	B. C. Evans,	D. W. Pendery,	C. M. Peak
	J M. Davis,	W. J. Allen.	

1878.

CITY OFFICERS.

R. E. Beckham, Mayor.

All of the other officers holding over.

I. C. Terry elected City Engineer on the 21st day of May. 1878.

John T. Brown appointed Recorder on the 15th day of October, 1878.

ALDERMEN.

Geo. Jackson,   S. H. Holmes,   Thos. Aston,

B. C. Evans, John Nichols, W. J. Allen, holding over.

1879.

CITY OFFICERS.

John S. Loving, Treasurer.
R. E. Maddox, City Assessor and Collector.
C. McDougall, City Secretary.
S. M. Farmer, City Marshal.
C. C. Hyde, City Engineer.

ALDERMEN.

S. Terry,   R. N. Hatcher,   E. W. Morten.

S. H. Holmes, Thos. Aston, E. W. Morten, holding over.

1880.

CITY OFFICERS.

John. T. Brown, Mayor.

ALDERMEN.

I. W. Rouse,   E. M Orrick,   W. A. Darter,   C. L. Pigman.
*John A. Thornton.

S. Terry holding over.

*L. A. Trimble elected Alderman on the 5th day of June, A. D. 1880. John A. Thornton resigned.

1881.

CITY OFFICERS.

R. E. Maddox, Assessor and Collector.
Jno. S. Loving, Treasurer.
Robert McCart, City Attorney.
C. M. McDougall, City Secretary.
S. M. Farmer, City Marshal.

ALDERMEN.

Jesse Jones,   H. P. Shiel,   H. B. Pitts,   L. A. Trimble.

I. W. Rouse, E. M. Orrick, H. B. Pitts, holding over.

1882.

CITY OFFICERS.

J. P. Smith, Mayor.
J. J. Goodfellow, City Engineer.

ALDERMEN.

Max Elser,   H. S. Broiles,   Sam Seaton,   J. T. Hickey.

N. C. Brooks elected Alderman April 20, 1882, in place of H. B. Pitts, resigned.

Henry Feild appointed Recorder May 2, 1882.

W. R. Haymaker, elected August 26, 1882, in place of H. S. Broiles, resigned.

1883.

CITY OFFICERS.

Jno. Nichols, Treasurer.
R. E. Maddox, Assessor and Collector.
J. W. Swayne, City Attorney.
Stuart Harrison, City Secretary.
W. M. Rea, City Marshal.
E. K. Smoot, City Engineer.

ALDERMEN.

T. T. Andrews,   J. R. Adams,   J. B. Askew.

Max Elser, J. T. Hickey and W. R. Haymaker holding over.

Henry Feild appointed Recorder April 10, 1883.

W. H. Aldridge and R. Flannigan were elected Aldermen of the newly-created Fourth ward on the 14th day of August, 1883.

1884.

CITY OFFICERS.

J. P. Smith, Mayor.

ALDERMEN.

J. B. Askew, J. R. Adams, T. T. D. Andrews and Richard Flannigan, held over.

ORDINANCES

OF THE

CITY OF FORT WORTH.

ORDINANCE NO. I.

An Ordinance opening an alley ten feet wide through block No. — known as the Peak Block.

Be it ordained by the City Council of the City of Fort Worth:

SECTION 1. That an alley ten feet wide be opened through the middle of block No. — known as the Peak block, said alley to run in a northerly and southerly direction, and from Weatherford to First street.

B. A.
O. 145
§ 1

SEC. 2. That the ordinance take effect and be in force from and after its passage.

B. A.
O. 145
§ 2

Approved April 13, 1878,

ORDINANCE NO. II.

An Ordinance creating the office of Assistant Assessor and Collector.

Be it ordained by the City Council of the City of Fort Worth:

B. A.
O. 62
§ 1
    SECTION 1. That the office of Assistant Assessor and Collector of this city is hereby created and established.

B. A.
O. 62
§ 2
    SEC. 2. That the Mayor have power to appoint some suitable person to said office, said appointment to be confirmed by the City Council before it takes effect.

B. A.
O. 62
§ 3
    SEC. 3. That the powers, duties, salaries and fees of said officer shall be the same as is now prescribed and authorized by law and by the charter of this city for the Tax Assessor and Collector.

B. A.
O. 62
§ 4
    SEC. 4. That this ordinance shall take effect and be in force from and after its passage.

Approved August 11, 1874.

ORDINANCE NO. III.

An Ordinance defining and prohibiting Assaults and Batteries.

Be it ordained by the City Council of the City of Fort Worth:

B. A.
O. 158
§ 1
    SECTION 1. The use of any unlawful violence upon the person of another, with intent to injure him, whatever be the means or the degree of violence used, is an assault and battery. Any attempt to commit a battery or any threatening gesture, showing in itself, or by words accompanying it, any immediate intention, coupled with the ability to commit a battery, is an assault.

B. A.
O. 158
§ 2
    SEC. 2. When an injury is caused by violence to the person, the intent to injure is presumed, and it rests with the person inflicting the injury to show the accident or innocent intention. The injury intended may be either bodily pain, constraint, a sense of shame, or other disagreeable emotions of the mind.

    SEC. 3. An assault or assault and battery may be committed by the use of any part of the body of the person committing the offense, as of the hand, foot, head, or by the use of any inanimate object, as a stick, knife or anything else capable of inflicting the slightest injury, or by the use of any animate object, as by throwing one person against another, or driving a horse or other animal against the person; any means used by the person assaulting, as by spitting in the face, or otherwise, which is capable of inflicting an injury, comes within the definition of an assault or assault and battery, as the case may be; and an assault or an assault and battery may be committed though the person injured thereby was not the person intended to be injured. B. A.
O. 158
§ 3

SEC. 4. Violence used to the person does not amount to an assault or battery in the following cases: 1. In the exercise of the right of moderate restraint or correction given by law to the parent over the child, the guardian over the ward, the teacher over the scholar. 2. For the preservation of order in a meeting for religious, political or other lawful purpose. 3. For the preservation of the peace or to prevent the commission of offenses. 4. In preventing or interrupting an intrusion upon the lawful possession of property. 5. In making lawful arrests and detaining the party arrested in obedience to the lawful order of a magistrate or court, and in overcoming resistance to such lawful order. 6. In self-defense or the defense of another against unlawful violence offered to his person or property, provided, that in all cases mentioned in this section, where violence is permitted to effect a lawful purpose, only that degree of violence must be used which is necessary to effect such purposes. B. A.
O. 158
§ 4

SEC. 5. No verbal provocation justifies an assault and battery, but insulting and abusive words may be given in evidence in mitigation of the punishment affixed to the offense. B. A.
O. 158
§ 5

SEC. 6. That any person who shall commit an assault or an assault and battery, as defined in this ordinance, shall, upon conviction thereof, be fined in any sum not less than five dollars, nor more than one hundred dollars. B. A.
O. 207
§ 1

SEC. 7. The word battery is used in this ordinance in the same sense as assault and battery. B. A.
O. 158
§ 7

SEC. 8. That this ordinance take effect and be in force from and after its publication as required by law. B. A.
O. 158
§ 8

Approved May 29, 1878.

Section 6 approved September 4, 1879.

ORDINANCE NO. IV.

An Ordinance fixing the amount of the official bonds of certain officers elected by the vote of the people.

Be it ordained by the City Council of the City of Fort Worth:

SECTION 1. That the City Marshal shall, before entering upon the discharge of his duties, enter into a bond with two or more securities, to be approved by the City Council, in the penal sum of one thousand dollars, payable to the city of Fort Worth, conditioned for the faithful discharge of his duties in accordance with the charter and ordinances of the city.

SEC. 2. That the City Assessor and Collector shall, before entering upon the discharge of his duties, enter into a bond with two or more securities, to be approved by the City Council, in the penal sum of twenty thousand dollars, payable to the city of Fort Worth, conditioned for the faithful discharge of his duties in accordance with the charter and ordinances of the city.

SEC. 3. The City Treasurer shall, before entering upon the discharge of his duties, enter into a bond with two or more securities, to be approved by the City Council, in the penal sum of fifty thousand dollars, payable to the city of Fort Worth, conditioned for the faithful discharge of his duties in accordance with the charter and ordinances of the city.

SEC. 4. The City Secretary shall, before entering upon the discharge of his duties, enter into bond with two or more good securities, to be approved by the City Council, in the penal sum of two thousand dollars, payable to the city of Fort Worth, conditioned for the faithful discharge of his duties in accordance with the charter and ordinances of the city.

SEC. 5. The City Attorney shall, before entering upon the discharge of his duties, enter into bond with two or more good securities, to be approved by the City Council, in the penal sum of five hundred dollars, payable to the city of Fort Worth, conditioned for the faithful discharge of his duties in accordance with the charter and ordinances of the city.

SEC. 6. The City Engineer shall, before entering upon the discharge of his duties, enter into a bond with two or more good sureties, to be approved by the City Council, in the penal sum of one thousand dollars, payable to the city of Fort Worth, conditioned for the faithful discharge of his duties in accordance with the charter and ordinances of the city.

B. B.
O. 302
§ 6

SEC. 7. That it shall be the duty of the City Secretary to properly record all official bonds of city officers in the city record book of bonds. etc.

B. B.
O. 302
§ 7

SEC. 8. That this ordinance shall take effect and be in force from and after its passage.

B. B.
O. 302
§ 8

Approved April 6, 1883.

ORDINANCE NO. V.

An Ordinance to provide for funding the indebtedness of the city incurred for the erection of a city hall.

Be it ordained by the City Council of the City of Fort Worth:

THAT WHEREAS, this city has incurred to J. Kane an indebtedness amounting to two thousand ($2,000) dollars for material furnished and labor performed by said Kane in erecting a public city hall for said city, and

Whereas, by an act of the Legislature of the State of Texas, passed March 15, 1875, entitled "An Act regulating the incorporation of cities of one thousand inhabitants or over, and to repeal all other acts," etc., it is provided that the city council of every such city shall have power to pass all necessary ordinances to provide for funding the whole or any part of the existing debt of the city, or of any future debt, by cancelling the evidences thereof, and issuing to the holders or creditors, notes, bonds or treasury warrants, with or without coupons, bearing interest at any annual rate not to exceed ten per cent., and

Whereas, it is desired to fund said indebtedness for said city hall in bonds without coupons, payable and issuable as hereinafter set forth, therefore,

SECTION 1. It is ordered that twenty bonds of the city of Fort Worth be issued and signed by the Mayor of said city, and that they be countersigned by the Secretary of said city in manner and form as hereinafter directed, and that the seal of the city be affixed to each bond.

B. A.
O. 104
§ 1

Sec. 2. That said bonds be for the sum of one hundred ($100) dollars each, and that they be made payable to J. Kane, or bearer, at the city of Fort Worth, and that they each bear interest from date at the rate of ten per centum per annum, and that they each be dated May 1, 1877.

Sec. 3. That ten of said bonds be made payable one year after date, and that the remaining ten thereof be made payable two years after date, and that they be numbered from one to twenty, inclusive.

Sec. 4. That as soon after the passage of this ordinance as may be practicable. the Mayor shall cause said bonds to be engraved or printed on good, substantial paper or parchment, and shall cause a copy of this ordinance to be printed either on the face or back of said bonds as he may deem best.

Sec. 5. That as soon as said bonds shall have been issued and signed as hereinbefore directed, it shall be the duty of the Mayor to forward the same to the Comptroller of the State, as directed by the act of the Legislature hereinbefore referred to, for registration and certification; and the Mayor shall request said comptroller to state in his certificate that no other bonds of the city of Fort Worth have before been registered in his office.

Sec. 6. That the Mayor at the time he shall so forward said bonds shall furnish the comptroller with a statement of the value of all taxable property, real and personal, in the city, as required by said act.

Sec. 7. That when said bonds shall be returned from the Comptroller's office the Mayor shall deliver them to J. Kane, or to such other person holding and owning the evidence of indebtedness issued by the city for the erection of said city hall, as fast as said Kane, or other person shall surrender and deliver up for cancellation an equal amount of said evidences of said indebtedness, and as soon as said evidences of indebtedness shall be delivered to said Mayor he shall report them to the City Council for cancellation.

Sec. 8. That there be, and the same is hereby appropriated, out of the revenue of the city, emanating from whatever source, for the present fiscal year, the sum of eleven hundred dollars for the purpose of paying off the first installment of said bonds and interest, and that the sum of twelve hundred dollars be and the same is hereby appropriated out of the revenue of the next fiscal year, from whatever source derived, for the purpose of paying off the second installment of said bonds and interest; and the City Treasurer is hereby directed to set apart said amounts out of the first moneys coming to his hands in said years respectively for said purpose.

SEC. 9. That this ordinance take effect and be in force from and after its passage.

Approved April 27, 1878.

B. A.
O. 104
§ 9

ORDINANCE NO. VI.

An Ordinance authorizing the issuing of bonds for the purpose of establishing and completing a system of sewerage and street improvement in the city of Fort Worth, and to provide for the interest and create a sinking fund for the principal of said bonds.

WHEREAS, a system of sewerage and street improvement have become a public necessity in this city, and the Council of said city have ordered certain streets in said city to be repaired, macadamized and improved and have perfected a system of sewerage, and

Whereas, it becomes necessary to create a debt and obtain the means for carrying out the plans for street improvement and sewerage, and

Whereas, by an official census ordered by the City Council, it has been ascertained that there are upwards of eleven thousand inhabitants in this city, and

Whereas, all cities in the state of Texas may issue bonds equal to six per centum of the property subject to an advalorem tax, and there is upwards of three million two hundred thousand dollars of said property in this city subject to such tax as shown by the assessment roll thereof, therefore

Be it ordained by the City Council of the City of Fort Worth:

SECTION 1. That the Mayor and City Secretary be and are hereby authorized to have prepared, and when prepared, to execute, under the corporate seal of this city, for the purposes hereinbefore set forth, one hundred and ninety bonds of one thousand dollars each payable to bearer at the financial agency of this city in the city

B. A.
O. 293
§ 1

of New York, on the first day of November A. D. 1912, with interest at the rate of seven per cent. per annum payable semi-annually on the first days of May and November in each year. The principal and interest of said bonds to be payable in gold coin of the present weight and fineness as fixed by the laws of the United States now in force. Said bonds to be designated as sewerage and street improvement bonds of the city of Fort Worth, and shall be numbered from one to one hundred and ninety inclusive, each bond to have sixty coupons signed by the City Secretary each coupon to represent one semi-annual installment of interest.

SEC. 2. The said city hereby reserves the right to redeem at par the said bonds or any of them at any time after ten years from the date thereof, upon giving notice by advertisement in any two newspapers of general circulation in the city of New York for thirty consecutive days exclusive of the days upon which said papers are not published; that, upon a day to be therein named, it will redeem at par, upon presentation at its financial agency in said city, the bonds described in such advertisement. The said notice shall be signed by the City Treasurer and shall give the number, date and amount of each of the bonds so to be redeemed. The bonds authorized by this ordinance shall be redeemed in the order in which they are numbered, that is to say, the bond being numbered one shall be first redeemed, and any bond so advertised for, and designated as aforesaid, and not being presented for redemption as aforesaid upon the day named in said notice shall cease to bear interest from and after such day.

SEC. 3. To provide for the payment of interest on said bonds and to create a sinking fund for the redemption of the same and payment of principal thereof there is hereby levied and set apart and specially appropriated an annual advalorem tax on all property, real and personal and mixed, within the said city of Fort Worth, not exempt from taxation by the Constitution and laws of the state, of and at the rate of five and three-eighths mills on the dollar valuation of said property, such tax to be collected annually until the principal and interest of said bonds are fully paid up and discharged; and if at any time such tax shall be insufficient to yield, for the payment of said interest and for said sinking fund, the amount required for said purposes, it shall be the duty of said Council to set apart and appropriate such additional amount and sum of the annual general revenue and from all other sources of revenue of said city, as may be necessary to supply such deficiency, until the principal and interest of said bonds is fully paid up and discharged. It shall be the duty of the City Treasurer to place all moneys collected and received from the advalorem tax and general revenue mentioned in the foregoing section to the credit of the interest and sinking fund of said bonds and shall divide said revenue between the said interest and sinking funds as follows: One and one-quarter mills to the sinking, and four and one-eight mills to the interest fund, and if at any time there shall be a surplus of the interest fund after provision is made for the payment of interest for the next six months thereafter, then this surplus shall be placed to the credit of the sinking fund.

SEC. 4. The said Council shall cause the said sinking fund and all accretions thereof to be invested in the bonds hereby authorized to be issued in bonds of the state of Texas or in bonds of the United States, as they may from time to time determine, upon the accumulation of each thousand dollars of said fund. B. A. O. 293 § 4

SEC. 5. The said interest and said sinking fund are hereby made special funds for special purposes and shall be disbursable only for the purposes for which they are especially created. B. A. O. 293 § 5

SEC. 6. That when said bonds are prepared and registered, as provided by law, the Mayor of the city is hereby empowered, in connection with the finance committee, to negotiate and sell the bonds authorized to be issued by this ordinance for the best interest of the city. B. A. O. 293 § 6

SEC. 7. That the Treasurer of said city shall, during the months of April and October of each year, not later than the twentieth of each of said months, transmit all money in said interest fund to the financial agents, as may be elected by said council as provided in this ordinance, for the purpose of paying the interest on said bonds in the city of New York, in such manner as the council shall direct. B. A. O. 293 § 7

SEC. 8. There shall be no compensation paid to any officer of the city for receiving and distributing the money realized from the sale of said bonds. B. A. O. 293 § 8

SEC. 9. That this ordinance take effect from and after its passage. B. A. O. 293 § 10

Approved Nov. 10, 1882.

ORDINANCE VII.

An Ordinance authorizing the issuing of bonds for the purpose of completing a system of sewerage and street improvement, and to provide for the interest and create a sinking fund for the principal of said bonds.

WHEREAS, a system of street improvements and sewerage has been begun in said city, and it being a public necessity that said work shall be prosecuted to its completion, and the Council of said city have ordered certain streets in said city to be repaired, macadamized and improved and have prepared a system of sewerage; and whereas, it becomes necessary to create a debt and obtain the means for carrying out the plans for street improvements and sewerage; and whereas, by an official census ordered by the City Council, it has been ascertained that there are upwards of twenty-two thousand inhabitants in this city; and whereas, all cities in the State of Texas accepting the general incorporation act, and having more than ten thousand inhabitants, may issue bonds equal to six (6) per centum of the property subject to ad valorem tax, and this city having accepted the provisions of the general incorporation act—and there is upwards of five million three hundred thousand dollars of said property in this city subject to such tax as shown by the assessment rolls thereof—and there having been only one hundred and ninety thousand dollars in bonds of said city isued; therefore,

Be it ordained by the City Council of the City of Fort Worth:

SECTION 1. That the Mayor and City Secretary be and are hereby authorized to have prepared, and when prepared to execute, under the corporate seal of this city, for the purposes hereinbefore set forth, one hundred and thirty bonds of one thousand dollars each, payable to bearer at the financial agency of this city in the city of New York, on the—day of—A. D.—with interest at the rate of seven per cent. per annum, payable semi-annually, on the first days of March and September of each year. The principal and interest of said bonds to be payable in gold coin of the present weight and fineness, as fixed by the laws of the United States, now in force; said bonds to be denominated as sewerage and street improvement bonds of the city of Fort Worth, and shall be numbered from one to one hundred and thirty, inclusive, and marked "second series." Said bonds to have forty coupons signed by the City Secretary, each coupon to represent one semi-annual installment of interest.

SEC. 2. To provide for the payment of interest on said bond, and to create a sinking fund for the redemption of the same and payment of principal thereof, there is hereby levied and set apart, and specially appropriated, an annual advalorem tax on all property real and personal and mixed, within the city of Fort Worth, not exempt from taxation by the laws of the State, of and at the rate of two and one-half mills on the dollar valuation of said property; such tax to be collected annually until the principal and interest of said bonds are fully paid up and discharged; and if at any time such tax shall be insufficient to yield for the payment of said interest and said sinking fund the amount required for said purposes, it shall then be the duty of said council to set apart and appropriate such additional amount and sum of the annual general revenue, and from all other sources of revenue of said city as may be necessary to supply such deficiency until the principal and interest of said bonds is fully paid up and discharged.

B. B. O. 345 § 2

SEC. 3. It shall be the duty of the City Treasurer to place all moneys collected and received from the advalorem tax and general revenue mentioned in the foregoing section to the credit of the interest and sinking fund as follows: Two-ninths to the sinking fund and seven ninths to the interest fund, after provision is made for the payment of interest for the next six months thereafter, then this surplus shall be placed to the credit of the sinking fund.

B. B. O. 345 § 3

SEC. 4. The said Council shall cause the said sinking fund all accretions thereof to be invested in the bonds of the city of Fort Worth in bonds of the State of Texas or in bonds of the United States as they may from time to time determine upon the accumulation of each thousand dollars of said fund.

B. B. O. 345 § 4

SEC. 5. The said interest and sinking fund are hereby made special funds for special purposes, and shall be disbursable only for the purposes for which they are respectively created.

B. B. O. 345 § 5

SEC. 6. That when said bonds are prepared and registered as provided by law, the Mayor of said city is hereby empowered, in connection with the finance committee, to negotiate and sell the bonds authorized to be issued by this ordinance for the best interest of the city.

B. B. O. 345 § 6

SEC. 7. That the Treasurer of said city shall, during the months of February and August of each year, not later than the 20th of each said months, transmit all moneys in said interest fund to the financial agents, as may be selected by said Council, as provided in this ordinance, for the purpose of paying the interest on said bonds in the city of New York, in such manner as the Council shall direct.

SEC. 8. That this ordinance take effect from and after its passage.

Approved August 12, 1884.

ORDINANCE NO. VIII.

An Ordinance providing for the pulling down of buildings and structures liable to fall down and injure persons or property, etc.

Be it ordained by the City Council of the City of Fort Worth:

SECTION 1. That whenever, in the opinion of the City Council, any building, fence, shed, awning or any erection of any kind, or any part thereof, is liable to fall down and endanger persons or property, the City Council shall order any owner or agent of the same, or any owner or occupant of the premises on which such building, shed, awning or other erection stands, or to which it is attached, to take down and remove the same or any part thereof, within ten days after notice is served them by the City Marshal to remove the same as directed by order of the City Council. In the event the said owner, agent or occupant shall fail or refuse to remove the same after notice, as directed by order of the City Council, then the said City Council shall have the power to remove the same at the expense of the city, on account of the owner of the property or premises, and assess the expense on the land on which it stood or to which it was attached.

SEC. 2. Be it further ordained by the City Council of the city of Fort Worth, that the mode and manner of giving notice to the owner, agent or occupant of the same, or any owner, agent or occupant of the premises, on which such building, shed, awning or other erection stands, or to which it is attached, to take down and remove the same, or any part thereof, shall be by entering an order of said council on its minutes directing the City Marshal to serve a certified copy of said order, and written notice, requiring said person or persons to remove said building, shed, awning or other erection within ten days from the time of serving said notice.

SEC. 3. Be it further ordained by the City Council of the city of Fort Worth that in the event said owner, agent or occupant of the premises on which said building, shed, awning or other erection stands, or to which it is attached, shall fail or refuse to take down or remove the same or any part thereof, after due notice served on him, the City Council shall at its first regular meeting proceed to assess the expenses of removing said building, shed, awning or other erection so taken down by them, as provided under § 1, of this ordinance, after giving five days notice in writing by the City Marshal to said owner, agents, or occupant of said premises to appear before the said City Council at its said regular meeting and contest the assessment of said expenses. B. A. O. 205 § 3

SEC. 4. Be it further ordained by the City Council of the city of Fort Worth, that in the event said owner, agent or occupant of said premises shall fail or refuse for a period of thirty days to pay off and discharge said expenses assessed by said Council then the city of Fort Worth may commence an action in any court having jurisdiction of the same, to recover said expenses so assessed by said Council. B. A. O. 205 § 4

SEC. 5. Be it further ordained by the City Council of the city of Fort Worth that in the event said owner's agent or occupant of such building, shed, awning, fence or other erection shall fail or refuse to comply with the order of said City Council and written notice served on him by the City Marshal, as directed in the second section of this ordinance, that said owner, agent or occupant shall be deemed guilty of a misdemeanor, and on conviction, be punished by a fine of not less than ten dollars nor more than fifty dollars. B. A. O. 205 § 5

SEC. 6. That this ordinance take effect and be in force from and after its publication as required by law. B. A. O. 205 § 6

Approved August 20, 1879.

ORDINANCE NO. IX.

An Ordinance prohibiting communications with prisoners while in the calaboose.

Be it ordained by the City Council of the City of Fort Worth:

B. A.
O. 38
§ 1
SECTION 1. That it be declared unlawful for any person, without the consent of the Marshal first obtained, to hold communication with any prisoner or prisoners confined in the city calaboose.

B. A.
O. 38
§ 2
SEC. 2. Any person delivering to a prisoner or prisoners confined in the city calaboose, liquors or any other article whatsoever, without the proper authority, shall be deemed guilty of a misdemeanor.

B. A.
O. 38
§ 3
SEC. 3. Any person violating any of the provisions of the above ordinance, shall, upon conviction, be fined not more than fifty dollars.

B. A.
O. 38
§ 4
SEC. 4. This ordinance shall be in force, and take effect from and after its publication, as required by law.

Approved June 10, 1873.

ORDINANCE NO. X.

An Ordinance prohibiting the running at large of cattle, sheep, goats, horses and mules.

Be it ordained by the City Council of the City of Fort Worth:

B. B.
O. 314
§ 1
SECTION 1. That it shall be unlawful for any person to allow any cow, calf, steer, bull, bullock, heifer, sheep, goat, horse, mare, or mule, belonging to him or her, or under the control of said person, to run at large, on or upon the streets of said city.

B. B.
O. 314
§ 2
SEC. 2. The city shall appoint a suitable person to act as pound keeper, and shall furthermore establish a suitable place for the keeping of stock found upon the streets of said city.

B. B.
O. 314
§ 3
SEC. 3. It shall be the duty of the pound keeper to catch and take up all stock, such as are mentioned in § 1, of this ordinance, that are found upon the streets of said city, and place the same in said pound. Any officer or citizen shall have the right to

catch any animal mentioned above, found upon the streets of said city, and delived the same to the pound keeper.

SEC. 4. Any person who may own any animal so caught up and placed in the pound, as stated above, shall have the right to take out his or her said animal by applying to the pound keeper, and paying the expenses and costs incurred up to the time such animal is taken out.
B. B.
O. 314
§ 4

SEC. 5. For such animal so taken up and placed in said pound, the pound keeper shall be entitled to a fee of one dollar for each day that such animal remains in said pound, the owner shall pay, for a horse, mare, or mule, jack or jennette, fifty cents, and for each cow, bull, bullock, steer, heifer or calf, twenty-five cents; and for each sheep or goat, twenty-five cents: and when the pound keeper shall sell any animal in accordance with this ordinance, he shall be entitled to the further sum of one dollar for the expense and trouble incurred in working said sale.
B. B.
O. 314
§ 5
B. B.
O. 338
§ 1

SEC. 6. If the owner of any animal so taken up and placed in said pound as mentioned in the predeeding sections, does not either by himself or agents, apply for the same in ten days, then the pound keeper shall sell said animal to the highest bidder at the gate of said pound.
B. B.
O. 314
§ 6

SEC. 7. It shall be the duty of the pound keeper, upon placing any animal in said pound, to immediately give notice in three public places in said city, one of which shall be at the city hall door, describing such animal, and stating that if the same is not called for in ten days it will be sold according to law.
B. B.
O. 314
§ 7

SEC. 8. The money so received by selling said animals shall be applied as follows: first, to the payment of the fees of the pound keeper, and costs incurred by keeping said animals in said pound. The balance, if any, shall be placed in the city treasury, and if the owner of such animal shall make suitable and sufficient proof within six months after the sale of such stock, that the same at the time of being placed in said pound, was the property of him or her, then the City Treasurer, upon the proper order shall pay to such owner the amount of money placed in the City Treasury arising from the sale of said stock.
B. B.
O. 314
§ 8

SEC. 9. Any person who shall allow any of the animals mentioned in § 1, of this ordinance under his or her control, to run at large into and upon the streets of said city, shall be deemed
B. B.
O. 314
§ 9

guilty of a misdemeanor, and fined in any sum not execeeding fifty dollars.

B. B.
O. 314
§ 10
SEC. 10. That this ordinance take effect from and after its publication.

Passed Dec. 18, 1883.

ORDINANCE NO. XI.

An ordinance regulating the City Cemetery of the City of Fort Worth, and establishing the office of Sexton.

Be it ordained by the City Council of the City of Fort Worth:

B. A.
O. 238
§ 1
SECTION 1. That the tract of land donated by J. P. Smith to the city of Fort Worth for the purpose of a cemetery be, and the same is hereby set apart for the burial of the dead, and shall be known as the City Cemetery.

B. A.
O. 238
§ 2
SEC. 2. The City Engineer, whenever directed by the City Council shall survey the City Cemetery into avenues, streets, walks and lots, and shall prepare a map thereof, on which the lots shall be represented and numbered, which map shall be kept in the City Secretary's office for public inspection at all times, and a copy thereof furnished to the City Sexton.

B. A.
O. 238
§ 3
SEC. 3. A portion of the City Cemetery shall be surveyed and set apart under the direction of the City Council for the interment of strangers and inhabitants of the city not owners of lots.

B. A.
O. 238
§ 4
SEC. 4. The Mayor and Cemetery Committee shall set a value not less than five dollars, upon every lot not set aside as provided by the foregoing section when surveyed, before the same shall be subject to sale, and may re-appraise all unsold lots from time to time, and no lot shall be sold for less than the appraised value.

SEC. 5. Any person desiring to purchase any unsold lot shall pay the appraised value thereof to the City Treasurer, who shall give to such purchaser a receipt therefor, in which shall be stated the number of lot proposed to be purchased, and on presentation of such certificate, the Mayor shall, at the expense of the purchaser, execute a deed for such lot to the purchaser, which may be in form as follows, to-wit: "The state of Texas, county of Tarrant, know all men by these presents, that the city of Fort

Worth in consideration of ———— dollars to said city paid by ————
————, doth hereby give, grant, release and convey unto said
————, lot number —, in block —, in that plot of the city cemetery as shown on the map of said cemetery, to have and to hold the
same with its appurtenances thereto belonging, to said ————, and
his heirs forever, for the purpose of burying therein his or their
dead, and for no other purpose or use whatever, and subject to such
general rules and regulations as the City Council may from time to
time hereafter establish for the government of the City Cemetery,
and the said city of Fort Worth hereby covenants with the said
———— and his heirs, that the said City Cemetery shall be kept
and preserved for the burial of the dead. In witness whereof the
Mayor of said city has hereunto set his hand and caused the seal of
said city to be affixed. This — day of ————, 18—.
Countersigned,   ————————,   { L. S. }
————————City Secretary.   Mayor.

B. A.
O. 238
§ 5

SEC. 6. The City Treasurer shall keep a record in which
shall be recorded the number of every lot and block hereafter conveyed, with columns ruled in his record book for the name of the
purchaser, the appraisal price sold for, and date of sale; also a
column for appraisal with date of appraisal. On the sale of any lot he
shall cause a proper entry to be made; he shall also keep a cemetery account in which shall be entered all moneys received and
expended on the account of the cemetery. the name of each purchaser, the date of purchase, the price paid, and shall report to the
Council monthly, and at such other times as directed, the condition of said fund, and the number of lots sold.

B. A.
O. 238
§ 6

SEC. 7. That the office of City Sexton is hereby created and
established, and that there shall be annually appointed by the
Council, a City Sexton, who shall have charge of the City Cemetery, and shall keep the grounds, walks and avenues in order
and free from obstructions; he shall enforce all ordinances of the
City Council respecting the City Cemetery and report violations
to the proper officers for prosecution; he shall prevent the burial
of any body in any lot sold to an individual without the written
consent of the owner, and shall prevent the burial of any body
on any unsold lot except in that part set apart for the burial
of strangers and others not owners of lots; he shall keep in a
well bound book, to be furnished by the city, a record in which

B. A.
O 65
§ 1

B. A.
O. 238
§ 7

shall be recorded the name, and description if the name is unknown, age, sex, nationality, date and cause of death as near as the same can be ascertained of every person interred in the City Cemetery, and the number of the grave beginning at the northwest corner of the lot and block on which such person was buried, and shall at the end of each month make a written report to the City Council embracing the above particulars.

B. A.
O. 238
§ 8

Sec. 8. It shall be unlawful for any person to dig or cause to be dug any grave in said cemetery upon any lot not the property of such person, unless the same be upon some lot in that portion of said cemetery set apart for the burial of strangers and others not owners of lots, or by the written consent of the owner of such lot, and any person violating the provisions of this section shall, upon conviction, be fined not less than five nor more than fifty dollars.

B. A.
O. 238
§ 9

Sec. 9. It shall be the duty of the City Sexton to cause all bodies buried in any lot without authority to be removed to that portion set apart for the burial of strangers and persons not owning lots; and the person or persons causing such unlawful interment, shall, in addition to the penalties hereinbefore imposed, be liable to the city for all costs and expenses of such removal.

B. A.
O. 238
§ 10

B. A.
O. 66
§ 3

Sec. 10. Any person who shall be found discharging firearms, unless a form of burial, hunting or tresspassing in any manner in the city cemetery, or other place of burial in this city, or who shall cause any disturbance or in any manner break the peace, or be guilty of any disorderly conduct, or shall turn any animals into said cemetery, or shall in any manner deface or remove any tombstone or memorial erected to commemorate the dead, or disturb any tree or shrub planted in said cemetery, or injure or deface any erections for the preservation of said cemetery, or the graves therein, or who shall disobey any lawful order or regulation of the City Sexton within said cemetery or place of burial, shall be deemed guilty of a misdemeanor, and upon conviction thereof shall be fined in any sum not less than five nor more than one hundred dollars, provided, that any person acting under orders from the trustees of and in regard to the county cemetery are hereby excepted from the penalties and fines of this ordinance.

Sec. 11. Any person who shall go or remain upon the grounds of the city cemetery, or other place of burial in this city, before sunrise in the morning or after sunset in the evening, without permission of the City Sexton or other person lawfully in charge of such cemetery, shall be deemed guilty of a misdemeanor, and upon conviction thereof shall be fined not less than ten nor more than one hundred dollars.

B. A.
O. 238
§ 11

SEC. 12. It shall be unlawful for any lewd woman or person of immoral character, or a person who is at the time intoxicated, to loiter or stroll upon the grounds enclosed in said cemetery; and any such person so offending shall be deemed guilty of a misdemeanor, and upon conviction thereof, shall be fined in any sum not less than ten nor more than fifty dollars. Provided, that this section shall not be so construed as to prohibit any person in an orderly manner visiting the grave of any deceased relative or friend by the most convenient route to said grave.

B. A.
O. 238
§ 12

SEC. 13. It shall be the duty of the City Sexton to dig, or cause to be dug, the grave of all interments in said cemetery, when requested so to do, and the City Sexton shall receive for his services, to be paid as other funeral expenses, the fees as follows, to wit: For digging graves, $3.00, for children of ten years of age and under; and others $5.00. For designating plat when he is not employed to dig grave, fifty cents. For keeping the records, numbering the graves, and placing the head-board, fifty cents.

B. A.
O. 238
§ 13

SEC. 14. All graves in the city cemetery shall be dug not less than five feet deep.

B. A.
O. 238
§ 14

SEC. 15. That this ordinance shall take effect and be in force from and after its publication as required by law.

Approved July 7. 1880.

B. A.
O. 238
§ 15

ORDINANCE NO. XII.

An Ordinance amending section 4 of Ordinance No. 11, entitled, "An Ordinance regulating the City Cemetery of the City of Fort Worth."

Be it ordained by the City Council of the City of Fort Worth:

SECTION 1. That section four, of ordinance No. 11, entitled "An ordinance regulating the city cemetery of the city of Fort

B. A.
O. 254
§ 1

Worth," be and the same is hereby amended so as to read as follows:

All lots in blocks three and four, shall be sold for not less than ten dollars each, and all lots in blocks five and six and eleven shall be sold for not less than twenty-five dollars.

B. A. O. 254 § 2

SEC. 2. That this ordinance take effect and be in force from and after its passage.

Passed June 21, 1881.

ORDINANCE XIII.

An Ordinance regulating the building of stacks and chimneys to mills and engines.

Be it ordained by the City Council of the City of Fort Worth:

B. A. O. 171 § 1

SECTION 1. It shall be the duty of any and all persons erecting mills or machinery of any kind, to be run by steam, to build or erect the smoke stack or chimney to their furnace, at least forty feet high from the level of the ground, and to cover the same with some good cap or spark arrester before he or they shall attempt to run their engine, and on failure to comply with the provisions of this section, shall, upon conviction thereof, be fined in any sum not less than ten nor more than one hundred dollars, and shall be liable to a like fine for each and every day that he or they shall so run their engine.

B. A. O. 171 § 2

SEC. 2. That all persons who have erected mills and machinery before the passage of this ordinance, and are running the same without having their chimneys forty feet high and covered with some good cap or spark arrester, shall, when notified by the Marshal, upon an order of the Mayor, or resolution of the City Council, stop said mill or machinery until their chimneys or stacks are raised to the height of forty feet, and until they shall cover the same with good caps or spark arresters, and for failure to comply with the provisions of this section shall be liable to a fine of not les than ten nor more than one hundred dollars, and shall be liable to a like fine for each and every day that he, she or they shall run said mill or machinery after said notice without complying with the provisions of this ordinance.

SEC. 3. That this ordinance take effect and be in force from and after its publication as required by law.
Approved Sept. 10, 1878.

B. A.
O. 171
§ 4

ORDINANCE NO. XIV.

An ordinance regulating the use of Stoves and to prevent fires.

Be it ordained by the City Council of the City of Fort Worth:

SECTION 1. That it shall be unlawful for any owner or person having control of any building within the corporate limits of said city to have or use any pipe or flue in connection with any stove unless constructed as hereinafter provided, viz : In all buildings where other than brick or stone flues are used, the pipe where passing through any ceiling or wood except the roof shall be enclosed by an outer pipe or air flue with an air chamber between the two of not less than two inches in diameter, which outer pipe shall extend not less than six inches below the ceiling, or from the wall and not less than one foot above the roof and where the pipe shall not pass through any wood other than the roof, the same shall be so constructed as to be not less than six inches at any point from the wood secured by sheet iron and shall extend not less than four feet above the roof; all pipes other than stone or brick shall be constructed of the best quality of sheet iron or galvanized iron with folded joints, and joints securely riveted together and braded. Provided, that within the fire limits of said city no pipe shall be used in connection with any stove except such as are constructed of brick or stone, and all brick or stone flues shall be laid in good mortar with the inside securely plastered, and the walls of which shall not be less than four inches thick, and all flues or pipes shall extend above the top of the roof. And any person who shall violate either or any of the provisions of this section shall, on conviction, be fined not less than ten nor more than one hundred dollars.

B. A.
O. 184
§ 1

SEC. 2. It shall be the duty of every person using any stove with any character of flue other than such as provided in the foregoing section, on notice from the Marshal, or any policeman, to remove the same, and on failure to comply with such notice, shall, on con-

B. A.
O. 184
§ 2

viction, be fined not less than five nor more than twenty-five dollars.

B. A. O. 184. § 4.
SEC. 3. That this ordinance take effect and be in force from and after its publication.

Approved Jan. 2, 1879.

ORDINANCE NO. XV.

An ordinance creating the office of Fire Warden, and regulating and determining the duties of the same, and regulating the construction of and repairing of Flues and Chimneys.

Be it ordained by the City Council of the City of Fort Worth:

B. A. O. 200. § 1.
SECTION 1. That the office of Fire Warden in and for the city of Fort Worth be and the same is hereby created and established.

B. A. O. 200. § 2.
SEC. 2. That it shall be the duty of said Fire Warden, and he shall have the right at all reasonable hours in the day time to enter all buildings now being built, and those hereafter to be built, and those now built, in the city of Fort Worth, and personally inspect all flues and chimneys, and to condemn such as in his judgment are unsafe in regard to fires, and to give the owners or agents of the same notice to repair the same and to place the same in a safe condition.

B. A. O. 200. § 3.
SEC. 3. That a notice in writing from said Fire Warden served by himself or any member of the police force upon the owners or agents of property to repair and make safe a flue or chimney condemned and pronounced unsafe by said Fire Warden shall be deemed sufficient notice.

B. A. O. 200. § 4.
SEC. 4. That it shall be the duty of all owners or agents notified as required by this ordinance within five days after the service of said notice to repair and make secure to the approval of said Fire Warden all such flues and chimneys, and it shall be unlawful for any owner or agent to use or permit any flue or chimney to be used after the expiration of said five days notice until the same has been repaired and made secure to the approval of said Fire Warden.

SEC. 5. That chimneys and flues shall in all cases, from and

after the passage of this ordinance, be built of stone or brick, and all brick flues shall be at least four inches thick and well plastered on the inside, and no joist or studing shall rest or be in any manner supported on said chimneys or flues.
B. A.
O. 200.
§ 5.

SEC. 6. That no chimney or flue shall hereafter be hung or suspended from the ceiling nor from the side walls, nor rest on the floor of any frame building, but in all cases shall be built or supported from the foundation or ground on stone, brick or wood, and shall have at least one foot of solid brick or rock and mortar before the thimble or pipe shall be inserted, and said thimble or pipe shall be inserted at least two feet six inches below the ceiling. Further that this ordinance is not to prevent the building of what is known as double galvanized iron flues which are allowed to be built without the above restrictions, except that they shall be built so as to come six inches below the ceiling, and one foot above the roof doubled— the balance to be built single if preferred.
B. A.
O. 200.
§ 6.
&
B. B.
O. 347.
§ 1.

SEC. 7. That any person or persons violating any of the provisions of this ordinance shall be deemed guilty of a misdemeanor and, upon conviction thereof, shall be fined in any sum not less than one dollar, nor more than ten dollars, and shall be liable to a like fine for each and every day that such violation may continue.
B. A.
O. 200.
§ 7

SEC. 8. That no isolated or detached building fifty feet or more from any other building shall be subject to the provisions of this ordinance.
B. A.
O. 200.
§ 8.

SEC. 9. That this ordinance take effect and be in force from and after its passage, but the penal portion thereof from and after its publication as required by law.
B. A.
O. 200.
§ 9.

Approved July 16, 1879.

ORDINANCE NO. XVI.

An Ordinance regulating the storing of combustible matter within the city.

Be it ordained by the City Council of the City of Fort Worth:

SECTION 1. That it shall be required of every person selling or dealing in or having in his possession, or on his premises, powder or other combustible matter, to report the same, together with the quantity or kinds thereof, and the houses in which the same is stored, to the City Secretary, for the guidance of the fire department.

SEC. 2. It shall be the duty of the Secretary to make a list of the said houses and the combustible material stored therein, and deliver the same to the Chief Engineer.

SEC. 3. Any person failing or refusing to make a correct report, as herein required, shall be fined in any sum not more than fifty dollars.

SEC. 4. That this ordinance take effect and be in force from and after its passage, but the penal part thereof after publication as required by law.

Approved Oct. 13, 1873.

ORDINANCE NO. XVII.

An Ordinance regulating the keeping and storing of powder and kerosene and other inflammable oils in the City of Fort Worth.

Be it ordained by the City Council of the City of Fort Worth:

SECTION 1. That it shall be unlawful for any person or persons to store or keep or permit to be stored or kept on their premises, or in any house or building under their control, in the city of Fort Worth, any powder over the quantity of twenty-five pounds, or any kerosene oil or other inflammable oil over the quantity of two hundred and fifty gallons; provided the provisions of this ordinance shall not be construed as to apply to or prevent the storing or keeping of powder, kerosene or other inflammable oils in a fire proof powder or oil magazine; provided further, that the provisions of this ordinance shall not be construed as to prevent any railroad or person from erecting safe and suitable buildings for the purpose of storing and distributing oil.

SEC. 2. That any person or persons violating the provisions of this ordinance shall be deemed guilty of a misdemeanor, and upon conviction thereof shall be fined in any sum not less than twenty-five dollars and not more than one hundred dollars, and shall be liable to a like fine for each and every day thereafter that such violation shall continue.

Sec. 3. That this ordinance take effect and be in force from and after its puplication as required by law.

Approved Feb. 7, 1878.

B. A.
O. 140.
§ 3.

ORDINANCE NO. XVIII.

An Ordinance regulating the operation and construction of cotton yards and for the prevention of fires.

Be it ordained by the City Council of the City of Fort Worth:

Section 1. That it shall be unlawful for any person or persons to keep or store any cotton in any yard, lot or other place nearer than twenty feet from any house or building where there is any fire kept or used, without the consent of the owner of said house or building, unless the said cotton be securely enclosed and covered so as to protect it from flying sparks of fire.

B. A.
O. 241
§ 1.

Sec. 2. It shall be unlawful for any person or persons to carry any lighted candle or lamp, torch, brand or other fire, lighted smoking pipes or cigars, in, through or near any place in this city where cotton, hay, straw, shavings or other combustible material is stored, unless said fire be securely enclosed and protected in a covered vessel.

B. A.
O. 241.
§ 2.

Sec. 3. Any person who shall violate any of the provisions of the foregoing sections shall be deemed guilty of a misdemeanor and on conviction shall be fined not less than five nor more than one hundred dollars.

B. A.
O. 241.
§ 3.

Sec. 4. That this ordinance shall take effect and shall be in force from and after its publication as required by law.

Approved August 18, 1880.

B. A.
O. 241.
§ 4.

ORDINANCE NO. XIX.

An Ordinance regulating the proceedings of the Council.

Be it Ordained that the City Council of the City of Fort Worth.

Section 1. That it shall be the duty of the Mayor to appoint Standing Committees, each to consist of one Alderman from

B. A.
O. 146.
§ 1.

each ward, which Committees shall be as follows:—

First, Committee on Finance.
Second, Committee on Claims.
Third, Committee on Police.
Fourth, Committee on Fire Department.
Fifth, Committee on Streets, Alleys, and Sidewalks.
Sixth, Committee on Printing.
Seventh, Committee on Hospital and Paupers.
Eighth, Committee on Public Printing.
Ninth, Board of Health
Tenth, Committee on Public Schools.

B. A.
O. 146.
§ 2.

SEC. 2. It shall be the duty of said committees to make reports to the City Council such facts as may be deemed important, and each committee shall promptly and thoroughly investigate and report in writing upon all matters referred to it by the Council.

SEC. 3. The order of business at all regular sessions of the Council shall be as follows:

First.—Reading minutes of previous meeting, and intervening special meetings and corrections thereof when necessary.

B. A.
O. 146.
§ 3.

Second.—Reports of Standing Committees in their order.
Third.—Report of Special Committee.
Fourth.—Unfinished business.
Fifth.—Petitions.
Sixth.—Resolutions.
Seventh.—Miscellaneous business.

SEC. 4. The following rules, until altered shall be observed in the deliberations of the City Council:

Rule 1. No member shall speak more than twice on any question, nor shall any member speak more than once before each member so desiring shall have been heard.

B. A.
O. 146.
§ 4.

Rule 2. All votes of the Council upon the election or appointment of any officer appointed by the Council shall be by ayes and noes and be entered on the minutes of the Council when demanded by any member of the Council.

Rule 3. All reports of committees shall be filed and presented by the Secretary.

Rule 4. All ordinances after being presented and read shall lie over until the next regular meeting after that on which it is presented before final action is taken thereon.

Rule 5. On all points or questions of order not specially provided for by law or ordinance, parliamentary usage shall be observed by members and required by the presiding officer.

Rule 6. These rules, or either of them, may be suspended at any time by a vote of two-thirds of the Aldermen present.

SEC. 5. That this ordinance take effect and be in force from and after the 6th day of May, A. D., 1878.

Approved April 18, 1878.

B. A.
O. 146.
§ 5.

ORDINANCE NO. XX.

An Ordinance fixing the time of holding the regular meetings of the City Council of the City of Fort Worth.

Be it ordained by the City Council of the City of Fort Worth.

SECTION 1. That the regular meetings of the City Council of the City of Fort Worth shall be held in the City Hall on the first and third Tuesday of each and every month at two o'clock, p. m.

B. B.
O. 330.
§ 1.

SEC. 2. That this ordinance take effect and be in force from and after its passage.

B. B.
O. 330.
§ 2.

Passed June 20, 1884.

ORDINANCE XXI.

An ordinance describing the burial grounds and place of deposit of filth, garbage, offal, dead animals, and regulating the burial of the same.

Be it ordained by the City Council of the City of Fort Worth.

SECTION 1. That the following described tract or parcel of land be and the same is hereby designated and appointed as the place of deposit and burial of filth, offal, garbage, dead animals and other things required by the ordinances of said city to be removed from the city, to-wit: Beginning at a point on the west bank of the Trinity river, about two hundred yards above what is know as the brick yard crossing, thence north with the west bank of said

B. A.
O. 234.
§ 1.

river, about two hundred and fifty yards to a blazed post oak tree, thence in a westernly direction with a line of blaze trees to the edge of the prairie, thence in a southerly direction about two hundred and fifty yards to a blazed tree, thence in an easterly direction with a line of blazed trees to the river and place of beginning. The same containing about five or six acres.

<small>B. A. O. 234. § 2.</small>
Sec. 2. It shall be the duty of all persons hauling off privy filth and substances of like offensive character, dead animals, fish or fowls, to bury or inter the same in said burial grounds in such a manner that it will not be offensive to persons passing over or near said grounds; and any person or persons failing to comply with the requirements of this section shall be deemed guilty of a misdemeanor, and, upon conviction thereof, shall be fined in any sum not less than ten nor more than one hundred dollars.

<small>B. A. O. 234. § 3.</small>
Sec. 3. It shall be the duty of such scavenger or persons engaged in cleaning privies to dig a ditch, one end to be kept open, not less than four feet deep and three feet wide in said grounds for the burial of all privy filth, etc., hauled off by him and to place on the ends of said ditch a board with the name of the party owning and depositing in said ditch plainly marked on said board, and that any person or persons failing to comply with the provisions of this section shall be deemed guilty of a misdemeanor. and, upon conviction thereof, shall be fined in a sum of ten dollars, and that any person or persons who shall bury, place or deposit any privy filth or other offensive matter or nuisances of any kind in any ditch not his own, shall be deemed guilty of a misdemeanor, and, upon conviction thereof, shall be fined in a sum not less than ten nor more than one hundred dollars.

<small>B. A. O. 234. § 4.</small>
Sec. 4. That this ordinance shall take effect and be in force from and after its publication as required by law.

Approved May 20, 1880.

ORNINANCE NO. XXII.

An ordinance relating to the Removal of Carcasses.

Be it ordained by the City Council of the City of Fort Worth:

SECTION 1. That the owner or possessor of any animal which may die within the corporate limits of the city shall, within twenty-four hours after the death of said animal cause the carcass to be removed beyond the limits of the city or to the place of deposit of filth, etc.
B. A. O. 20. § 1.

SEC. 2. Any persons failing to comply with the provisions of this ordinance shall be deemed guilty of a misdemeanor, and upon conviction thereof, shall be fined not less than two nor more than ten dollars for each and every offence.
B. A. O. 20. § 2.

SEC. 3. This ordinance shall take effect and be in force from and after its publication as required by law.
B. A. O. 20 § 3.

Approved April 10, 1873.

ORDINANCE NO. XXIII.

An Ordinance providing for the killing of horses mules and asses diseased with glanders or farcy and for the removal and confinement of all such animals where there are good reasons to believe that they are taking either of said diseases.

Be it ordained by the City Council of the City of Fort Worth:

SECTION 1. That it shall be the duty of the City Marshal to seize and kill all animals of the horse or ass species, diseased with glanders or farcy in all cases where the owner or person in charge of said animal shall fail or refuse to immediately place and keep said animal in secure confinement separate and apart from all other stock at least two hundred yards.
B. A. O. 242. § 1

SEC. 2. That in all cases where there is good reason to believe that any animal of the horse or ass species are taking or liable to take, from contact, glanders or farcy, or have any disease liable to run into any of said diseases, it shall be the duty of the City Marshal, upon the refusal or failure of the owners, to have said
B. A. O. 242. § 2,

animal placed and kept in secure confinement separate and apart at least two hundred yards from all other stock at the expense of the owner of said animal, until said animal shall be thoroughly cured or declared to be diseased.

B. A
O. 242.
§ 3.
SEC. 3. That for the purpose of determining whether any animal is diseased with farcy or glanders, or any disease liable to run into either of said diseases, it shall be the duty of the City Marshal to employ a competent veterinarian to examine and condemn said animal, at the expense of the city.

B. A.
O. 242
§ 4.
SEC. 4. That it shall be the duty of every person or persons owning any yard, lot, stable or other building, in which animals diseased with farcy or glanders may have been fed or kept, to immediately thoroughly disinfect and cleanse said yard, lot, stable or building, whenever notified by the City Marshal so to do; and that any person or persons violating the provisions of this ordinance shall be deemed guilty of a misdemeanor and upon conviction thereof shall be fined one hundred dollars and that each day that such violation shall continue shall constitute a separate offence.

B. A.
O. 242.
§ 5.
SEC. 5. That whereas a public necessity exists for the immediate enforcement of this ordinance, therefore that this ordinance shall take effect and be in force on and after its passage, and without ten days publication.

Approved Sept. 3, 1880.

ORDINANCE NO. XXIV.

An Ordinance levying a tax on the keeping or owning of dogs in the city, and providing for the collection of the same, and regulating, restraining and prohibiting the running at large of dogs in this city.

Be it ordained by the City Council of the City of Fort Worth:

B. A.
O. 283.
§ 1.
SECTION 1. There is hereby levied upon each and every dog or bitch kept or owned within this city, an annual tax of two dollars and fifty cents, which tax is due and payable on the first day of August in each year, and it is hereby made the duty of every owner or keeper of any dog or bitch, to pay over to the Assessor and Collector the said tax, on or before the first day of August in each year and get a collar, and every person failing to comply with the pro-

visions of this section shall be fined in any sum not more than ten dollars.

SEC. 2. Upon the payment of said tax the Assessor and Collector shall furnish the owners of said animals with a collar on which is stamped the words "tax paid" with the year for which the tax is paid, and while said collar is around the neck of said animal, said animal may run at large in the city except as hereinafter prescribed.

<small>B. A. O. 236 § 2.</small>

SEC. 3. That when any bitch may become proud and in heat her owner or keeper shall confine said bitch in a suitable pen or building, and any owner or keeper of any bitch who shall fail to comply with the provisions of this section shall be fined in any sum not less than ten dollars, and said bitch, while so running at large, may be taken and killed by the City Marshal or any policeman.

<small>B. A. O. 236 § 3.</small>

SEC. 4. It shall be the duty of the police officers to capture and impound in a pen, to be provided by the City Council of said city, and called the "dog pound," any dog or bitch found running at large within the corporate limits of the city of Fort Worth without a collar as prescribed by section two of this ordinance, and it shall be the duty of the City Marshal to kill all dogs or bitches remaining in the dog pound twenty-four hours after their respective capture and impounding, being unclaimed and unredeemed as hereinafter prescribed.

<small>B. A. O. 236. § 4.</small>

SEC. 5. The owner or keeper of any dog or dogs, or bitches, captured and impounded under the provisions of this ordinance shall be permitted and allowed to redeem, reclaim and again receive possession of said dogs or bitches, upon payment to the City Marshal of the sum of one dollar and fifty cents for each dog, which said sum, so paid, shall by him, the said City Marshal, be paid over to the City Treasurer for the use and benefit of the city, as well as all other money received under the provisions of this ordinance; provided, there may be allowed to the City Marshal, out of the money received by him under the provisions of this section, a sum not to exceed two dollars per day, to be paid to the police officer, or to any person, to be employed by the City Marshal to capture and impound dogs; provided further, that the city shall in no case be held responsible for any part of the wages to be paid to said party so employed by the City Marshal.

<small>B. A. O. 236. § 5.</small>

SEC. 6. It shall be the duty of the City Marshal to see that

B. A.
O. 236.
§ 6.

this ordinance is strictly enforced; provided, that this ordinance shall not apply to dogs following countrymen in the city.

SEC. 7. The Marshal and police officers, or any other person,

B. A.
O. 236.
§ 7.

shall have the right to shoot or kill any rabbid dog, or any dog in the streets which shall manifest a disposition to bite.

SEC. 8. That this ordinance shall take effect and be in force

B. A.
O. 236.
§ 8.

from and after its publication, as required by law.

Approved July 7, 1880.

ORDINANCE NO. XXV.

An Ordinance relating to Dogs.

Be it ordained by the City Council of the City of Fort Worth:

SECTION 1. Any person taking a collar from a dog upon which the tax has been paid, or placing the figures of the year as

B. A.
O. 52
§ 3

aforesaid upon the collar of a dog upon which the tax has not been paid, shall, upon conviction thereof before the Mayor, be fined not less than twenty-five dollars.

SEC. 2. This ordinance to be in force and take effect from

B. A.
O. 52
§ 6

and after its publication as required by law.

Approved April 29, 1874.

ORDINANCE NO. XXVI.

An Ordinance regulating the running at large of Dogs, and punnishing the Owners thereof, etc.

Be it ordained by the City Council of the City of Fort Worth:

SECTION 1. It shall be unlawful hereafter for any person to allow and permit any dog or dogs belonging to them, or under their control, to run at large on the streets of said city, between the first day of June and the fifteenth day of October without having placed on the said dog's mouth a muzzle made of wire or other substance that will prevent said dog from biting.

SEC. 2. If any dog shall be hereafter caught or be on the

streets of said city after the first day of June, and prior to the fifteenth day of October, without having a muzzle over his mouth as stated in § 1, of this ordinance, then it shall be the duty of the city Marshal or any policeman of said city to immediately take pos- of said dog, and immediately kill the same.

SEC. 3. Any person violating § 1, of this ordinance shall be deemed guilty of a misdemeanor and fined in any sum not exceeding fifty dollars.

SEC. 4. That this ordinance take effect from and after its publication according to law.

Passed July 15, 1884.

ORDINANCE XXVII.

An Ordinance regulating Hotel Drummers.

Be it ordained by the City Council of the City of Fort Worth:

SECTION 1. That every porter, runner, or person soliciting patronage of any traveler or person for any hotel or public house within the City of Fort Worth, while engaged in soliciting patronage, wear conspicuously on some part of his person a badge or plate, with the name of the hotel or house for which he is soliciting, painted or engraved thereon in legible characters, and any person violating the provisions of this section shall, on conviction thereof, be fined five dollars. B. A.
O. 159
§ 1

SEC. 2. Any person pursuing the calling of a porter or runner of any hotel or public house, or other person soliciting patronage for such house, or the driver or manager of any carriage, omnibus or other vehicle, who shall speak in a loud or boisterous tone or manner, or who shall use any profane or obscene language, or who shall touch any traveler or person or any article of baggage unless by permission of the possessor or owner thereof, or who shall harrass, disturb or importune any person shall, on conviction thereof, be fined not less than five nor more than fifty dollars. B. A.
O. 159
§ 2

SEC. 3. Any porter, hotel runner or other person who shall go upon the platform of any railroad company on the arrival of passenger trains, and when passengers are leaving the same, for the B. A.
O. 159
§ 3 purpose of soliciting the custom or patronage of any passenger for any hotel, public house, omnibus, carriage or other vehicle, or who shall make representations of any kind to induce passengers to go to any particular house or vehicle shall, upon conviction thereof, be fined not less than five nor more than fifty dollars.

B. A. O. 159 § 4

SEC. 4. That this ordinance take effect and be in force from and after its publication as required by law.

Approved May 29, 1878.

ORDINANCE NO. XXVIII.

An Ordinance regulating and restraining Street Drummers.

Be it ordained by the City Council of the City of Fort Worth:

B. A. O. 161 § 1

SECTION 1. That it shall be unlawful for any person engaged in soliciting custom for any person, firm or association engaged in the sale of goods, wares or merchandise of any kind to stop or detain any person upon the streets, sidewalks or public place, or in any manner to harrass, disturb or importune any person or to take hold of any person or any article belonging to or possessed by such person, and any person so offending shall, on conviction thereof, be fined not less than five nor more than twenty dollars.

B. A. O. 161 § 2

SEC. 2. It shall be the duty of the Marshal and policemen to arrest with or without warrant any person violating the provisions of this ordinance.

B. A. O. 161 § 3

SEC. 3. That this ordinance take effect and be in force from and after its publication as required by law.

Approved June 7, 1878.

ORDINANCE NO. XXIX.

An Ordinance defining and regulating the powers and duties of the presiding officers, judges and clerks of elections held in the city of Fort Worth.

Be it ordained by the City Council of the City of Fort Worth:

SECTION 1. That it shall be the duty of the presiding officer of elections of each of the wards in this city to appoint two judges and two clerks, who, together with the presiding officer, shall be managers of elections; provided, that if the presiding officer is unable, fails, refuses or neglects to act, it shall be the duty of the Mayor to appoint another, and in case no appointed presiding officer appear to open the polls, the qualified electors may appoint such officer, who shall perform the same duties and have like power and authority to act as a first appointee; but in that case, the managers, in their returns, shall certify that the presiding officer failed to attend, or neglected to act, and that the person acting as such was duly chosen by the electors present.

B. A.
O. 102
§ 1

SEC. 2. The managers of elections shall be sworn to well and truly conduct the election without partiality and prejudice, and agreeable to law and according to the best of their skill and understanding, which oath shall be administered by the Mayor or any justice of the peace. The presiding officers and judges thus qualified, shall have power to administer oaths necessary to the performance of their official duties. When any person offering a vote shall be objected to by any one qualified to vote at such election, the managers shall examine him on oath touching the points objected to, and if he fail to establish his qualification to their satisfaction, his vote shall be rejected, and if he satisfy the managers that he is qualified to vote, he shall be allowed to cast his ballot and the clerk shall write opposite his name "sworn."

B. A.
O. 102
§ 2

SEC. 3. That it shall be the duty of the managers of elections, in each of the wards of the city, to open the polls at 8 o'clock a. m., and keep the same open until 6 o'clock p. m., with the privilege of a recess of one hour from 12 to 1 o'clock. Should the polls not be promptly opened by 8 o'clock a. m., the time thus lost shall be extended beyond the hour of 6 p. m., so as to secure the full period of nine hours for voting purposes; that each of the clerks write and number the name of each voter at the time of voting, and one of the judges in every case at the time of receiving the ticket or ballot shall write on it the voter's number corresponding with the number on the clerk's list; and no manager or other officer of election shall unfold or examine the vote received, nor shall they examine the endorsement on the ticket by comparing it with the clerks list of voters when the votes are counted out, nor shall they examine nor permit to be examined, by any other person, the tickets subsequent to their being received into the ballot box, except as provided by the laws of the state of Texas. That immediately after closing the polls the managers of election shall proceed to count the votes in the presence of two voters of their ward, of good repute, and shall continue such count, without interruption, until all the ballots voted at such election are counted; provided, that no ticket not numbered as provided in this section shall be counted or noticed in counting the vote, nor shall either of two or more tickets folded together be counted, they shall make up, certify and sign the returns in duplicate, one of which shall be sealed up and retained by the presiding officer for future use as a reference, in case of a contested election; the other copy shall be sealed up with the name of the presiding officer written across the seals and by the presiding officer, or in his absence or inability by one of the judges or clerks, delivered in open session to the City Council on the next day, or as soon thereafter as practicable. The officer so delivering the same shall make oath before the Mayor, or one of the Aldermen, that the returns by him delivered have not been altered or opened since being signed and sealed as aforesaid.

SEC. 4. That each of the presiding officers, judges and clerks of elections, shall be paid by the City Council the sum of two dollars per day while engaged in holding said election.

SEC. 5. That any person violating the provisions of this ordinance shall be deemed guilty of a misdemeanor, and upon conviction thereof, shall be fined in any sum not less than fifty nor more than one hundred dollars.

SEC. 6. That this ordinance take effect and be in force from and after its passage; but the penal portion thereof from and after its publication as required by law.

Approved March 22, 1877.

ORDINANCE NO. XXX.

An ordinance regulating the duties of City Engineer.

Be it ordained by the City Council of the City of Fort Worth:

SECTION 1. The City Engineer shall keep an office at the

City Hall, and shall preserve in his office all maps, plats and surveys of the city, and all records and papers relating thereto, and all profiles and maps showing grades and lines of streets and alleys established by order of the Council, and all plans and specifications of all structures built by the city.

B. A.
O. 176
§ 1

SEC. 2. It shall be his duty when required by the City Council to ascertain the established monuments of the city, and from them when required so to do to locate, establish and survey all private property, streets or alleys of the city, and to give grades of streets or alleys to persons desiring to build or construct sidewalks or curbings.

B. A.
O. 176
§ 2

SEC. 3. It shall be his duty when directed by the City Council to superintend all work done by the City Council upon the streets, alleys and public grounds or sidewalks.

B. A.
O. 176
§ 3

SEC. 4. That whenever called upon by the owner, agent or lessee of any property within the corporate limits of the city to do so; it shall be the duty of the City Engineer to survey the same, measuring from the nearest established monument of the city, and shall give to such parties when required field notes and plots of such surveys.

B. A.
O. 176
§ 4

SEC. 5. He shall have for all services performed by order of the City Council, and for which no fees are provided, such compensation as the Council may from time to time allow, or may be agreed upon by the Council and City Engineer.

B. A.
O. 176
§ 5

SEC. 6. That this ordinance take effect and be in force from and after its passage.

B. A.
O. 176
§ 6

Approved October 4, 1878.

ORDINANCE NO. XXXI.

An ordinance defining the duties and autnority of City Engineer.

Be it ordained by the City Council of the City of Fort Worth:

SECTION 1. That the City Engineer elect shall, before entering upon the duties of his office, qualify in the manner prescribed by the charter of the city.

B. A.
O. 294
§ 1

SEC. 2. He shall be the custodian of all papers, petitions, contracts, maps of the city and additions thereto, plans and specifications of public buildings and improvements and of such other matters as may pertain to public impovements, receiving from his predecessor and receipting therefor such papers as may have accrued and passing them in like manner to his successor in office.

B. A. O. 294 § 2

SEC. 3. He shall be *ex-officio* a member of all committees appointed to consider the opening of streets, alleys, or roads, or other public improvements, the removal of obstructions to public travel, sewerage and drainage and shall receive due notice of their meeting.

B. A. O. 294 § 3

SEC. 4. He shall have the sole superintendence of all improvements, shall at the request ef the Council furnish such plans, specifications and general professional information as may be necessary to assist the Council in its deliberations, shall have charge of all lettings and the making of contracts, subject, however, to the approval of the council, shall report from time to time the progress of such improvements as may be in execution, and without his approval no contractors shall receive pay for work done or alleged to be done.

B. A. O. 294 § 4

SEC. 5. The City Engineer shall, when required by the Council, and in accordance with the ordinances at such time made, furnish property owners having frontage on proposed street improvements, the grade and alignment of such improvements, and it shall be his duty to report to the City Council at the earliest meeting thereafter any wilful neglect or refusal to comply with instructions given in regard to the same. He shall furnish estimates of the value and costs of sidewalks, crossings, etc., and complete lists of the property-holders fronting thereon, showing their frontage and the amount to be assessed against them.

B. A. O. 294 § 5

SEC. 6. It shall be his duty, upon receiving notice of any obstructions to travel streets or alleys, or of any want of proper drainage thereof, to investigate the same promptly and report the most advantageous method of speedy relief to the Council, or proper Committee, and in case such obstructions shall be caused by private parties, his notice to abate the same shall have the effect of an order of the Council.

B. A. O. 294 § 6

SEC. 7. All surveys necessary to be done in the interest of the city shall be made under his charge.

B. A. O. 294 § 7

SEC. 8. All private parties desiring surveys made of their premises shall receive at the hands of the City Engineer prompt attention, and those requesting it shall receive from him a certificate of such survey. The fees for such work done for private parties shall in no case exceed these set forth in ordinance No —.

B. A. O. 294 § 8

SEC. 9. It shall be his duty to see that all buildings built in Fort Worth are erected in accordance with the provisions of the ordinance governing grades, fire limits, etc., and such other ordinances as may from time to time be enacted, and he shall issue building permits to all parties desiring to build within the corporate limits.

B. A. O. 294. § 9

SEC. 10. He shall keep books showing the number and nature of permits, grade certificates, etc., issued, which shall be open to inspection during ordinary business hours.

B. A. O. 294 § 10

SEC. 11. He shall have charge of the sewerage and drainage, and all matters connected therewith, shall issue permits for the connection of house drains with the sewers, shall inspect such connections when made and ascertain that they are in accordance with the prescribed form,

B. A. O. 294. § 11

SEC. 12. In conjunction with the Mayor and the City Council, he shall have charge of the removing of garbage and night soil, prepare the contracts and supervise the performance of the same.

B. A. O. 294. § 12.

SEC. 13. He shall have the power to appoint an assistant whose authority, until evaded, shall be similar to his own, and official acts of the assistant shall be when certified to by the Engineer, of the same effect as his own.

B. A. O. 294. § 13

SEC. 14. The City Engineer shall either in person or by his assistant be present at the regular meetings of the City Council.

B. A. O. 294. § 14

SEC. 15. This ordinance shall take effect immediately at the date of its passage.

B. A. O. 294. § 15.

Approved Oct. 23, 1882.

ORDINANCE NO. XXXII.

An Ordinance to prohibit fast midnight driving and running horse races.

Be it ordained by the City Council of the City of Fort Worth:

SECTION 1. Any person who shall ride or drive any horse, mule or other animal in, along or across any public square, street, alley or public place in this city in a gait faster than an ordinary or moderate gait shall be deemed guilty of a misdemeanor, and on conviction shall be fined not less than two nor more than fifty dollars.

B. A. O. 221. § 1.

SEC. 2. Any person who shall ride or drive any horse, mule or other animal around any street corner lying on the public square or on or across any bridge or causeway within the city in a gait faster than an ordinary walk, shall be deemed guilty of a misdemeanor, and on conviction shall be fined not less than two nor more than fifty dollars; provided, that this section and § 1, of this ordinance, shall not apply to the fire companies when going to a fire.

B. A. O. 221. § 2.

SEC. 3. Any person who shall run or be in any way connected in running any horse race in, along or across any public square, street or alley in this city, shall be deemed guilty of a misdemeanor, and on conviction shall be fined not less than twenty-five nor more than one hundred dollars.

B. A. O.221. § 3.

SEC. 4. This ordinance shall take effect and be in force from and after its publication as required by law.

B. A. O. 221. § 4.

Passed Jan. 6, 1880.

ORDINANCE NO. XXXIII.

An Ordinance for the protection of the lives and property of the citizens on the public streets of the City of Fort Worth.

Be it ordained by the City Council of the City of Fort Worth:

SECTION 1. That it shall be unlawful for any person or persons to leave standing upon the public square, or any public street or alley of the city of Fort Worth, any horse or horses, mule or mules, harnessed to any wagon, carriage, buggy or other vehicle, unless said horse or horses, mule or mules, shall be well and securely fastened to a post firmly set in the ground or sidewalk, or to a ring and staple securely and firmly placed in the sidewalk for that purpose, or to a cast iron weight, with ring attached, weighing not less than thirty pounds.

SEC. 2. It shall be unlawful for any person or persons to

hitch or fasten any horse or horses mule or mules or any other animal to any awning post, fence, lamp post or shade tree in the city of Fort Worth.

SEC. 3. Any person or persons violating §§ 1 and 2 of this ordinance, or either of them shall be guilty of a misdemeanor and upon conviction thereof, shall be fined in any sum not less than five dollars nor more than twenty-five dollars for each and every offence.

SEC. 4. This ordinance shall take effect on and after its publication according to law.

Passed Aug. 11, 1884.

ORDINANCE NO. XXXIV.

An ordinance establishing the Fees and Salaries of the Officers of the City of Fort Worth.

Be it ordained by the City Council of the City of Fort Worth :

SECTION. 1. That in every case of a violation of the city ordinances of the city, or for a violation of any of the penal laws of the state, of which the Mayor or Recorder has jurisdiction, the defendant upon conviction shall pay costs according to the following rates to-wit: The Mayor of said city shall be allowed an annual salary of six hundred dollars, and shall receive no other compensation.

B. B. O. 299 § 1

SEC. 2. The Marshal shall receive the following fees to-wit:
For each arrest with or without warrant, $1.00.
For each witness summonsed, 50 cents.
For taking and approving bond, $1.00.
For each commitment, 75 cents.
For summonsing a jury, $1.00.
For each case tried before the Recorder's court, a jury fee of 50 cents.
For executing a search warrant, $1.00
For levying execution, 70 cents.
For returning execution, 40 cents.
For all cases for carrying deadly weapons, the fee for making arrests shall be, $2.50.

B. B. O. 299 § 2

And that in addition to the above fees the marshal shall be allowed an annual salary of ten dollars only.

B. B. O. 305. § 1.

SEC. 3. To the Recorder of said city there shall be allowed a monthly salary of seventy-five dollars and no other compensation.

B. B. O. 299. § 4

SEC. 4. There shall be allowed in each case tried by a jury a jury fee to each person serving as a juror, to be taxed as cots and to be paid by the defendant only upon conviction, the sum of fifty cents.

B. B. O. 299 § 4½

SEC. 5. To the policemen there shall be allowed a monthly salary of sixty dollars, and said policeman shall receive no other compensation whatever.

SEC. 6. The City Attorney shall receive as a compensation for his services : 1st, For every conviction under the ordinances of said city, a fee of three dollars, except in cases of carrying concealed weapons, and, in said cases he shall be allowed a fee of five dollars, to be taxed as costs against the defendant. 2d, And for writing ordinances, all bonds required by said city or its officers, defending said city in the county and district court of Tarrant county, in the supreme court and in the court of appeals, and in the federal courts in this state, and in defending the officers of said city and the aldermen of said city in any and all cases arising out of their official duties, and in performing all other duties required by the City Council he shall receive a salary of ten dollars per annum.

B. B. O. 299 § 5

SEC. 7. The City Secretary shall be clerk of the Mayor's court and custodian of all the records, papers and documents of said court, and shall record the judgment and proceedings of said court, and shall receive the following fees to be taxed as a part of the costs in each case tried and convicted before said court to-wit :

B.B. O. 305 § 2

For taxing costs including copy thereof to defendant, 10 cents.

For docketing each cause, 10 cents.

For recording judgment in each cause, 50 cents.

For receiving fine and cost, and paying over same to proper officer, $1.30.

As Secretary for the Council the City Secretary shall receive an annual salary of ten dollars.

B. B. O. 299 § 7.

SEC. 8. To the Aldermen, for attending each regular meeting of the Council, $4.00.

For attending each called meeting of the Council, $2.00.

SEC. 9. That the fees of the City Engineer for making surveys for private individuals shall be as follows: per lineal mile necessary to arrive at ground to be surveyed starting from fixed point, $3.00.

For survey of ordinary lot, $4.

For survey of ordinary block not exceeding five acres, $5.00.

For surveying block exceeding five acres for each additiona acre, 25 cents.

Establishing grade of lot, $2.50.

Provided that maps and plots shall be furnished at prices mutually agreed upon, and, provided further, that the cost of the requisite chainmen shall be borne by the party desiring the survey, and shall receive from the city a salary of one hundred dollars per month.

<small>B. B. O. 299. § 8.</small>

SEC. 10. The City Treasurer shall receive as compensation for his services an annual salary of ten dollars and shall receive no other compensation, fees or perquisites.

<small>B. B. O. 299 § 9</small>

SEC. 11. The assessor and collector shall receive as a compensation for his services as follows: For assessing the ad-valorem tax one and one-half per cent on the amount of taxes assessed by him. For collecting occupation or other taxes five per cent on all amounts collected by him.

<small>B. B. O. 299. § 10.</small>

SEC. 12. In no case shall the city be liable for any costs allowed in this ordinance when not actually collected in money from the defendant, nor shall the city pay any costs which may be worked out by the defendant on the streets or otherwise.

<small>B. B. O. 299. § 11.</small>

SEC. 13. That this ordinance shall take effect and be in force from and after the first day of April A. D., 1883.

<small>B. B. O. 299. § 12.</small>

Passed Dec. 28, 1882.

ORDINANCE NO. XXXV.

An Ordinance prohibiting the leaving of wagons, and erection of sheds or structures of any kind on the Public Square, and the hitching of horses or other animals to the Court House fence.

Be it ordained by the City Council of the City of Fort Worth:

SECTION 1. That it shall be unlawful for any vehicle, boxes,

B. A.
O. 160.
§ 1.
barrels, lumber, wood, or material of any kind, or any article for sale, to be or remain upon the Public Square for a longer time than twelve hours, and any person owning, possessing or having the control of such article who shall permit the same to remain upon said square for a longer time than twelve hours shall, on conviction thereof, be fined not less than one nor more than twenty dollars.

SEC. 2. That it shall be unlawful for any person to erect upon the Public Square of the City of Fort Worth any tent, shed,

B. A.
O. 160.
§ 2
advertising boards, structures of any kind, and any person violating the provisions of this Section, shall, on conviction thereof, be fined not less than five nor more than twenty dollars.

SEC. 3. That it shall be unlawful for any person to hitch any horse or other animal to the fence enclosing the Court House, or to

B. A.
O. 160.
§ 3.
post any notice, bills, or advertisements on the same in any manner, and any person violating the provisions of this Section, shall, on conviction thereof, be fined not less than one nor more than twenty dollars.

B. A.
O. 160
§ 4.
SEC. 4. That this ordinance take effect and be in force from and after its publication as required by law.

Approved May 29, 1878.

ORDINANCE NO. XXXVI.

An Ordinance relating to the fire department, the election of officers thereof, and the appointment of a fire police, and defining the duties thereof.

Be it ordained by the City Council of the City of Fort Worth:

ARTICLE I.

SECTION 1. The fire department of the city of Fort Worth shall consist of officers and members of all engine, hook and ladder

B. B.
O. 340.
Art. 1, § 1.
and hose companies now organized and admitted to the fire department under the rules and regulations provided therefor.

SEC. 2. The officers of the fire department shall consist of one Chief, one First Assistant Chief, one Second Assistant Chief,

B. B.
O. 340.
Art. I, § 2.
one Third Assistant Chief, to be elected annually by ballot, on the first Monday in May, to be chosen from the members of the fire department, subject to confirmation by the City Council, and when

so elected and confirmed, shall hold their respective offices until their successors are duly elected and qualified.

SEC. 3. When any vacancy shall occur by death, removal or otherwise the companies shall meet and select such persons as they desire to fill the unexpired term and report the name of the person so selected, to the Council for appointment, and if the City Council should refuse to appoint the person so selected, then they shall select some other person, and so continue until the person so selected is confirmed by the Council; provided, that no person shall be elegible to the office of Chief or Assistant Chief unless he shall have been a member of the fire department at least one year next preceeding his election. _{B. B. O. 340. Art. 1, § 3}

SEC. 4. Each Company shall elect annually one foreman, one first assistant foreman, one second assistant foreman and such other officers as they may desire; a certificate of which election shall be furnished by the Secretary of the Company to the Mayor, that the officers so elected may be duly commissioned by him. _{B. B. O. 340. Art. 1, § 4.}

ARTICLE II.

SECTION 1. In case of fire or other assembling of the fire department the Chief shall assume control and be obeyed in all things pertaining thereto. In the absence of the Chief the highest in rank of the Assistant Chiefs present shall assume his authority and responsibility. The officers of the respective companies shall yield prompt and cheerful obedience to the orders of the officer in charge, and members of companies shall promptly obey the orders of their company officers. _{B. B. O. 340. Art. 2, § 1.}

SEC. 2. It shall be the duty of the Chief, or other officer acting as Chief, in command at fires, to establish a post of observation, to be designated in day time by a red flag and at night by a red lantern, at which post he shall remain during the progress of the fire, and direct the operations of the department, except when his presence at some other portion of the field is temporarily indispensible. _{B. B. O. 340. Art. 2, § 2.}

ARTICLE III.

FIRE POLICE.

SEC. 1. The police committee shall appoint, subject to approval

by the Council, six good men not members of the fire department,
to constitute and be known as the "Fort Worth Fire Police."

SEC. 2. The Fort Worth Fire Police shall elect their own Chief and Assistant Chief, who shall be commissioned by the Mayor and shall hold their offices until the first Monday in May next after date of their commission and until their successors are elected and commissioned.

SEC. 3. The Fort Worth Fire Police shall be independent of but act in conjunction with the fire department of Fort Worth, under the orders of its own officers.

SEC. 4. The duties of the members of the Fire Police shall be to attend at all fires, and under the orders of their officers to preserve the peace and protect property, to prevent robbery and crime, to prevent interference or meddling, if necessary, of persons not belonging to the premises or interested therein, and not belonging to the regular police or fire department. They shall be vested with authority and power to arrest persons charged with committing crime at fires generally, to do all that may be deemed necessary for the protection and safety of persons and of property at fires. They shall also have the power and authority to prevent incendiarism and to arrest parties committing or charged with committing the same.

SEC. 5. The Mayor, when present at fires, shall have command of the fire police and shall issue orders thereto through its officers, but in the absence of the Mayor the officer of the Fire Police in command shall make such disposition of his men as he may deem best.

SEC. 6. Each member of the Fire Police shall be furnished with a badge marked with the words "Fire Police Fort Worth," to be worn on the left breast. The said badge shall be sufficient evidence that the person wearing the same is a member of said police. Each member of the Fire Police shall be furnished with a rope thirty feet long with a ring at one end and a hook at the other by means of which, through the order of their commanding officer streets may be closed or goods saved may be enclosed and secured. Each member of the Fire Police shall be responsible for the safe keeping of his rope and have it with him at all fires.

SEC. 7. Each member of the Fire Police, shall receive, for each fire at which he may do duty, the sum of two dollars; provided, however, that no member shall receive more than four dollars for any one day's service. _{B. B. O. 340. Art. 3, § 7.}

Sec. 8. Any person not a member of the Fire Police wearing a Fire Police badge shall be guilty of a misdemeanor, and upon conviction thereof, shall pay a fine of not less than five nor more than twenty-five dollars. _{B. B. O. 340. Art. 3, § 8.}

ARTICLE IV.

GENERAL PROVISIONS.

Section 1. It shall be the duty of the Chief of the fire department, at least once a week, to make a thorough inspection of the houses, apparatus, buildings and other public property in the use of the various companies, to see that they are at all times in good condition and ready for use, and to make a full report of the condition of the department on the first days of January, April, July and October in each year. _{B. B. O. 340. Art. 4, § 1.}

Sec. 2. No person shall use any of the tools or apparatus belonging to the fire department without first obtaining the consent of the Chief of the fire department; and it shall be the duty of every fireman, knowing of any such offence, to report the same to his foreman, and said foreman to make complaint to the City Marshal, who shall take action in the matter, and any person convicted for violation of this article shall pay a fine of not less than one nor more than five dollars. _{B. B. O. 340. Art. 5, § 2.}

Sec. 3. Racing to and from fires is not allowed under any circumstances, under penalty of dismissal; and if the apparatus of several companies are proceeding on the same street to or from any fire, they shall do so in single file. _{B. B. O. 340. Art. 4, § 3.}

Sec. 4. Any driver of a steam fire engine, hose cart, hook and ladder company, or any other apparatus belonging to the fire department, who may carelessly or willfully come into collision with any other vehicle while going to or from a fire, shall be responsible for all damages that may occur. _{B. B. O. 340. Art. 4, § 4.}

Sec. 5. Drivers shall see that their horses are at all times properly secured and attended to, and any driver neglecting or ill-treating his horses shall be dismissed. _{B. B. O. 340. Art. 4, § 5.}

Sec. 6. All drivers of city teams, when the same are hitched to fire apparatus of any kind, going to or from fires, or alarms of fires, or on parade, drill or other exercise or assemblage of the fire department, or any part of the some, shall be and considered and treated as a member of the fire department, subject to the rules, regulations and by-laws of the same, and shall at such time promptly obey th officers of said department.

<small>B. B. O. 340. Art. 4, § 6.</small>

SEC. 7. Drivers shall be appointed by the fire committee, subject to confirmation by the Council, upon the recommendation of their company. Drivers refusing to obey orders of their officers, or for other misconduct, may be suspended by the Chief of the department, who shall immediately report the same to the committee on fire department; and if said committee approve of the Chief's action in the premises, said suspension shall be final and a new driver shall be appointed. In case of suspension of a driver by the Chief he may select a driver to act temporarily until the case is decided by the committee on fire department.

<small>B. B. O. 340 Art. 4, § 7.</small>

SEC. 8. All drivers of city teams, when driving their teams, hitched to wagons on street works, shall be subject to the street and alley committee, and shall not be considered as firemen, but merely as employees of the city, and the chairman of the committee on streets and alleys may dismiss any driver on duty under his committee at any time, for refusal to obey orders, or other misconduct, and if all of his committee concur with him, the dismissal shall be absolute, but if the committee disagree the case must be referred to the Council. In case of a dismissal of a driver by the street and alley committee, the chairman thereof shall immediately notify the chairman of the committee on fire department to appoint a temporary driver.

<small>B. B. O. 340. Art. 4, § 8.</small>

SEC. 9. Drivers while on duty as firemen shall be considered volunteers and receive no pay for their services. But for their services on the street each driver shall receive the sum of fifty dollars per month.

<small>B. B. O. 340. Art. 4 § 9.</small>

SEC. 10. In case of an alarm of fire when out on the streets, drivers shall instantly, without awaiting orders, unhitch their teams, leave their wagons on the spot, when they hear the alarm, and hurry to their apparatus, and resume their work after the fire is extinguished.

<small>B. B. O. 340. Art. 4.§ 10.</small>

SEC. 11. It shall be the duty of the Chief of the fire department, in addition to his duties in fire department, to inspect all flues,

chimneys and fire-places in the city limits, notify property owners when the same are dangerous and order them to change the same so that they will not be dangerous to adjoining property.

B. B. O. 340. Art. 4, § 11.

SEC. 12. That all ordinances and parts of ordinances in conflict with this ordinance, be and the same are hereby repealed.

B. B. O. 340. Art. 4, § 12.

SEC. 13. That this ordinance shall take effect from and after its publication.

Passed July 15, 1884.

ORDINANCE NO. XXXVII.

An Ordinance allowing the Chief Engineer of the Fire Department a salary and causing him to give bond, etc.

Be it ordained by the City Council of the City of Fort Worth:

SECTION 1. That the Chief Engineer of the fire department of said city be allowed a salary of seventy-five dollars per month for his services as such Chief.

B. B. O. 331. § 1.

SEC. 2. The Chief of the said department shall be the custodian of all the property under the control of the department which belongs to the said city and for the safe handling, careful management and protection of the hose carriage, hook and ladder truck, engines and appurtenances belonging to each of the above, the horses, harness, etc., belonging to each. He shall be required to give a bond payable to the city of Fort Worth, in the sum of twenty-five hundred dollars, which said bond shall be conditioned as above, and approved by the Mayor of said city.

B. B. O. 331. § 2.

SEC. 3. That this ordinance take effect and be in force from and after its passage.

B. B. O. 331 § 3.

Passed July 2, 1884.

ORDINANCE NO. XXXVIII.

An Ordinance establishing the Fire Alarm Bell and regulating the ringing of the same, and prescribing the duties, etc., of the Fire Department.

Be it ordained by the City Council of the City of Fort Worth:

SECTION 1. That the bell erected on the City Hall, and Engine-room be, and the same is hereby defined to be, the fire-alarm bell of the City of Fort Worth.

B. A.
O. 135
§ 1

SEC. 2. That in case of fire it shall be lawful, and is hereby made the duty of any and all persons to sound the fire-alarm by a continuous and rapid ringing of the fire bell for ten minutes, and, also, in case of riot, the Mayor may ring the fire bell to call out the citizens to quell the same.

B. A.
O. 135
§ 2 & O. 113
§ 1

SEC. 3. That it shall be lawful, and it is hereby made the duty of the engineer of the engine company, or some other person by his permission, to give the following signals for meetings of the Fire Department and Fire Companies, viz: For a regular or call meeting of the M. T. Johnson Hook and Ladder Company, No. 1., two quick taps of the fire-alarm bell, with an interval of ten seconds; for a regular or call meeting of the Panther Engine Company No. 2, three quick taps of the fire alarm bell, with an interval of ten seconds; for a regular or call meeting of the Fire Department, four quick taps with an interval of ten seconds.

B. A.
O. 135
§ 3

SEC. 4 That it shall be unlawful for any person or persons to ring the fire bell except for the purposes provided in the first and second Sections of this ordinance, and that any person violating the provisions of this ordinance shall be deemed guilty of a misdemeanor, and upon conviction shall be fined in any sum not less than ten nor more than one hundred dollars.

B. A.
O. 135.
§ 4

SEC. 5. Each of the fire companies respectively may adopt such constitution, By-laws, and regulations for their government, subordinate to the ordinances of the city, as they may deem best calculated to accomplish the objects hereby contemplated, to adopt, fix and impose reasonable fines and penalties for nonattendance at meetings regular or special, for disobedience, want of discipline or any other offence against the law, rule or regulation of such company, and each of said companies shall annually choose from among its own members such officers as they may require in accordance with their respective constitutions and in the same manner provided therein.

B. A.
O. 96.
§ 6.

SEC. 6. The different fire companies under the control and direction of their respective officers, shall, upon an alarm of fire, repair to the place of the fire with the engines and other fire apparatus under their care, and there work and manage under the chief engineer and his assistants, and in case of their absence, place and work the engines and other apparatus in the most effectual manner until the fire shall be extinguished, and shall not remove therefrom but by permission of an engeneer if any should be present, and on such permission they shall return their engines and fire apparatus to their respective places of deposit.

B. A.
O. 96.
§ 7.

SEC. 7. The engineer in command, or in the absence of all engineers, the Mayor, or in the absence of the Mayor, two Aldermen, may direct the Hook and Ladder men to cut down and remove any building or buildings, erection or erections, or fence or fences, for the purpose of checking the progress of the fire, and the engineer in command, with the advice and concurrence of the Mayor, or in the absence of the Mayor, two Aldermen shall have the power to blow up or cause to be blown up with powder or otherwise, any building or buildings or other erections during the progress of the fire, for the purpose of extinguishing or checking the same.

B. A.
O. 96
§ 8

SEC. 8. The Chief Engineer and assistant engineers shall while on duty wear a leather hat or cap painted white with gilded front, and carry a bright metal speaking trumpet. On the front of the leather cap of the Chief Engineer, also of those of the assistants, shall be painted the rank of office which they respectively hold. And this shall take effect from and after its passage.

B. A.
O. 96
§ 9

Approved Dec. 31, 1877.

ORDINANCE NO. XXXIX.

An Ordinance establishing Fire Limits, and regulating the character of Buildings to be placed therein.

Be it ordained by the City Council of the City of Fort Worth:

SECTION 1. All that property, blocks and lots bounded on the north by Weatherford street and the public square, and on the west by Throckmorton street, and on the east by Rusk street, and on the south by Seventh street, including all blocks and lots on Main, Houston and cross streets between said boundaries, and that certain block on the west side of the public square, bounded on the

B. B.
O. 318
§ 1
&
B. B.
O. 320.
§ 1.

north by Belknap street, on the west by Throckmorton street, and on the south by Weatherford street, and also the west half of that certain block situated on the east side of the public square, bounded on the north by Belknap street, the east by Calhoun street, south. by Weatherford street; also that certain property and blocks and lots situated between the following boundaries; bounded on the south by the railroad donation, on the north by Fifthteenth street, on the west by Throckmorton street, and on the east by Calhoun street; all of the above lots and blocks embraced within the boundaries herein mentioned, shall and do hereby constitute the fire limits of the city of Fort Worth.

B. B.
O. 318
§ 2.

SEC. 2. That any person or persons who shall build or plaee in or upon any blocks or lots within any of the boundaries described above to-wit: within the fire limits as laid out in § 1, of this ordinance, or be concerned in building or placing therein any building or structure of wood or combustible material or erect any wooden frame work to be covered with tin, sheet iron or any other material shall be fined in the sum of fifty dollars.

B. B.
O. 318.
§ 3

SEC. 3. It shall be the duty of the City Marshal to remove any such structure as mentioned in §. 2, of this ordinance that may hereafter be built within the fire limits of said city.

B. B.
O. 318
§ 4

SEC. 4. That all ordinances in conflict with this ordinance or appertaining to the fire limits be and the same are hereby repealed.

B. B.
O. 318
§ 5

SEC. 5. That this ordinance take effect and be in force from and after its publication, according to law.

Passed February 5, 1884.

ORDINANCE NO. XL.

An Ordinance prohibiting the shooting off, firing or discharging of Fire-arms; the firing, exploding or setting off of Squibs, Firecrackers, Torpedoes, Roman Candles, Sky-rockets or other things containing powder or other explosive matter, or the throwing of any fire balls, or making of any bon-fires in the corporate limits of the City of Fort Worth.

Be it ordained by the City Council of the City of Fort Worth:

SECTION 1. It shall be unlawful for any person or persons to shoot off, fire, or discharge any gun, pistol, revolver or any firearm of any description, or to fire, explode or set off any squib, firecracker, torpedo, roman candle, sky-rocket, or other thing containing powder or other explosive matter, or to throw any fire-ball or make any bon-fire in the corporate limits of this city, and that any person or persons violating the provisions of this ordinance, shall be deemed guilty of a misdemeanor, and, on conviction thereof, shall be fined in any sum not less than one dollar nor more than one hundred dollars. Provided that this shall not apply to any licensed shooting gallery nor to the shooting of dogs running at large in violation of the city ordinances.

B. A. O. 233 § 1

Approved May 20, 1880.

ORDINANCE XLI.

An Ordinance prohibiting the sale of Unwholesome Food or Drink.

Be it ordained by the City Council of the City of Fort Worth:

SECTION 1. That whoever shall sell or offer for sale within this city any milk produced from any sick or diseased cow shall, for each offence, be fined in any sum not less than twenty nor more than one hundred dollars.

B. A. O. 278 § 1.

SEC. 2. Whoever shall sell or offer to sell or keep or expose for sale within said city any tainted, unhealthy or unwholesome meat or other substance for food shall be fined not less than twenty nor more than one hundred dollars.

B. A. O. 278 § 2.

SEC. 3. Whoever shall sell, offer to sell or keep or expose for sale within this city any impure or unhealthy ice shall, for each offence, be fined not less than twenty nor more than one hundred dollars.

B. A. O. 278 § 3

SEC. 4. Whoever shall sell, offer to sell, or keep or expose for sale within this city, any ice shipped or brought into this city for the purpose of cooling and preserving beer or any other substance, shall be fined not less than twenty nor more than one hundred dollars.

B. A. O. 278. § 4.

SEC. 5. That this ordinance shall take effect and be in force from and after its publication as required by law.

B. A. O. 278. § 5

Passed June 13, 1882.

ORDINANCE NO. XLII.

An Ordinance regulating the sale of Corrupted and Unwholesome Substances, and prohibiting the sale of same.

Be it ordained by the City Council of the City of Fort Worth:

B. B.
O. 325
§ 1

SECTION 1. If any person shall, knowingly, sell the flesh of any animal dying otherwise than by slaughter, or slaughtered when diseased, or shall sell any kind of corrupted, diseased or unwholesome substance, whether for food or drink, without making the same fully known to the purchaser, he shall be fined not less than twenty dollars nor more than one hundred dollars.

B. B.
O. 325
§ 2

SEC. 2. If any person shall sell any milk which has been adulterated in any way by water or otherwise, or any liquid pretended to be milk which has been so compounded as to resemble milk, but in fact made out of some other substances and not milk, shall be deemed guilty of a misdemeanor, and fined in any sum not less than five dollars nor more than twenty-five dollars.

B. B.
O. 325
§ 3.

SEC. 3. If any person shall fraudulently adulterate for the purpose of sale any substance indicated for food or any liquid or spiritous, vinous or malt liquids intended for drink with any other substance injurious to health, he or she shall be fined in any sum not exceeding one hundred dollars.

B. B.
O. 325.
§ 4.

SEC. 4. It shall be the duty of the City Physician at any time he may see proper to examine any and all meats sold in the city, and at any time examine milk which may be for sale, and the City Physician shall at any time requested by an officer or citizen make an examination of any meats and milk that may be taken to him for examination, and upon his failure to so examine said meats and milk he shall be deemed guilty of a misdemeanor and fined in any sum not exceeding fifty dollars. And any party or parties refusing to allow the City Physician at any time to examine meats and milk which he or they have for sale, shall be deemed guilty of a misdemeanor, and fined in any sum not less than five nor more than twenty-five dollars.

B. A.
O. 325.
§ 5.

SEC. 5. This ordinance to take effect from and after its publication.

ORDINANCE NO. XLIII.

An Ordinance granting Right of Way to the Fourth Street, Union Depot and Lake Park Street Railway Company, to construct and operate a street railway in the City of Fort Worth.

Be it ordained by the City Council of the City of Fort Worth.

SECTION 1. That in consideration of the faithful performance of the conditions hereinafter set forth by the Fourth Street, Union Depot and Lake Park Street railway company, a corporation duly and legally chartered under the laws of this State, the right of way be and is hereby granted to the street railway company to build, construct and operate in the City of Fort Worth a line of street railway, with the necessary switches, turn-outs and side tracks, along and upon the following streets, to wit: from the western terminus of Fourth Street near the Weldon school-house along and upon said Fourth Street to Calhoun Street, thence south upon Calhoun Street to Front Street, thence south-east on Front Street, as the said Street Railway Company may elect, to Henrietta Street, thence east on Henrietta Street to Missouri Avenue, thence south on Missouri Avenue to the corporate line of the City of Worth.

B. B. O. 329 § 1.

SEC. 2. That the said right to construct and operate the said line of railway as aforesaid, is granted to the said Fourth Street, Union Depot and Lake Park Street Railway Company upon the following conditions:—

B. B. O. 329. § 2.

First,—The said street railway company shall keep in good repair all street crossings along its line and shall so construct its track as not to obstruct tarvel on the streets used by it.

Second.—The said street railway company shall commence the work of construction at their beginning point or some other point of said line within thirty days from the granting of this right of way by the City Council, and the same shall be completed and equipped within four —— from said beginning to the Texas and Pacific reservation, and completed to their terminus within six months, provided, the right of way is granted and a street opened across the said reservation within twenty days from the passage of this ordinance.

Third.—All the track of said street railway north of the said reservation shall be laid with the tram or Johnson rail, and the road-bed and eighteen inches on either side shall be paved with the Telford-Macadam, and all tracks south of the Texas and Pacific track, the ordinary T rail may be used, and the paving or road-bed and the eighteen inches on either side with gravel eight inches thick.

Fourth.—Good and substantial crossings shall be made on all cross streets not less than thirty feet wide and at a grade of one to ten. No sidings shall be constructed longer than one hundred and seventy-five feet and shall not cross any street.

SEC. 3. Said street railway company shall at all times be subject to all police ordinances and regulations adopted by the City Council under and by virtue of the authority vested in them by the laws of this State.

SEC. 4. That this ordinance take effect and be in force from and after its passage.

Approved June 20, 1884.

ORDINANCE NO. XLIV.

An Ordinance giving certain parts of Prince street to the Fort Worth and Denver City Railway Company.

Be it ordained by the City Council of the City of Fort Worth:

SECTION 1. That so much of Prince street, or any other street having no name, as extends from Morgan street south through Adamson's addition to Luella avenue between blocks 144 and 145 of said City of Fort Worth be and the same is hereby vacated and the use of the same granted to the Fort Worth and Denver City Railway Company for depot and railroad purposes.

SEC. 2. This ordinance to take effect from and after its passage.

Passed June 13, 1882.

ORDINANCE NO. XLV.

An Ordinance granting certain privileges to the Fort Worth Street Railway Company.

(This repealed, except as to Main street, Aug. 19, 1884.)

Be it ordained by the City Council of the City of Fort Worth:

SECTION 1. That the Fort Worth Street Railway Company, a corporation duly organized and authorized by charter under the laws of Texas, certified to by the Secretary of State, under the great seal of the State of Texas, bearing date Jan. the 8th, 1874, be, and the said company is hereby fully authorized and empowered with the right to construct, equip, operate and maintain, own and control, in accordance with the conditions and terms in their said charter contained, one or more lines of street railway, together with all necessary switches, turnouts, sidings, stables, offices and depots, on either or all of the following named streets and their extensions in said city, to-wit: Belknap and Weatherford streets, running east and west; Jennings avenue, Houston, Main and Rusk streets, running north and south, and to such other streets or avenues in said city as may on application be designated by ordinance by the said City Council aforesaid; provided, said company shall construct and operate at least one line of street railway on one of the above named streets running from the public square to the Texas Pacific Railway Depot, or vicinity thereof, within eighteen months from the date of this ordinance, or within six months from and after the completion of the Texas Pacific Railway to the said city of Fort Worth; and provided further, that said Fort Worth Street Railway Company shall fix a rate of passenger fare not to exceed ten cents per mile or less, and a freight tariff not to exceed fifty cents per one hundred pounds per mile or less.

B. A.
O. 60
§ 1.

SEC. 2. That the City Council of the city of Fort Worth reserve the right to determine when the requirements of traffic necessitates any further track than the one selected and built by the company in pursuance of the right granted it the first instance, and shall then notify the company of their judgment, and specify the street on which they deem the railway desirable, and if the company

B. A.
O. 60
§ 2.

shall not comply with said notice within twelve months, then the right to those streets shall be forfeited.

B. A.
O. 60
§ 3.
SEC. 3. That on the filing by said Fort Worth Street Railway Company of a duly certified copy of their said charter and the written acceptance of said company of this ordinance with the Secretary of said city, said company shall be authorized to act hereunder without further ordinance or permit by the City Council.

B A.
O. 60
§ 4
SEC. 4. That this ordinance take effect and be in force from and after its passage.

Passed July 15, 1874.

ORDINANCE NO. XLVI.

An Ordinance granting certain rights and privileges to the Fort Worth Street Railway Company.

Be it ordained by the City Council of the City of Fort Worth:

B. A.
O. 262
§ 1.
SECTION 1. That the Fort Worth Street Railway Company be, and it is hereby authorized to construct, equip and operate a line of street railway over and along the following route: Beginning at the center of the intersection of either Eleventh or Twelfth and Main streets, on the railway constructed on said Main street, thence along the center of said Eleventh or Twelfth streets to the center of Jones street, to the railroad donation and to the Union Depot.

B. A.
O 262
§ 2
SEC. 2. That said railway shall be constructed on such grades as the city or its authorities may fix or prescribe, and it shall be constructed in such manner as to not interfere with travel on said streets, and the said company shall keep the street between the rails of said railway and eighteen inches on each side, graded up to the grade of said street as established by the city or its authorities.

SEC. 3. Said right of way privileges are granted upon the following conditions:

B. A.
O. 262
§ 3
1st. That said corporation shall construct and have in operation and in good running order all of said line within —— days from the 1st day of Feb., 1882.

2nd. That said corporation shall keep level the space between their tracks and for two feet on each side thereof with similar material to that with which the balance of the streets over which it passes shall be constructed, and they shall have the top of the rails on a level with the surface of said street.

3rd. That said corporation shall at all times be subject to all police regulations and ordinances now existing or which may be adopted by the City Council under and by virtue of their power and authority to pass ordinances for the regulation and government of street railways.

SEC. 4. That this ordinance take effect and be in force from and after its passage.

Approved Dec. 20, 1881.

B. A.
O. 262
§ 4

ORDINANCE NO. XLVII.

An Ordinance granting the right of way to the Fort Worth Street City Railway Company over and upon certain streets in the City of Fort Worth.

Be it ordained by the City Council of the City of Fort Worth:

SECTION 1. That the Fort Worth Street Railway Company shall have the right to extend its lines on Seventh street to Taylor, down Taylor to the reservation of the Texas and Pacific Railway Company, and on Hemphill and Lipscomb, Broadway and Main streets on the south side of said reservation.

B. A.
O. 277
§ 1.

SEC. 2. Said right of way and privilege are granted upon the following conditions: 1st, That said corporation shall construct and have in operation and in good running order, all of said line within ninety days from the passage of this ordinance. 2d, That said corporation shall keep in good repair all street crossings along the line of their track, and the track of said railway shall be laid in such a manner as not to obstruct travel. 3d, That said corporation shall keep level the space between their track, and for eighteen inches on each side thereof, with similar material to that with which the balance of the streets over which it passes shall be constructed, and they shall keep the top of their rails on a level with the surface of said streets.

B. A.
O. 271.
§ 2.

SEC. 3. That said corporation shall at all times be subject to all police ordinances and regulations now existing, or which may be adopted by the City Council under and by virtue of their power and authority to pass ordinances for the regulation and government of streets and railways.

B. A.
O. 271
§ 3

SEC. 4. That this ordinance take effect and be in force from and after its passage.

B. A.
O. 271
§ 4

Passed May 7, 1882.

ORDINANCE NO. XLVIII.

An Ordinance granting the right of way to the Fort Worth Street Railway Company over and upon certain streets in the City of Fort Worth upon certain conditions, etc.

Be it ordained by the City Council of the City of Fort Worth:

SECTION 1. That in consideration of the stipulations and agreement hereinafter contained to be kept and performed by the Fort Worth Street Railway Company, a corporation duly incorporated under the laws of Texas, the said corporation is hereby granted the right of way over and along and upon the streets of said city as are hereinafter specified and designated for the purpose of laying the track of a street railway and operating the same thereon.

B. A.
O. 296.
§ 1

SEC. 2. Said street railway shall run over and upon the following streets and in the following manner, namely: Beginning at the railroad donation, and from thence running north on Taylor to Third street, thence east on Third to Rusk street, thence north on Rusk street to Public Square, thence across the Public Square to Weatherford or Belknap street, and from thence to the track of the Trans-continental branch of the Texas and Pacific Railway, provided that said line need not be completed beyond the west end of block three, Moore, Thornton & Knight's addition to the city of Fort Worth, unless a station or a place for the taking on and off of passengers is established by said Texas and Pacific Railway or the Missouri Pacific Railway Company.

B. A.
O. 196
§ 2

SEC. 3. Said corporation shall have the right to lay, erect, construct and put down their track in the center of said streets together with such a number of switches, spurs, turning tables and

B. A.
O. 296.
§ 3.

side tracks as may be necessary for the proper and advantageous conduct of the said street railway line.

Sec. 4. Said right of way and privileges are granted upon the following conditions:

1st. That said corporation shall construct and have in operation and in good running order all of said line within ninety days from the passage of this ordinance.

2d. That said corporation shall keep in good repair all street crossings along the line of their track, and that the track of said railway shall be laid out in such manner as not to obstruct travel.

3d. That said corporation shall keep level the space between the tracks, and for eighteen inches on each side thereof with similar material to that with which the balance of the streets over which it passes shall be constructed, and they shall have the top of their rails on a level with the surface of said streets.

4th. That said company within and during the year 1883 extend, build, equip and keep in good running order said street road across the Texas and Pacific road and across the Texas and Pacific donation, and for at least one-half mile south of the south line of the said Texas and Pacific ralroad donation.

5th. That said corporation shall at all times be subject to all police ordinances and regulations now existing, or which may be adopted by the City Council under and by virtue of their power and authority to pass ordinances for the regulation and government of streets and railways.

Sec. 5. That this ordinance shall take effect and be in force from and after its passage.

Passed November 4, 1882

B. A. O. 296 § 4.

B. A. O. 296. § 6

ORDINANCE XLIX.

An Ordinance granting the Right of Way to the Fort Worth Street Railway Company, and upon certain Streets in the City of Fort Worth upon certain condittions, etc.

Be it ordained by the City Council of the City of Fort Worth:

Section 1. That in consideration of the stipulations and agreements hereinafter contained to be kept and performed by the Fort Worth Street Railway Company, a corporation duly incorporated under the laws of Texas, the said corporation is hereby granted the right of way over, along and upon the streets of said City as are hereinafter specified and designed for the purpose of laying the track of a street railway and operating the same thereon together with all necessary sidings, switches and turn-outs. Beginning at the center of the intersection of Hemphill Street and Pennsylvania Avenue, thence east along Pennsylvania Avenue to Jennings Avenue, thence along Jennings Avenue to Hattie Street, thence east along Hattie Street to Missouri Street, thence north along Missouri Street to Henrietta Street, thence along Henrietta Street to Pecan Street, thence north along Pecan Street to the Texas and Pacific donation, thence to Jones Street on north line of said donation, thence north on Jones Street to Third Street, thence west on Third Street to the west line of Rusk Street.

B. B. O. 328 § 1

SEC. 2. Said right of way and privileges are granted upon the following conditions. First, that said company shall construct and have in operation and good running order their said road from Hemphill Street to Grove Street within ninety days from passage of this ordinance, and the balance of said line within four months after the opening of a street across the said Texas and Pacific Railroad reservation. Second, That said company shall keep in good repair all street crossings along the line of their track, and that the track of said railway shall be laid in such manner as not to obstruct travel.

B. B. O. 328. § 2.

SEC. 3. That said company shall construct all of their said track north of the Texas and Pacific reservation of Tram or Johnson rail, and that the road-bed and eighteen inches on either side of the rail shall be paved with Telford-Macadam on all their road north of said donation. That said company may use trail and road bed, and eighteen inches on either side of said track, of gravel south of said donation. On all cross streets, good and substantial crossings shall be constructed by said company, not less than thirty feet wide with a grade of one to ten. No siding shall be constructed longer than one hundred and seventy-five feet, and shall extend across no street; that all of said railway north of said donation shall be completed in three months from the passage of this ordinance.

B. B. O. 328 § 3.

SEC. 4. That said said corporations shall at all times be subject to police ordinances and regulations now existing or which may be adopted by the City Council under and by virtue of their power

B. B. O. 328. § 4

and authority to pass ordinances for the regulation and government of streets and railways.

SEC. 5. That this ordinance take effect and be in force from and after its passage.

Passed June 20, 1884.

B. B.
O. 328.
§ 5

ORDINANCE NO. L.

An Ordinance creating a special Fund for payment of expenses of Calaboose and Salaries of Recorder, and Policemen and Engineer of the Fire Department.

Be it ordained by the City Council of the City of Fort Worth:

SECTION 1. That all moneys paid into the City Treasurer from the proceeds of the Recorder's court from fines or forfeitures be, and the same is hereby set apart as a special fund for the payment of accounts that may be hereafter allowed by the City Council for board of prisoners in the city prison and for salaries of the Recorder, Policemen and Engineer of the Fire Department of the City of Fort Worth.

B. A.
O. 290.
§ 1

SEC. 2. That this ordinance take effect and be in force from and after its passage.

Passed Sept., 1882.

B. A.
O. 279
§ 2.

ORDINANCE NO. LI.

An Ordinance prohibiting gambling and gambling houses.

Be it ordained by the City Council of the City of Fort Worth:

SECTION 1. A gambling house, is any house, room or place in which any gambling table or bank of any name whatever, or any table, bank or device used for gambling, which has no name, is kept or exhibited for the purpose of gaming, or in which any game or play, whatsoever, at which any money or thing of value or representation of value may be bet, won or lost, is played, dealt or exhibited.

B. A.
O. 153.
§ 1.

SEC. 2. Any person who shall keep or maintain or be in any manner interested in the keeping or maintaining of any gambling house as defined in the first section of this ordinance shall be deemed guilty of a misdemeanor and upon conviction thereof shall be fined in any sum not less than ten nor more than one hundred dollars for each offence.

B. A. O. 153. § 2.

SEC. 3. It is intended by the first section of this ordinance to include keno, faro, monte, pool, rondo, roulette, rouge et noir, chuck-a-luck, and every species of gaming device whatever, which in any common language is said to be dealt, kept, established or played, but the special enumeration herein of any game shall not exclude any other properly within the meaning of the first section of this ordinance.

B. A. O. 153. § 3.

SEC. 4. Any person who shall knowingly permit any game, prohibited by the above provisions of this ordinance, to be played in his house, or in any house under his control, shall be fined in any sum not less than ten nor more than one hundred dollars.

B. A. O. 153. § 4.

SEC. 5. If any person shall rent to another a room or house for the purpose of being used as a place for playing, dealing, keeping or exhibiting any of the games prohibited by the provisions of this ordinance, he shall be fined not less than twenty-five nor more than one hundred dollars. It shall be presumed a room or house was let for the purpose of being used for gaming whenever the lessor knew that to be the purpose for which it was rented.

B. A. O. 208. § 1

SEC. 6. If any person shall bet at any gaming table, or bank, or pigeon hole, or Jenny Lind table, or nine or ten pin alley, or such as are mentioned in the preceeding sections, he shall be fined not less than ten nor more than twenty-five dollars.

B. A. O. 208. § 2.

SEC. 7. If any person shall play at any game with cards at any house used for retailing spiritous liquors, store house, tavern, inn, or in any other public house or in an any street, highway or other public place, or in any out-house where people resort, he shall be fined not less than ten nor more than twenty-five dollars.

B. A. O. 208. § 3

SEC. 8. All houses commonly known as public, and all gambling houses as defined by the provisions of this ordinance, are included within the meaning of the seventh section of this ordinance; any room attached to any public house and commonly used for gambling is also included, whether the same be kept closed or

B. A. O. 153. § 8

open; a private room of an inn or tavern is not within the meaning of public place, unless such room is commonly used for gaming.

SEC. 9. In the proceedings before the Mayor or Recorder's court on the trial of offences under the second and seventh sections of this ordinance, it is sufficient to prove that the game was played, kept, dealt or exhibited without proving that money or other articles of value were bet, won or lost thereon; the offence is complete without such proof. <small>B. A. O. 153. § 9.</small>

SEC. 10. Any person keeping a gambling house as defined in this ordinance, or dealing or playing any game prohibited by this ordinance, who shall permit any minor or any person who is at the time intoxicated, to loiter or idle in any place where such games are being dealt or played, or who shall permit such minor or intoxicated person, to play or bet at any game herein prohibited, shall, on conviction, be fined not less than fifty nor more than one hundred dollars. <small>B. A. O. 153. § 10</small>

SEC. 11. That this ordinance take effect and be in force from and after its publication as required by law. <small>B. A. O. 153. § 11</small>

Approved April 24, 1878.

ORDINANCE NO. LII.

An Ordinance amending Ordinance No. 198 dated July 1, 1879, created an Ordinance in relation to Gas Works.

WHEREAS, July 1st, A. D. 1879, the City Council of the City of Fort Worth passed an ordinance, No. 198, being an ordinance in relation to gas works, and thereby granted and secured to J. P. Smith, his associates, their successors and assigns, certain rights and privileges, and

WHEREAS, Since that time the said J. P. Smith has sold and transferred said gas works, and is desirous of transferring said rights and privileges to the Fort Worth Gas Light Company, its successors and assigns, and

WHEREAS, Said Fort Worth Gas Light Company is desirous of laying many miles of additional pipe and of making arrangements with the City of Fort Worth for lighting the streets, public buildings, etc., and for other purposes, and for these purposes additional legislation is needed, therefore

Be it ordained by the City Council of the City of Fort Worth:

That ordinance No. 198 be amended so as to read as follows:

B. A. O. 287. § 1

SECTION 1. There is hereby given and granted to the Fort Worth Gas Light Company the exclusive right and privilege for the term of seven years from the date of the adoption of this ordinance, of supplying the City of Fort Worth and the inhabitants thereof, with gas for domestic and other uses, and for illuminating the streets of said city.

B. A. O. 287. § 2.

SEC. 2. The said company is hereby authorized to establish, construct, maintain and operate said works in the City of Fort Worth, to receive, take and store, conduct and distribute gas through the city, to construct and extend mains and pipes through all the streets, alleys, lanes, public grounds and all places under the control of said City of Fort Worth: to erect and maintain all engines, machinery and other appliances necessary for the proper conducting of said works, and for supplying said city and the inhabitants thereof with gas of good illuminating power for domestic, manufacturing and other purposes. The said Fort Worth Gas Light Company shall have the right to take up all pavements or side walks on streets, alleys, lanes or public grounds or places, and make such excavations thereon as may be necessary to lay, repair and maintain gas pipes below the surface of the ground for conveying and distributing said gas aforesaid, provided that said company shall within reasonable time replace and repair all such pavements and sidewalks in as good condition as they were before as near as practicable.

B. A. O. 287. § 3

SEC. 3. Said company shall be liable for all damages occasioned by a failure to protect and guard persons and property from injury by reason of the removal of such pavements and sidewalks and the making of such excavations as aforesaid.

B. A O. 287 § 4

SEC. 4. The said Fort Worth Gas Light Company shall lay pipes and mains sufficient to supply at least fifty street lamps, said street lamps to be located as the City Council may direct; said lamps to be placed upon iron posts, and to be furnished with Bartlett's corporation style of globe, and frame of the pattern hereto attached and similar thereto in all respects.

SEC. 5. The Fort Worth Gas Light Company shall furnish

gas of good illuminating power for the said fifty lamps, and as many more as may be ordered erected by the City Council of the City of Fort Worth. B. A.
O. 287
§ 5

SEC. 6. The City of Fort Worth agrees to pay said Fort Worth Gas Light Company a monthly rental of three dollars for each of said street lamps, for the purposes contemplated in this contract, which said rental shall be payable semi-annually, on the first days of June and December of each year in a warrant drawn on the City Treasurer, that is to say at the end of each six months of each year, during the full time specified in this contract, the first payment or a pro rata proportion thereof for each of said street lamps to become due and payable on the first day of June and December, as the case may be, after said street lamps are placed in a position and ready for use, and for the purpose of providing for the payment of all street lamp rental becoming due under the provisions of this contract, the said city shall annually make an appropriation sufficient to pay the same out of the first moneys not otherwise appropriated, arising from the general revenue of the city. B. A.
O. 287.
§ 6.

SEC. 7. For all extensions of pipes or mains which the gas company may hereafter make in addition to those contemplated in this contract, the said company shall erect such number of street lamps and posts of the same kinds specified in § 4, of this ordinance as the City Council shall order at the place designated or located by said City Council, and for all street lamps and posts in excess of fifty herein contracted for, the monthly rental shall be three dollars per month, payable as hereinafter provided. B. A.
O. 287
§ 7

SEC. 8. The said city shall have the right to use gas free of charge for the City Hall, City Jail and all Fire Department buildings, and shall have the right to paint on the globes of such lamps in legible letters the names of the street or streets on which said lamps may be located. B. A.
O. 287.
§ 8.

SEC. 9. The rates and charges to all persons and consumers other than the said city shall not exceed three and one-half dollars per thousand cubic feet, the same to be payable monthly under such regulations as said company or its Board of Directors may prescribe, the quantity to be ascertained by meters of accurate and proved pattern and action. B. A.
O. 287.
§ 9.

SEC. 10. The said company shall not be required to extend its mains or supply pipes as aforesaid unless the demand

B. A.
O. 287.
§ 10.
to be supplied shall afford a reasonable prospect of a fair remuneration.

B. A.
O. 287.
§ 11.
SEC. 11. The said company shall in addition to the furnishing of the gas lamps, posts, etc., light, extinguish, clean and keep in repair all lamps, and paint all lamp posts, and have the exclusive control of the same, subject to the use of the said lamps by the City of Fort Worth for illuminating purposes.

B. A.
O. 287
§ 12.
SEC. 12. The City of Fort Worth shall have the right at its option to acquire by purchase and become the sole owner of said works, including all grounds, machinery, mains, pipes, buildings, franchises and property thereto appertaining, at the expiration of five years or at any time thereafter upon giving one year's notice of such intention upon, paying therefor to the owners thereof, the value of said property to be ascertained by appraisal, as follows, viz: The said city shall select one competent person and the owners of the gas works another, and the two so selected shall select a third, or in case they cannot agree upon such third person, a third person shall be appointed by the district judge of Tarrant county, and the three men so determined upon shall appraise the value of said property, exclusive of franchises, at its then cash value, which appraisal shall be binding upon said Fort Worth Gas Light Company as to the value thereof, but shall not be binding upon the city unless said appraisal shall be ratified by the City Council, and the city shall have the right to become the owner of said works and property at the appraised value when said appraisement shall have been ratified by the City Council. In case the said city shall not purchase and become the owners of said works and property as aforesaid at the expiration of seven years then all the rights, franchises and privileges in this contract granted to the said Fort Worth Gas Light Company shall (except the exclusive rights) be extended to said company for a further period of twenty-five years thereafter, subject to all the duties, liabilities, obligations and penalties herein, provided, that if at the time of said purchase by the city said works and franchises shall be encumbered by mortgage or otherwise, the city shall assume and pay such liability as part of the appraised value as aforesaid made and ascertained.

SEC. 13. It is hereby agreed by and between the City of Fort

Worth on the one part and the Fort Worth Gas Light Company on the other part, that in the event the said company deem it necessary to issue first mortgage bonds upon the said gas works, property or extensions, either or all for the purpose of aiding in the extensions of the same that so much of the aforesaid street lamp rental to be paid to the said Gas Light Company under the provisions of this ordinance as will pay the interest on such bonds, as the same may become due and payable, shall be paid to the owners or holders of such bonds by and through the trustee of such bonds at the time when such street lamp rental is due from the city, and such sum shall be paid as long as the interest on such bonds remain due and unpaid. Provided, however, that nothing herein contained shall be construed as to require the said City of Fort Worth at any time to pay any amount greater than the amount due the said Fort Worth Gas Light Company, it being understood that so much of the street lamp rental as is necessary to pay the interest on such bonds shall be paid to the trustee of said bonds, and by him used exclusively to pay the interest on said bonds as long as the same remains unpaid. When the same shall be paid and cancelled then all of the street lamp rental in excess thereof shall be paid to the said Fort Worth Gas Light Company.

B. A. O. 287. § 13.

SEC. 14. Said City Council with said Gas Light Company, shall agree upon a time table or schedule of time during which said lamps shall be lighted and kept burning, but said company shall not be required to light or keep said lamps burning during clear moonlight nights, said schedule or time to be made a part of this contract.

B. A. O. 287. § 14.

SEC. 15. Any person or persons who shall wilfully or maliciously injure or destroy any portion of the works, fixtures or other property appertaining or pertaining to said gas works, or shall wrongfully interfere with or open any lamps or waste any gas therefrom, or shall hitch or tie any horse, horses or other animal to any lamp post shall be deemed guilty of a misdemeanor, and upon conviction thereof, shall be punished by a fine of not less than ten or more than one hundred dollars, and costs of prosecution.

B. A. O. 287 § 15.

SEC. 16. Said City of Fort Worth shall make all ordinances, appropriations, etc., necessary to secure the said Fort Worth Gas Light Company in the rights and privileges granted in this agreement, so long as the same may be in force. That said gas pipes

B. A. O. 287. § 16

shall be laid at least two feet below the grade established by the city.

SEC. 17. This ordinance shall be a contract by and between the City of Fort Worth and the Fort Worth Gas Light Company, its successors and assigns, and shall be binding upon both parties thereto. Provided said company shall file with the City Clerk its acceptance of the same in writing within ten days after the passage of the same.

Passed November 15, 1882.

B. A.
O. 287.
§ 17

ORDINANCE NO. LIII.

An Ordinance establishing the Grade of Throckmorton, Houston, Main and Rusk streets, in the City of Fort Worth.

Be it ordained by the City Council of the City of Fort Worth:

B. A.
O. 78.
§ 1

SECTION 1. That the grade lines of Throckmorton, Houston, Main and Rusk streets be and the same are hereby established as follows, to-wit:—

THROCKMORTON STREET.

Commencing at the south line of Weatherford Street.

Station	0,		Elevation	112
"	9,	900°	"	103
"	14,	500°	"	101
"	30,	1,600°	"	103
"	38,	800°	"	101
"	40,	200°	"	103–5

HOUSTON STREET.

Commencing at the south line of Weatherford Street.

Station	0,		Elevation	113
"	9,	900°	"	104
"	14,	500°	"	99
"	19,	500°	"	97
"	29,	1,000°	"	100
"	34,	500°	"	99
"	36,	200°	"	99
"	40,	400°	"	99

MAIN STREET.

Commencing at the south side of Weatherford Street.

Station	0,		Elevation	109
"	8,	900°	"	103
"	19,	1,000°	"	93
"	29,	1,000°	"	98
"	34,	500°	"	97
"	44,	1,000°	"	102

RUSK STREET.

Commencing at the south line of Weatherford Street.

Station	0,		Elevation	107
"	9,	500°	"	101
"	17,	800°	"	89
"	18,	100°	"	89
"	24,	600°	"	93
"	39,	1,500°	"	96
"	49,	1,000°	"	98

SEC. 2. That any person who shall build or erect sidewalks on a street on which the grade has been established by the first section of this ordinance, or shall cause the same to be built or erected of any material whatsoever, and shall fail to build or erect or cause the same to be built or erected in accordance with the grades as established by § 1, of this ordinance, shall be deemed guilty of a misdemeanor, and upon conviction thereof, shall be fined in any sum not less than twenty-five nor more than one hundred dollars, and shall be subject to a like fine for each and every day thereafter that said sidewalk shall be allowed to remain not in comformity to said grade.

B. A.
O. 118.
§ 1..

SEC. 3. This ordinance to be in force and take effect from and after its publication as required by law.

Approved July 15, 1876.

B. A.
O. 78.
§ 3.

ORDINANCE NO. LIV.

An Ordinance granting the Gulf, Colorado & Santa Fe Railway Company the right of way through the City of Fort Worth and the right to locate and maintain a depot and other buildings and structures therein.

Be it ordained by the City Council of the City of Fort Worth:

SECTION 1. That the right of way, one hundred feet in width, through the city of Fort Worth be, and the same is hereby granted, of the Gulf, Colorado and Santa Fe Railway Company on the line of its railway, as the same is located through said city, with the right to construct, maintain and forever operate and use its said railway with tracks, turn-outs and switches, over and along all streets and alleys within said right of way.

B. A. O. 266. § 1.

SEC. 2. That the right is hereby granted to said railway company to locate, construct, maintain and forever use such buildings, structures, turn-tables, switches and sidings, as it may deem necessary or convenient for the transaction of its business anywhere upon the ground on their present right of way, situated between Nichols, Bluff, Belknap, Weatherford, Elm, First, Second, Third, Fourth, Fifth, Sixth, Pecan, Eighth, Ninth, Luella avenue, Twelfth, Thirteenth, Fourteenth, Grove, Jones, Callahan, Fifteenth, Sixteenth, and Eighteenth streets, also all streets occupied by them in Daggett's and Tucker's additions south of Texas & Pacific donation, running east and west.

B. A. O. 266. § 2.

SEC. 3. That this ordinance take effect and be in force from and after its passage.

B. A. O. 266. § 3.

Passed March 7, 1882.

ORDINANCE NO. LV.

An Ordinance regulating street hacks and other vehicles carrying passengers in the city.

Be it ordained by the City Council of the City of Fort Worth:

SECTION 1. That it shall be the duty of all persons running carriages, hacks, coaches, buggies or other vehicles after dark in this city, to have on said vehicles two good lights, in such position that they can be seen by other persons passing in the streets of said city.

B. A. O. 88 § 1.

SEC. 2. That any person convicted of a violation of the foregoing section of this ordinance shall be fined in any sum not less than five nor more than fifty dollars for each night said vehicle is so run.

B. A. O. 88. § 2.

SEC. 3. That this ordinance take effect and be in force from and after its publication as required by law.

B. A. O. 88. § 4.

Approved Nov. 30, 1876.

ORDINANCE NO. LVI.

An Ordinance regulating street hacks.

Be it ordained by the City Council of the City of Fort Worth:

SECTION 1. That it shall be unlawful for any persons owning or using a street carriage, hack or other vehicle for the purpose of conveying passengers from one place to another in said city, to charge more than fifty cents for each passenger, including one trunk.
B. A.
O. 274.
§ 1.

SEC. 2. That it shall be unlawful for any person or persons owning or using a street carriage, hack or other vehicle from one place to another in said city, to charge more than two dollars for the first hour and one dollar and fifty cents for each and every subsequent hour.
B. A. O. 274. § 2.

SEC. 3. The owner, driver or person running any street carriage, hack or other vehicle, used for the transportation of persons for hire, shall keep on the inside of each street carriage, hack or other vehicle, hung up in a conspicuous and prominent manner, so as to be easily seen and read, a printed card of the tariff of rates fixed in this ordinance.
B. A. O. 274. § 3.

SEC. 4. That any person who shall be found guilty of violating this ordinance, or any section of said ordinance, shall be deemed guilty of a misdemeanor, and shall be fined in any sum not less than five dollars nor more than twenty-five dollars.
B. A. O. 274. § 4.

SEC. 5. Every person owning, keeping or using any licensed vehicle who shall refuse to transport any person when applied to, at the rates established by ordinances of the city, or who shall extort or demand any greater sum for carrying any person than herein allowed, shall, on conviction thereof, be fined not less than five nor more than twenty-five dollars for each offence.
B. A. O. 183. § 6.

SEC. 6. Any person refusing to pay the fare established by ordinances of the city, after being carried to his or her destination, or place where they may wish to leave such licensed vehicle, if demanded, without delay, by the owner or driver of such vehicle, shall be deemed guilty of disorderly conduct, and on conviction, shall be fined not less than one nor more than ten dollars for each offence.
B. A. O. 183. § 7.

SEC. 7. Any owner or driver of any licensed vehicle, who

B. A.
O. 183.
§ 8.
shall, by any misrepresentation or device, induce another to employ his vehicle, or who shall carry any passenger without his or her request to any house of ill-fame or bad repute, or shall deceive any passenger in any manner, or shall, under any pretext, whatever, assault, threaten, insult or otherwise abuse any passenger, shall be fined not less than five nor more than one hundred dollars.

B. A.
O. 183.
§ 9.
SEC. 8. That this ordinance take effect and be in force from and after its publication.

Approved Dec. 28, 1878.

ORDINANCE NO. LVII.

An Ordinance regulating Hawkers and other itinerant Venders, of Merchandise by out-cry.

Be it ordained by the City Council of the City of Fort Worth:

B. A.
O. 31.
§ 1.
SEC. 1. That it shall be unlawful for any hawker or other itinerant vender of merchandise to expose his goods, or cry the same on or near any sidewalk in this city.

B. A.
O. 31.
§ 2.
SEC. 2. That it shall be unlawful for any person to sell at public auction on any of the sidewalks of the city, any goods, wares, merchandise, or household furniture.

B. A.
O. 31.
§ 3.
SEC. 3. That it shall be unlawful for any hawker or other vender of merchandise to obstruct the streets of this city by the outcry or exposition of his goods.

B. A.
O. 31.
§ 4.
SEC. 4. That any person violating any of the provisions of this ordinance shall, upon conviction, be fined not more than twenty-five dollars for each and every offence.

B. A.
O. 31.
§ 5.
SEC. 5. That this ordinance shall take effect and shall be in force from and after its publication as required by law.

Approved April 17, 1873.

ORDINANCE NO. LVIII.

An Ordinance relating to the Health of the City.

Be it ordained by the City Council of the City of Fort Worth:

SECTION 1. That it shall be the duty of the Board of Health

to make a personal inspection of the city, as often as once a week during the months of June, July, August and September of each year, and at such other times as may be ordered by the City Council, for the purpose of examining the sanitary condition of the city.

B. A.
O. 16.
§ 2.

SEC. 2. That under the direction of the City Council or the Board of Health, the Marshal shall by written notice require all nuisances calculated to affect the health of the city to be removed, cleaned or abated by the occupant or owner of said premises.

B. A.
O. 16
§ 3

SEC. 3. It shall be the duty of the occupant or owner of any building or lot within the corporate limits of the city to use upon said premises as often as directed by said Board of Health, chloride of lime or other disinfectant.

B. A.
O. 16
§ 4

SEC. 4. That this ordinance shall take effect and be in force from and after its publication, as required by law.

B. A.
O. 16.
§ 6.

Approved April 10, 1873.

ORDINANCE NO. LIX.

An Ordinance requiring the Board of Health to cause certain persons to be vaccinated and quarantined.

Be it ordained by the City Council of the City of Fort Worth:

SECTION 1. That the City Physician shall upon the order or demand of the Board of Health, vaccinate or cause to be vaccinated any and all persons in said city who in the judgement of the Board of Health it may be necessary to vaccinate to prevent the spreading of small-pox.

B. A.
O. 267.
§ 1

SEC. 2. That it shall be the duty of the Marshal of said city to arrest and cause to be vaccinated by the City Physician all persons who have been ordered to be vaccinated by the Board of Health.

B. A.
O. 267.
§ 2.

SEC. 3. That the Board of Health shall have the power and authority, and it is made their duty to send any person or persons to the pesthouse established by said city, who has or may have the smallpox, and the said Board of Health shall have the power and authority to quarantine any person or persons who are suspected of being infected with smallpox.

B. A.
O. 267.
§ 3

SEC. 4. That it shall be the duty of the Board of Health to destroy any and all furniture, wearing apparel or property of any kind suspected of being tainted or infected with smallpox, or shall be likely to pass into such a state as to generate or propagate the said disease, and from time to time to do all acts and make all regulations which they shall deem expedient for the preservation of the health and the suppression of the spread of the smallpox in said city.

B. A. O. 267. § 4.

SEC. 5. Whereas, there is an urgent necessity for the passing of said ordinance, that said ordinance be in force and take effect from and after its passage.

B. A. O. 267 § 5

Approved March 13, 1882.

ORDINANCE NO. LX.

An Ordinance relating to houses of ill-fame and inmates thereof.

Be it ordained by the City Council of the City of Fort Worth.

SECTION 1. Any person who shall keep and maintain in this city, a brothel, bawdy-house or house of ill-fame, or of assignation shall, upon conviction thereof, be fined in a sum not less than ten dollars nor more than fifty dollars.

B. A. O. 11. § 1

SEC. 2. Any person, whether male or female, being an inmate or resident of any brothel, bawdy-house or house of ill-fame, shall, upon conviction thereof, be fined in a sum not less than five dollars nor more than fifty dollars.

B A. O. 11. § 2.

SEC. 3. The general reputation of any such house mentioned in the foregoing sections, or of its inmates and residents, shall be *prima facie* evidence of the character of such house and persons.

B. A. O. 11. § 3

SEC. 4. This ordinance to take effect and be in force from and after its publication as required by law.

B. A. O. 11. § 4.

Approved April 9, 1873.

ORDINANCE NO. LXI.

An Ordinance defining dance houses and punishing the keepers thereof.

Be it ordained by the City Council of the City of Fort Worth:

SECTION 1. That any house or part thereof kept for lewd, loose or immodest women or women of ill-fame or bad repute to assemble and dance, or at which such persons may live for that purpose, or where such is permitted, shall be considered as a dance house within the meaning of this ordinance.

<small>B. A.
O. 110
§ 1</small>

SEC. 2. That any person who shall keep such a house as is described in the first section hereof, shall be fined in any sum not less than ten nor more than fifty dollars.

<small>B. A.
O. 110
§ 2.</small>

SEC. 3. That this ordinance take effect and be in force from and after its publication as required by law.

Approved May 31, 1877.

<small>B. A.
O. 110.
§ 4</small>

ORDINANCE NO. LXII.

An Ordinance licensing dance houses.

Be it ordained by the City Council of the City of Fort Worth:

SECTION 1. That every keeper of a dance house within the city of Fort Worth shall pay a license tax of one hundred dollars per quarter in advance for the privilege of keeping the same.

<small>B. A.
O. 165.
§ 1</small>

SEC. 2. It shall be unlawful for any person or persons to keep a dance house within the city of Fort Worth unless he, she or they shall obtain a permit or license in writing from the City Council; provided, however, that no permit or license shall be given for more than three months, and shall specify the time and place of holding the same.

<small>B. A
O. 165
§ 2</small>

SEC. 3. No permit or license shall be sold or transferred and the City Council may at any time revoke any license or permit issued under this ordinance on repayment of any amount which may have been paid by the holder of said license or permit, after deducting the amount due on the time expired.

<small>B. A.
O. 165.
§ 3</small>

SEC. 4. It shall be the duty of any person or persons keeping a dance house within the City of Fort Worth to execute and file with the City Council, a bond with two or more sureties to be approved by them, payable to the City of Fort Worth in the sum of two hundred dollars, conditioned that the said dance house shall be conducted in an orderly manner.

B. A. O. 165 § 4

SEC. 5. Should any riot or disturbance of good order take place at any such dance house, unless it shall be immediately suppressed, it shall be the duty of the officers of the city to cause the same to be closed forthwith.

B. A. O. 165 § 5.

SEC. 6. This ordinance shall not repeal or effect ordinance No. 61 except in cases where a permit or license has been issued under the provisions of this ordinance.

B. A. O. 165. § 6.

SEC. 7. Any person or persons who shall violate this ordinance or any section of this ordinance, shall, on conviction thereof, be fined in any sum not less than ten dollars nor more than fifty dollars.

B. A. O. 165 § 7.

SEC. 8. This ordinance shall take effect and be in force from and after its publication according to law.

B. A. O. 165 § 8.

Passed Aug. 13, 1878.

ORDINANCE NO. LXIII.

An Ordinance prohibiting disorderly houses and punishing prostitutes.

Be it ordained by the City Council of the City of Fort Worth:

SEC. 1. A disorderly house is one kept for the purpose of prostitution, or as a common resort for prostitutes and vagabonds.

B. A. O. 193. § 1

SEC. 2. Any room or part of a building occupied by one or more persons, or appropriated by one or more persons, for either of the purposes above mentioned, is a disorderly house within the meaning of this ordinance.

B. A. O. 193 § 2.

SEC. 3. Any person who shall keep a disorderly house as defined above, within the limits of this city, shall, upon conviction, be fined not less than ten dollars nor more than fifty dollars.

B. A. O. 193. § 3

SEC. 4 Any person who shall be found an inmate of a disorderly house, as herein defined, for the purposes of prostitution, shall, upon conviction thereof, be fined in any sum not less than five dollars nor more than fifty dollars.

B. A.
O. 193
§ 4

SEC. 5. Any courtesan, prostitute or lewd woman who shall be found wandering, or promenading the streets, alleys, or public places, or visiting beer houses or places of public resort, in the night time, shall be deemed guilty of a misdemeanor, and upon conviction thereof shall be fined not less than five nor more than twenty-five dollars. The general reputation of any person mentioned in this section of this ordinance, shall be *prima facie* evidence of the character of such person, and it shall be the duty of the City Marshal and policemen to arrest, without process, any person found violating the provisions of this section.

B. A.
O. 239.
§ 1.

SEC. 6. Any prostitute, courtesan or lewd woman who shall ply, or seek to ply, her avocation by word, sign or action, while upon the streets, alleys or public places of said city, or from the door or window of any house, or window of any room or house that may be seen from any street, alley or public place in said city, or from any private residence of said city, shall be fined upon conviction thereof, not less than five dollars nor more than twenty-five dollars.

B. A.
O. 193
§ 6

SEC. 7. That this ordinance take effect and be in force from and after its publication as required by law.

B. A.
O. 193
§ 7

Approved May 21, 1879.

ORDINANCE NO. LXIV.

An Ordinance defining and punishing offences against Public Decency.

Be it ordained by the City Council of the City of Fort Worth:

SECTION 1. Any person who shall within the corporate limits in any public place or in any place exposed to the public view, appear in a state of nudity or in a dress or costume not appropriate to his or her sex, or in an indecent or lewd dress, or who shall make an indecent exposure of his or her person, or be guilty of any lewd or indecent act or behavior, shall, on conviction thereof, be fined not less than five nor more than one hundred dollars.

B. A.
O. 157.
§ 1

SEC. 2. Any person who shall within the corporate limits of the City of Fort Worth exhibit or perform, or shall assist in exhibiting or performing any indecent, obscene or lewd play, exhibition or other representation shall, upon conviction thereof, be fined not less than five nor more than one hundred dollars.

SEC. 3. This ordinance to take effect and be in force from and after its publication as required by law.

Approved May 22, 1878.

ORDINANCE NO. LXV.

An Ordinance to limit the Time in which Prosecutions shall be commenced.

Be it ordained by the City Council of the City of Fort Worth:

SECTION 1. That for all violations of any ordinance of the City of Fort Worth, an information or complaint may be made within one year from the commission of the offence and not afterwards.

SEC. 2. That this ordinance take effect and be in force from and after its passage.

Passed Oct. 21, 1879.

ORDINANCE NO. LXVI.

An Ordinance establishing a market place for the selling, buying, trading and exhibiting horses, mules and other animals.

Be it ordained by the City Council of the City of Fort Worth:

SECTION 1. The market place for the buying, selling, trading and exhibiting of horses, mules or other animals, shall hereafter be upon Belknap Street, between Main and Houston Streets, and upon the east side of the Public Square, between Weatherford and Belknap Streets.

SEC. 2. Whoever shall be found guilty of violating § 1, of the above ordinance, shall be fined not less than one dollar and not more than fifty dollars.

B. A.
O. 251.
§ 2.

SEC. 3. That this ordinance shall take effect and be in force from and after its publication according to law.

B. A.
O. 251
§ 3.

Approved June 8, 1881.

ORDINANCE NO. LXVII.

An Ordinance regulating the Conduct and prescribing the Duties of the Marshal, Deputy Marshal, and Policemen of the City.

Be it ordained by the City Council of the City of Fort Worth :

SECTION 1. That the Marshal of the city shall be *ex-officio* Chief of Police, and may appoint one or more deputies, and shall in person or by deputy attend upon the Recorder's or Mayor's court while said court is in session, and shall promptly and faithfully execute all writs and process issued from said court.

B. A.
O. 125.
§ 1.

SEC. 2. It shall be and is hereby made the duty of the Marshal, Deputy Marshal, and policemen, to be active in quelling riots, disorder and disturbances of the peace within the limits of the city, and they shall take into custody all persons offending against the peace of the city, and authority is hereby given them to take suitable and sufficient bail for the appearance before the Mayor or Recorder's court of any person charged with an offence against the ordinances of the city. To prevent a breach of the peace, or to preserve quiet or good order, the Marshal shall have authority to close any theatre, bar room, ball room, drinking house or any other place or building of public resort, and for said purposes and for the purpose of arresting any offender, the Marshal, Deputy Marshal and policemen shall have power to make forcible entry into any house where entry is denied them.

B. A.
O. 125
§ 2.

SEC. 3. It shall be and is hereby made the duty of the Marshal, Deputy Marshal and policemen of the city to return, arrest, prosecute, and make complaint against, before the Mayor or Recorder, any and all persons violating any ordinance of the city within their view or knowledge. And when they shall be informed by any credible person that any offence against any of the ordi-

B. A.
O. 125
§ 3

nances of the city has been or is about to be committed, they shall be active in preventing the same and bringing the offenders to trial.

B. A.
O. 125.
§ 4.
SEC. 4. If any Marshal, Deputy Marshal or policeman shall wilfully neglect to return, arrest or prosecute any person who has violated any of the ordinances of the city within his view or knowledge, or shall wilfully and knowingly absent himself from any place where such violation of any ordinance is taking place, or is about to take place, for the purpose of avoiding seeing or having a knowledge of the same, or who after having been credibly informed that such violation of an ordinance is being committed or is about to be committed, shall fail or refuse to take steps to prevent the same and for the arrest of the offenders, he shall be guilty of a misdemeanor, and, upon conviction thereof, shall be fined not less than ten nor more than one hundred dollars.

B. A.
O. 125.
§ 5
SEC. 5. If any Marshal, Deputy Marshal or policeman shall while on duty drink any intoxicating liquor in any bar-room or public place he shall be guilty of a misdemeanor, and upon conviction thereof shall be fined not less than five nor more than twenty-five dollars.

B. A.
O. 125
§ 6.
SEC. 6. If any Marshal, Deputy Marshal or policeman shall use any profane, indecent or offensive language while on duty, he shall be deemed guilty of a misdemeanor, and upon conviction thereof, shall be fined not less than one nor more than ten dollars.

B. A.
O. 125.
§ 7
SEC. 7. If any Marshal, Deputy Marshal or policeman shall get drunk, or shall conduct himself in a riotous or disorderly manner, or shall provoke a breach of the peace while on duty, he shall be fined not less than twenty-five nor more than one hundred dollars.

B. A.
O. 125.
§ 8.
SEC. 8. The Marshal, Deputy Marshal or policemen are prohibited to frequent, while on duty, places of any kind where intoxicating liquors are sold unless for the purpose of preventing a breach of the peace or to preserve quiet or good order, and for a violation of this section the fine shall be not less than five nor more than twenty-five dollars.

SEC. 9. It shall be and is hereby made the duty of the Marshal, with the approval of the Mayor, to prescribe the hours for duty of each policeman of the city, and he shall file with the Secretary, who shall place the same on file among the records of the city, a schedule, which said schedule shall contain the names of the respective policemen and the hours during which they are assigned to duty, and it shall be his duty to report all changes that may be made in said schedule as soon as the same shall be made to said Secretary who shall enter said changes on said schedule.

SEC. 10. That it shall be the duty of the Mayor or Recorder upon a conviction of any Marshal, Deputy Marshal or policeman for a violation of any section in this ordinance contained, to report the same to the City Council for their action at the next regular meeting of said Council.

SEC. 11. That this ordinance take effect and be in force from and after its publication as required by law.

Approved Sept. 13, 1877.

ORDINANCE NO. LXVIII.

An Ordinance in regard to the duties of City Marshal and the collection of Fines.

Be it ordained by the City Council of the City of Fort Worth:

SECTION 1. That the City Marshal shall attend all sittings of the Recorder's or Mayor's court and shall always assist the City Attorney, when so required, in the discovery and preparation of testimony in all cases in which the city is interested.

SEC. 2. The Marshal shall have no right to release any prisoner before conviction without bond, nor after conviction until such fine and costs as have been assessed shall be paid. The Marshal shall be subject to dismissal from office if he allows parties after conviction to go without satisfaction of judgment of the court as provided herein.

SEC. 3. That this ordinance take effect and be in force from and after its passage.

Passed Dec. 6, 1881.

ORDINANCE NO. LXIX.

An Ordinance relating to the resisting of Officers in discharge of Duty.

Be it ordained by the City Council of the City of Fort Worth:

B. A.
O. 22
§ 1.
SECTION 1. Whoever in the city shall by forcible means resist, or by threats, menaces, or gestures, or other means hinder or delay the City Marshal or any policeman in making any arrest or serving any process, or doing any other act required by him by the ordinances of this city, he or she shall be deemed guilty of a misdemeanor, and on conviction shall be fined any sum not less than five nor more than fifty dollars.

B. A.
O. 22.
§ 2.
SEC. 2. That this ordinance shall take effect and be in force from and after its publication as required by law.

Approved April 10, 1873.

ORDINANCE NO. LXX.

An Ordinance relating to Misdemeanors.

Be it ordained by the City Council of the City of Fort Worth:

B. A.
O. 14.
§ 1.
SECTION 1. That the several acts and offences specified in this ordinance are hereby prohibited in this city, and any person found guilty of any or either of them shall be subject to the penalties provided for by one or either of them respectively.

B. A.
O. 14.
§ 2.
SEC. 2. For disturbing the quiet of the city or any lawful assembly of persons, or any church or religious meeting, or any house, family or neighborhood, or person or persons, for any assault, battery or affray, a sum of not less than three nor more than fifty dollars.

B. A.
O. 14.
§ 3.
SEC. 3. For lighting a cigar or pipe, or match in any barn, stable or cellar, or any building containing straw or any combustible material, a fine of not less than five dollars.

SEC. 4. That any person who shall get drunk or be found in a state of intoxication in any public place in this city shall be

deemed guilty of a misdemeanor, and on conviction before the Mayor's or Recorder's court, shall be fined in a sum of not more than one hundred dollars for each and every such offence. A public place within the meaning of this section is any public road, street, alley, public square, inn, tavern, store, grocery, work-shop, or any place to which people commonly resort for purposes of business, recreation or amusement.
B. A.
O. 163.
§ 1.
&
B. A.
O. 209.
§§ 1 & 2.

SEC. 5. For unnecessarily obstructing any sidewalk or passage, or any street or alley, or any walk or public ground in this city with any boxes, barrels, vehicles, horse or beast of any kind, lumber, wood or any material, or for placing dirt or rubbish therein, or riding or driving over or upon any sidewalks, or digging holes in the same, any sum not exceeding twenty dollars. Provided that any person erecting buildings may for the time occupy a reasonable portion of the street in front of such building, and if any person shall continue any obstruction of any street, alley or sidewalk after he shall have been notified by the City Marshal to remove the same he shall be fined in any sum not less than five dollars for every day he shall continue the obstruction.
B. A.
O. 14.
§ 7.

SEC. 6. For beating, injuring, or treating any animal in an immoderate, cruel or unnecessary manner, a fine not exceeding fifty dollars.
B. A.
O. 14.
§ 8.

SEC. 7. That every person who shall refuse to assist the Marshal or any policeman to make an arrest or suppress any disturbance when called upon so to do, shall be fined, upon conviction, not less than three nor more than ten dollars for each offence.
B. A.
O. 14.
§ 9.

SEC. 8. That this ordinance take effect and be in force from and after its publication as required by law.
B. A.
O. 14.
§ 12.

ORDINANCE NO. LXXI.

An Ordinance prohibiting the Obstruction of Street Railways.

Be it ordained by the City Council of the City of Fort Worth:

SECTION 1. That any person who shall place obstructions of any kind on the track or rails of any street railway shall be guilty of a misdemeanor, and upon conviction thereof, shall be fined in
B. A.
O. 122.
§ 1.

any sum not less than twenty-five nor more than one hundred dollars.

B. A. O. 122. § 2.
SEC. 2. This ordinance shall take effect from and after its publication as required by law.

Approved Sept. 13. 1877.

ORDINANCE LXXII.

An Ordinance prohibiting the use of Rubber Slings or "Nigger Shooters" and the throwing of Stones or missiles of any kind in or across any street or in any public place or upon or against any building in the City of Fort Worth.

Be it ordained by the City Council of the City of Fort Worth:

B. A. O. 250. § 1.
SECTION 1. That it shall be unlawful for any person or persons to use any rubber sling or "nigger shooter" within the limits of the City of Fort Worth, or to throw any stone or missile of any kind in or across any street, alley or public place, or upon or against any house or building in the City of Fort Worth, and that any person or persons violating either of the provisions of this ordinance shall be deemed guilty of a misdemeanor, and upon conviction thereof, shall be fined in any sum not exceeding twenty-five dollars.

B. A. O. 250. § 2.
SEC. 2. That this ordinance shall take effect and be in force from and after its publication as required by law.

Approved July 18, 1881.

ORDINANCE NO. LXXIII.

An Ordinance relating to mobs.

Be it ordained by the City Council of the City of Fort Worth:

B. A. O. 25. § 1.
SECTION 1. That if any two or more persons shall, in this city assemble together with an intent, or being together shall mutually agree to do any unlawful act with force or violence against the property of this city, or against the person or property of another, or against the peace, or to the terror of another, or shall make any move-

ment or preparation therefore, and every person present at such meeting or assembly who shall directly or indirectly encourage by not endeavoring to prevent, or otherwise, the commission or perpetration of such unlawful act, such person shall be deemed guilty of a misdemeanor, and upon conviction, shall be fined not less than one nor more than fifty dollars.

SEC. 2. That this ordinance shall be in force and take effect from and after its publication as required by law.

B. A.
O. 25.
§ 2.

Approved April 10, 1873.

ORDINANCE NO. LXXIV.

An Ordinance granting right of way to the Missouri, Kansas and Texas Railway Company over and upon the streets known as Arizona avenue, Daggett's avenue and Grove street in the City of Fort Worth.

Be it ordained by the City Council of the City of Fort Worth:

SETION 1. That the Missouri, Kansas and Texas Railway Company is hereby fully authorized and empowered with the right to equip, construct and forever operate and maintain, own and control railway together with all necessary switches, turn-outs, sidings and depots on either or all of the following named streets and their extensions in said city, to wit: On Daggett's avenue and extension one block in length from Grove to Park street, on Grove street from the Texas and Pacific grounds to Arizona avenue on south line of Daggett's addition, on and over Arizona avenue to the south line of the city limits and on the streets connecting with said Arizona avenue within the limits of fifty feet from each side of the center of the tract.

B. A.
O. 247.
§ 1.

SEC. 2 This ordinance to take effect and be in force from and after its passage.

B. A.
O. 247.
§ 2.

Passed Jan. 19, 1881.

ORDINANCE NO. LXXV.

An Ordinance defaming and prohibiting certain nuisances and providing for the abatement of the same.

Be it ordained by the City Council of the City of Fort Worth:

SECTION 1. All dead, decaying or putrid carcasses, flesh, fish, fowls or vegetables, all deposits of manure or other unwholesome substances or flesh of any kind or description whatever, all filthy or offensive water or slops when thrown or conducted into or upon any street, alley, public ground or any enclosure so as to be unwholesome or offensive or liable to become unwholesome or offensive, all privies, slaughter-houses or slaughter-pens that are offensive from use, all markets, cellars, stores or other buildings or places which are not kept clean and free from filthy or unwholesome substances, all deposits or substances that are offensive or liable to engender disease ; every trade, business or occupation injurious to the health or comfort of those who reside in the vicinity, any lots, barrel or receptacle containing water or slops until it becomes stagnant, offensive or unwholesome from any cause, any article or substances placed upon any street, sidewalk, alley, gutter, drain or public ground except such as are permitted by ordinances of the city so as to obstruct the same, the throwing of glass, tin, queensware, crockery or other rubbish into or upon the streets, alleys, public thoroughfares, commons, drains or gutters, persons found asleep upon the sidewalk or on the streets, alleys or public thoroughfares, any unwholesome food, liquor, or adulterated medicines, all cattle, horse or hog pens, stable or enclosure in which any cattle horse or hog may be kept or confined which from use have become offensive, the printing, pasting, sticking or placing of any advertisement, hand bill, placard of any printed, pictured or written matter upon any house, wall, building, fence or other property private or public without the permission of the owner or person in charge thereof, any nauseous, foul or putrid liquors or substances likely to be nauseous, foul, offensive or putrid, discharged, placed, thrown or conducted into or upon any street, alley, public ground or common, the wrongful casting, throwing or depositing of any filth, substance or thing into any public or private well or cistern, all gates or doors

B. A.
O. 229
§ 1.

opening upon any public street or sidewalk upon which it opens unless such gates or door be so constructed or hung as to be self-closing, the keeping or leaving open of any cellar or trap-door or the grating of any vault in or upon any sidewalk, street, thoroughfare, or public passway, the making, keeping or permitting any uncovered opening or hole in or across any sidewalk or public passway, street or public thoroughfare, unless the same is with proper authority, and is sufficiently guarded and protected to insure the safety of all persons passing by, over or near the same ; the sweeping or depositing of paper, filth or rubbish of any kind from business houses or from private premises into the drains or gutters, or into or upon any sidewalk, street or alley or public thoroughfare, and failing to burn or remove the same, the burning of any hair, leather, rags, or substance of any kind in the city which may cause or produce an offensive smell, smoke or odor to the annoyance of persons living in the vicinity or to persons passing the same, on any public thoroughfare in said city ; defecating or urinating upon the streets, alleys, or public grounds or in any place that may be seen from a private residence or by persons passing along the streets, alleys or public thoroughfares, be and the same are each and all hereby held and declared to be nuisances, and as such are liable to be abated, and the person or persons causing, creating or keeping the same, liable to punishment as hereinafter provided.

SEC. 2. That any person or persons who shall cause, create, keep, permit or otherwise be guilty of a nuisance as defined in the first section of this ordinance, shall be deemed guilty of a misdemeanor, and upon conviction thereof, shall be fined in a sum of not less than five dollars nor more than one hundred dollars, and that each day that said nuisance shall continue shall constitute a separate offence. B. A. O. 229. § 2.

SEC. 3. In all cases arising under this ordinance whenever it shall appear to the court trying said cause that the nuisance continues at the time of conviction, the court shall order and adjudge the removal, abatement or destruction of such nuisance as the case may require and shall issue a separate warrant therefor, and the court shall inquire into the probable cost of such removal, abatement or destruction, and shall tax the costs thereof against the defendant, with the proviso that the same be remitted if the defendant obey the commands of said warrant B. A. O. 229. § 3.

without delay, without the interference of the Marshal or a policeman, such costs shall be collected by the Marshal or any policeman in the same manner that other costs are collected.

SEC. 4. It shall be the duty of the owner or his agent or the occupant of any lot, building or place of any kind in this city where any nuisance may exist, to remove, abate or destroy the same without delay, and it shall be the duty of the Marshal Deputy Marshal, policeman, or any member of the Board of Health who may be cognizant of any nuisance either of his own knowledge or from creditable information, to make complaint against the author thereof before the Mayor's court, and any officer above mentioned, failing to comply with the provisions of this section shall be deemed guilty of a misdemeanor and neglect of official duty, and upon conviction thereof, shall be fined in any sum not less than ten dollars nor more than one hundred dollars.

_{B. A.
O. 229.
§ 4.}

SEC. 5. Whenever any nuisance as defined in the first section of this ordinance is found in any place in this city, for the removal, abatement or destruction of which no one can be held liable under the provisions of this ordinance, it shall be the duty of the Marshal to remove, abate or destroy the same at the expense of this city.

_{B. A.
O. 229.
§ 5}

SEC. 6. It shall be unlawful for any scavenger or other persons to remove the contents of any privy, or other material of like offensive character situated within the city at any other hour of the day than between the hours of ten o'clock in the afternoon of any day and four o'clock in the morning of the day following, or to deposit the same at any other place than that designated by the City Council for the burial of filth, offal and dead animals, or to leave the same until he shall have properly buried or interred the same so that it shall not be offensive to persons passing said burial grounds, and that any person or persons violating either of the provisions of this section shall be fined the sum of ten dollars.

_{B. A.
O. 229
§ 6.}

SEC. 7. Every vehicle used to transfer or haul off dung, filth, offal or any offensive matter or material through the streets, alleys or public thoroughfares of the city shall be fitted with a tight box to be so constructed and loaded that no portion of the offensive matter or material therein conveyed shall escape or be scattered or left upon the street, alley or public thoroughfare, and when necessary to prevent the escape of offensive odors such box shall be tightly covered ; any scavenger or other person engaged in hauling off

_{B. A.
O. 229.
§ 7.}

dung, filth, offal or other offensive matter or material, who shall use in the business any vehicle not of the construction herein specified or who shall scatter, leave, or deposit any dung, filth, offal or offensive matter or material upon any street, alley or public thoroughfare or common, within the city, shall be fined the sum of ten dollars.

SEC. 8. That this ordinance shall take effect and shall be in force from and after its publication as required by law.

Approved April 26, 1880.

B. A.
O. 229.
§ 8.

ORDINANCE LXXVI.

An Ordinance defining and prohibiting certain nuisances.

Be it ordained by the City Council of the City of Fort Worth:

SECTION 1. Whoever shall, in this city, suffer or permit any cellar, vault, drain, pool, privy, sewer, yard, grounds or premises belonging to or controlled by him, to become from any cause nauseous, foul, offensive or injurious to the public health, or unpleasant and offensive to adjacent residents or persons, shall be deemed guilty of a nuisance, and on conviction, be fined not less than ten nor more than one hundred dollars.

B. A.
O. 255.
§ 1.

SEC. 2. The owner or occupant of any premises in the city upon which there is located a privy, shall, every third day during the months of May, June, July, August and September, of each and every year, thoroughly disinfect said privy with lime or other disinfectant.

B. A.
O. 255
§ 2.

SEC. 3. Whoever fails, refuses or neglects to comply with § 2 of this ordinance, shall, on conviction thereof, be fined not less than ten nor more than one hundred dollars.

B. A.
O. 255.
§ 3

SEC. 4. Whereas there is an urgent necessity for said ordinance, the same shall take effect and be in force from and after its passage.

B. A.
O. 255.
§ 4

Approved Aug. 3, 1881.

ORDINANCE NO. LXXVII.

An Ordinance prohibiting opium smoking.

Be it ordained by the City Council of the City of Fort Worth:

B. B.
O. 309.
§ 1.
SECTION 1. That it shall be unlawful for any one to smoke opium within the corporate limits of said city.

B. B.
O. 309.
§ 2.
SEC. 2. Any person violating section one of this ordinance shall be deemed guilty of a misdemeanor and fined not less than five nor more than fifty dollars.

B. B.
O. 309.
§ 3.
SEC. 3. Any person who shall keep a house, room or place where opium smokers visit, or a place of resort for opium smokers, in said city, shall be fined in any sum not less than ten nor more than one hundred dollars.

B. B.
O. 309.
§ 4.
SEC. 4. Any person visiting an opium den in said city for the purpose of opium smoking, shall be fined in any sum not exceeding fifty dollars nor less than five dollars.

B. B.
O. 309.
§ 5.
SEC. 5. Any place where opium smoking is carried on is an opium den.

B. B.
O. 309.
§ 6.
SEC. 6. That this ordinance take effect from and after its publication.

Approved Aug. 3, 1883.

ORDINANCE NO. LXXVIII.

An Ordinance to prevent the keeping, raising and breeding of pigeons in said city.

Be it ordained by the City Council of the City of Fort Worth:

B. A.
O. 297.
§ 1
SECTION 1. It shall hereafter be unlawful for any person or persons to keep, raise or breed pigeons within the corporate limits of said city.

B. A.
O. 297.
§ 2
SEC. 2. Any person or persons keeping, raising or breeding pigeons, and any person or persons having in their possession, or having in or about their premises any pigeons with intent to keep, raise or breed the same, within the corporate limits of said city,

shall be deemed guilty of a nuisance, and on conviction thereof, shall be fined in any sum not less than five dollars nor more than twenty-five dollars.

Sec. 3. That this ordinance shall take effect and be in force from and after its publication by law.

Passed November 29, 1882.

B. A.
O. 297.
§ 3.

ORDINANCE NO. LXXIX.

An Ordinance regulating the Duties of the Police of the City of Fort Worth.

Be it ordained by the City Council of the City of Fort Worth:

Section 1. The regular police force of this city shall consist of the Marshal as Chief of Police, and of such number of policemen as the City Council may from time to time authorize and by resolution appoint.

B. A.
O. 155.
§ 1

Sec. 2. That upon the appointment of any policeman by the Council, the Mayor shall issue to him a commission as such, and upon receipt of such commission the person so appointed shall before entering upon the duties of his office take and subscribe the oath of office prescribed by the Constitution of the State and the Charter of the city, and shall execute to the City of Fort Worth a bond with one or more sufficient securities, to be approved by the Mayor, in the sum of five hundred dollars for the faithful performance of his duties.

B. A.
O. 155.
§ 2.

Sec. 3. It shall be the duty of the policemen to keep a faithful watch, and work in the district assigned them, and to arrest and detain without warrants all offenders against the peace and all persons who may obstruct, hinder or endanger them or either of them in the discharge of their duties, or who shall be guilty of any disorderly conduct, or engage in a riot, unlawful assembly, outcries, noises or other disturbances, and for this purpose said Marshal and policemen are authorized to enter any house where any person may take refuge or be, to arrest any person who has in their presence or hearing been guilty of any offence against the peace of the city, or may enter any house where any breach of the peace is about to be

B. A.
O. 155.
§ 3

committed, or where any unusual noise, alarm, outcry, or disturbance shall be made.

B. A.
O. 155
§ 4.
SEC. 4. The Marshal shall with the approval of the Mayor, assign to each policeman his particular district and the hours of duty.

B. A.
O. 155.
§ 5.
SEC. 5. It shall be the duty of each and every member of the police force to arrest without warrant all persons found in suspicious places or under circumstances which reasonably show that such persons have been guilty of some felony or breach of the peace.

B. A.
O. 155.
§ 6.
SEC. 6. In all cases of the arrest of any person or persons without warrant, the officer making the arrest shall take the person arrested forthwith before the Mayor's court if in session. If said court is not in session the officer shall commit the person or persons arrested to the city prison or calaboose, there to be kept securely in custody until said court shall be in session. Provided that the Marshal or his deputy or any member of the regular police force may take good and sufficient bail for the appearance of such offenders before the Mayor's court.

B. A.
O. 155.
§ 7.
SEC. 7. No person shall be appointed a member of the police force who does not possess a good moral character.

B. A.
O. 155.
§ 8.
SEC. 8. It shall be the duty of every policeman to arrest without warrant any person who in his presence violates any ordinance of the city, or when informed by any credible person that another has violated any ordinance or State law and is about to escape.

B. A.
O. 155.
§ 9.
SEC. 9. The Marshal shall devote his whole time to the discharge of his duties, and shall see that the laws and ordinances are enforced as far as possible by those under his command, and shall see that policemen are on duty during the whole time of their watch, and shall in no case absent himself from the city without notifying the Mayor of his intended absence. He shall keep a record in a book to be provided by the Council, of all persons committed to the prison, the offence with which such person is charged, the date of his committment and release, and a description of such property, money or valuables as the arrested party may have, and and he shall at the first regular meeting of the Council in each month, and as often as may be required by the Mayor, make a report in writing of the doings of his department during the month perceeding. Said report shall set forth all arrests made, the nature of the charge and

how disposed of, and a statement of all property received by him and how disposed of.

SEC. 10. The Marshal, Deputy Marshal and all policemen shall obey all orders of the Mayor or of the City Council when in session, and shall to the best of their ability preserve order, quiet, and peace throughout the city, and enforce all ordinances of the city. Every policeman shall report to the Marshal all persons known or suspected to be gamblers, receivers of stolen property, theives, burglars, or disorderly persons, and all unlawful or disorderly houses or places within the city, and when it shall come to the knowledge of any member of the police force that any ordinance has been violated, such member shall forthwith report the same to the City Attorney, who shall cause a proper complaint to be made and evidence procured for the prosecution of the offender. <small>B. A. O. 155. § 10.</small>

SEC. 11. The Mayor or Council may, on application being made to them, appoint any suitable person in the employ of any corporation, association, firm, or individual, a special policeman, in and for the city. Special policemen shall have all the qualifications of the regular police, shall take and subcribe the same oath, and may exercise the same powers, subject to the same regulations of the regular police. But special policemen shall not be paid anything by the city for their services. <small>B. A. O. 155. § 11.</small>

SEC. 12. The Mayor shall at the time of appointing policemen assign each a number, said members shall rank according to their number, one being the highest, two, next, and so on, and in all cases the policeman present having the highest number (in the absence of the Marshal) shall be obeyed by subordinates. <small>B. A. O. 155 § 12.</small>

The following rules for the general government of the police department are adopted:

First.—No member of the police force shall follow any other business or occupation.

Second.—All members of the force must be prepared to act whenever their services are demanded by a superior officer is in view of a violation of any ordinance or law, at all times.

Third.—No member of the police force shall, while on duty, drink any intoxicating liquor, wine or beer, or enter any place where such liquors are sold, or any billiard hall, gambling house or house of ill-fame, except to execute process, or to make an arrest in cases herein authorized to be made without warrant

Fourth.—No member of the force shall, while off duty, frequent any saloon, gambling house, or house of ill-fame or prostitution.

Fifth.—Members of the force shall be civil and respectful to the public, and shall not while on duty, use any violent, intemperate, or abusive language.

Sixth.—Each member shall always have with him a memorandum book, in which he shall enter the names and residences of persons who may be necessary for evidence against the party.

Seventh.—Policemen must report to the Marshal or City Attorney all houses where idlers, gamblers, prostitutes, or other disorderly persons are in the habit of congregating.

Eighth.—Policemen shall caution strangers and others against going into places where idlers, gamblers, or prostitutes congregate, and against all vicious persons. They shall also direct strangers and others needing directions the nearest and safest way to their destination.

B. A. O. 155. § 13.
Sec. 13. That this ordinance take effect and be in force from and after its passage.

Approved May 11, 1878.

ODINANCE NO. LXXX.

An Ordinance creating the office of pound keeper and regulating the powers and duties thereof and prohibiting the running at large of hogs, shoats and pigs, and punishing persons breaking into pound or hindering keeper.

Be it ordained by the City Council of the City of Fort Worth:

Section 1. There shall be appointed by the City Council, in and for said city, a pound keeper who shall, before entering on the duties of his office, execute a bond to the City of Fort Worth in the sum of two hundred dollars, with one or more sureties, to be approved by the Mayor, conditioned for the faithful performance of the duties of pound keeper and the observance of all ordinances and regulations of the City Council relating to the impounding of animals, which bond shall be filed with the City Secretary.

B. A. O. 162. § 1.

Sec. 2. The City Pound Keeper shall provide within the city

a pound suitably constructed for impounding of such animals, and shall designate the location of said pound and report the same to the City Council at the first meeting after providing the same, and shall also post on the door of the engine room of the City Hall a notice stating the location of such pound, naming the lot and street on which located.

SEC. 3. It shall be the duty of the Pound Keeper to take up and impound all animals found running at large in violation of any ordinance of this city and also to receive and impound any such animal when taken up by any other authorized person, and shall during the time such animal shall remain in the pound, feed and water the same; the cost of which as also the impounding fees, the claimant of such animal shall pay to the Pound Keeper before such animal shall be released.

SEC. 4. It shall be the duty of the Marshal and policemen to forthwith take up and drive to the pound any hog, shoat or pig found running at large in violation of the ordinances of the city.

SEC. 5. Any person who is injured or is in danger of being injured in his property by reason of the unlawful running at large of any hog, shoat or pig, may drive the same to the pound or may confine the same in some safe place until he can notify the Pound Keeper or a policeman of the fact, and the officer so notified shall forthwith take such animal and impound the same.

SEC. 6. The owner or person entitled to the possession of any impounded hog, shoat or pig, may redeem the same by paying to the Pound Keeper the impounding fees and cost of feeding and sustenance up to the time of redemption, but if no person appear and redeem such impounded animal within forty-eight hours after the impounding of the same, it shall be the duty of the Pound Keeper to advertise and sell such animal at public auction at the City Pound for cash in hand, after giving five days' notice by posting written or printed notices of the time and place of such sale at the door of the engine room and at one public place in each ward of the city, which notice shall contain a full description of the animals to be sold, and each animal shall be sold separately and the money arising therefrom shall, after the expenses of impounding, feeding and selling are deducted, be paid over to the treasurer, and shall by him be kept for the benefit of the owner and paid to such owner by order of the Mayor, on satisfactory proof of ownership; provided, that should no owner appear and claim the same within sixty days from the date of such sale, the same shall be transferred to the current expense fund of the city.

B. A.
O. 162.
§ 7
SEC. 7. The Pound Keeper shall keep a book which shall be open to the inspection of all persons, in which he shall record a discription of all animals impounded, giving size, color, sex and marks, with the date of impounding each animal, by whom impounded and the disposition made of such animal, when and by whom redeemed, and in case of sale, the date of the sale, name of the purchaser, and amount for which same was sold and each animal shall be numbered in the order in which impounded.

B. A.
O. 162
§ 8.
SEC. 8. No animal impounded as herein provided shall be released by the Pound Keeper unless the claimant shall make affidavit before some officer authorized by law to administer oaths, that he is the rightful owner or entitled to the possession of such animal, in which the number of the animal, as it appears on the record of the Pound Keeper shall be stated, which affidavit shall be returned with the receipt of such claimant by the Pound Keeper to the City Council.

B. A.
O. 162
§ 9.
SEC. 9. The Pound Keeper shall, at the first regular meeting of the City Council, in each month, make a written report, under oath, of the number of animals impounded and the disposition made of each.

B. A.
O. 162
§ 10.
SEC. 10. The following fees shall be allowed for impounding and feeding animals at large contrary to ordinances: To the Pound Keeper or policeman for taking up and impounding each hog, shoat or pig, fifty cents; to the Pound Keeper for keeping and feeding each hog, shoat or pig, fifteen cents per day; to the Pound Keeper for receiving each hog, shoat or pig taken up and driven to the pound by any policeman, ten cents; to the Pound Keeper for advertising and selling any animal as herein provided, five per cent. of the proceeds of such sale.

B. A.
O. 109
§ 5
SEC. 11. That if any person or persons shall break open or in any manner, directly or indirectly, aid or assist in breaking open any pen or enclosure with the intent of releasing any hog, shoat or pig or other animal therein impounded, pursuant to the provisions of any ordinance of this city, he, she or they shall be deemed guilty of a misdemeanor, and upon conviction thereof, shall be fined in any sum not less than fifty nor more than one hundred dollars.

SEC. 12. If any person or persons shall hinder, delay or obstruct any officer in the performance of any duty herein enjoined, or enjoined by any other ordinance of this city in regard to impounding animals, he, she or they shall be deemed guilty of a misdemeanor, and on conviction shall be fined in any sum not less than ten nor more than fifty dollars. B. A. O. 109 § 6.

SEC. 13. That it shall be unlawful for the owner of any hog, shoat or pig to allow the same to run at large within the corporate limits of the city, and any person violating the provisions of this section, shall, on conviction thereof, be fined in any sum not less than one nor more than one hundred dollars. B. A. O. 109 § 8 & B. A. O. 149. § 1

SEC. 14. That this ordinance shall take effect and be in force from and after its passage.

Approved July 17, 1878.

ORDINANCE NO. LXXXI.

An Ordinance in relation to the Poor and Dead.

Be it ordained by the City Council of the City of Fort Worth:

SECTION 1. That it shall be lawful, and it is hereby made the duty of the Mayor that whenever it shall come to his knowledge that any person or persons in said city are sick or in destitute condition he shall furnish such person or persons with the necessary means of support and such medical aid as may be deemed requisite by him, until such time as they shall be otherwise provided for, the expenses of which shall be borne by the city. B. A. O. 18 § 1

SEC. 2. Whenever any person shall die within the limits of this city who has not at the time of his or her death means sufficient to defray their burial expenses, the Mayor, at his discretion, may furnish the means to defray the expenses of such burial, provided that the same shall be done in a plain and inexpensive but decent manner. B. A. O. 18. § 2.

SEC. 3. This ordinance to take effect and be in force from and after its passage. B. A. O. 18. § 3

Approved April 10, 1873.

ORDINANCE NO. LXXXII.

An Ordinance to prohibit male persons from riding, walking or prominading the streets, alleys or other public grounds of the city with any prostitute or woman of ill-fame, commonly denominated whores.

Be it ordained by the City Council of the City of Fort Worth:

B. A. O. 99 § 1.

SECTION 1. That it shall be unlawful for any male person or persons to ride or drive in any hack, buggy or other vehicle, or ride on horseback with any prostitute or woman of ill-fame, commonly denominated as whores, in or upon any street, alley or other public ground of the city between the hours of four o'clock a. m. and nine o'clock p. m. Provided that the drivers of licensed hacks or passage vehicles shall not be included in the provisions of this ordinance.

B. A. O. 92 § 2.

SEC. 2. That it shall be unlawful for any male person or persons to walk or prominade with any prostitute, or woman of ill-fame, commonly denominated whores, in or upon any street, alley or other public ground of the city.

B. A. O. 92. § 3

SEC. 3. That any person or persons violating the provisions of this ordinance shall be deemed guilty of a misdemeanor, and upon conviction, thereof, shall be fined in any sum not less than ten nor more than fifty dollars.

B. A. O. 92. § 4

SEC. 4. That this ordinance shall take effect and be in force from and after its publication, as required by law.

Approved Dec. 27, 1876.

ORDINANCE NO. LXXXIII.

An Ordinance prohibiting lewd women or women of bad repute being employed in Saloons or other Public Places as Waiters or Bar-tenders.

Be it ordained by the City Council of the City of Fort Worth:

B. A. O. 211. § 1

SECTION 1 That it shall be unlawful for the proprietor or keeper of any saloon, beer house, or other place of public resort to employ any lewd women or women having the reputation of a prostitute as a carrier of beer or other article sold in such place, or to permit any lewd woman of bad repute to act as a carrier of beer or as a bartender in such place, and any person violating any of the provisions of this ordinance, shall, on conviction thereof, be fined not less than ten dollars nor more than fifty dollars.

SEC. 2. That this ordinance take effect and be in force from and after its publication as required by law.

Approved Sept. 17, 1879.

B. A.
O. 211.
§ 2.

ORDINANCE NO. LXXXIV.

An Ordinance relating to the Public Peace.

Be it ordained by the City Council of the City of Fort Worth:

SECTION 1. That if any person shall, in this city, by violent, tumultuous, offensive or obstreperous conduct, or carriage, or by loud or unusual noise, or by unseemly, profane, or offensive langauge, calculated to provoke a breach of the peace, or by assaulting, striking or fighting each other, wilfully disturb the peace of the city or of others, he or she shall be deemed guilty of a misdemeanor.

B. A.
O. 24.
§ 1

SEC. 2. That if any person shall, in this city, permit such conduct in or upon any house or premises owned or possessed by him, or under his management or control, so that others in the vicinity are disturbed thereby, he or she shall be deemed guilty of a misdemeanor.

B. A.
O. 24.
§ 2

SEC. 3. That any person violating either of the provisions of this ordinance shall be fined in any sum not less than five nor more than fifty dollars upon conviction thereof.

B. A.
O. 24.
§ 3.

SEC. 4. That this ordinance take effect and be in force from and after its publication as required by law.

B. A.
O. 24.
§ 4.

Approved April 10, 1873.

ORDINANCE NO. LXXXV.

An Ordinance defining and punishing Affrays and Disturbances of the Peace.

Be it ordained by the City Council of the City of Fort Worth:

SECTION 1. If any two or more persons shall fight together

in a public place they shall be punished by fine not exceeding one hundred dollars.

SEC. 2. If any person shall go into any public place, or into or near any private house, or along any public street or highway near any private house, and shall use loud and vociferous, or obscene, vulgar, or indecent language, or swear or curse, or expose his person, or rudely display any pistol or other deadly weapon in such public place, or upon such public street or highway, or near such private house, in a manner calculated to disturb the inhabitants thereof, he shall be fined in a sum not exceeding one hundred dollars.

SEC. 3. A public place, within the meaning of the two preceding sections, is any public road, street or alley, inn, tavern, store, grocery, workshop, or any place to which people resort for purposes of business, recreation or amusement.

SEC. 4. That this ordinance take effect and be in force from and after its publication as required by law.

Passed Sept. 4, 1879.

ORDINANCE NO. LXXXVI.

An Ordinance prohibiting the ringing of Bells, blowing of Horns or Bugles, or other noisy practices or performances tending to annoy persons passing in the streets or sidewalks, or frighten horses or teams.

Be it ordained by the City Council of the City of Fort Worth:

SECTION 1. That it shall be unlawful for any person or persons to ring any bell or blow any horn or bugle, or beat any drum or to make any loud noise, or to be guilty of any practice, performance or amusement tending to annoy other persons passing in the streets or sidewalks, or tending to frighten horses or teams within this city.

SEC. 2. That any person or persons violating the provisions of the first section of this ordinance shall be deemed guilty of a misdemeanor, and upon conviction thereof, shall be fined in any sum not less than five dollars nor more than one hundred dollars.

SEC. 3. That nothing in the first section of this ordinance

shall be so construed as to prevent the mayor from granting permits for the playing of bands in parades or processions. Provided, that whenever any accident or damage to person or property is occasioned by reason of the playing of any band, the parties engaged in such playing shall be held responsible and not the city.

B. A.
O. 291
§ 3.

SEC. 4. That this ordinance shall take effect and be in force from and after its publication as required by law.

B. A.
O 291.
§ 4

Passed Oct. 19, 1882.

ORDINANCE NO. LXXXVII.

An Ordinance establishing Quarantine Regulations.

Be it ordained by the City Council of the City of Fort Worth:

SECTION 1. There shall be appointed by the Mayor with the advice and consent of the City Council a quarantine physician, who shall be a regular graduate of some medical school, and at the time of his appointment engaged in the pursuit of his profession.

B. A.
O. 167.
§ 1.

SEC. 2. A point on the Texas and Pacific railroad, ten miles east of Fort Worth is hereby established as a quarantine station for the City of Fort Worth, and the same shall be subject to the regulations herein prescribed or that may be prescribed.

B. A.
O. 167.
§ 2

SEC. 3. All passenger coaches, freight cars, mail or baggage cars, and all persons arriving at said station from any place or places beyond the limits of the county of Tarrant, shall immediately upon their arrival stop at the place assigned for quarantine, and shall there remain with their officers, employees or passengers during the time prescribed by the quarantine physician, not exceeding twenty days.

B. A.
O. 167.
§ 3

SEC. 4. The quarantine physician shall forthwith upon the arrival of any train at said station cause such train and each car with freight and clothing to be disinfected and purified under such rules as said physician may prescribe, and said physician may, if in his discretion necessary to prevent spreading of any infectious disease, cause all freight or clothing to be destroyed or securely stored.

B. A.
O. 167.
§ 4.

SEC. 5. It shall be the duty of the conductor or persons in

charge of any train on arriving at said station to make report to the quarantine physician of the place from whence such train and each coach thereof came, of each and every person on board, and the place from which each person, baggage, freight, or package may have come, and when required by the physician shall exhibit all tickets taken by him from those on board his train, or bills showing from what points any freight or baggage or package have been shipped, and no person, freight or baggage or package of any kind shall be allowed to leave such train or quarantine station without the written permission of the quarantine physician.

SEC. 6. It shall be unlawful for any conductor or person in charge of any train to put off any passenger or person, baggage, mail or package, or to unload or tranship any freight before his train shall have been examined by the quarantine physician.

SEC. 7. It shall be the duty of every conductor or person in charge of a train to stop his train only at the place assigned for quarantine, to submit his train, cargo, freight, passengers and employees to the examination of the quarantine physician, and to furnish all necessary information to enable that officer to determine the right of quarantine, to remain with his train, freights or passengers at quarantine during the time assigned by the quarantine physician, and to comply with the directions, regulations or orders given by the quarantine physician.

SEC. 8. All expenses incident to the removal and care of persons, freights or baggage at said quarantine station, shall be paid by such persons or owners of such baggage or freight.

SEC. 9. All persons are prohibited leaving any train or coach upon arrival at said station without permission of the quarantine physician.

SEC. 10. All persons coming from Memphis, New Orleans or other places infected with yellow fever or other infectious diseases since the first day of August, 1878 are prohibited coming into the City of Fort Worth without written permission of the quarantine physician.

SEC. 11. The quarantine physician may appoint one or more assistants, who shall possess the same qualifications, and while acting under his authority or directions shall have the same power and authority.

SEC. 12. No driver of any kind of vehicle shall transport

or deliver any person, baggage, mail or freight brought from any place or places infected with yellow fever or other infectious diseases.

B. A. O. 167 § 12

SEC. 13. It shall be the duty of all keepers of hotels, boarding houses, to report the arrival of all persons coming from places infected with yellow fever or contagious diseases who may apply for board or lodging, to the mayor.

B. A. O. 167 § 13.

SEC. 14. Any person violating any or either of the provisions of this ordinance, shall on conviction thereof, be fined not less than fifty nor more than one hundred dollars, and in addition thereto be liable to fifteen days imprisonment.

B. A. O. 167 § 14.

SEC. 15. That the provisions of this ordinance shall be in force, on proclamation to that effect, by the Mayor of the City of Fort Worth, without further publication than the notice contained in such proclamation, and the Board of Health are authorized and empowered to pass such additional rules, not inconsistent with the laws of the state, as they may deem expedient, to prevent contagion, and for the government of quarantine stations.

B. A. O. 167. § 15

SEC. 16. That this ordinance take effect and be in force from and after its publication.

B. A. O. 167. § 16.

Approved Aug 21, 1878.

ORDINANCE NO. LXXXVIII.

An Ordinance regulating trials before the Mayor's Court and proceedings therein.

Be it ordained by the City Council of the City of Fort Worth:

SECTION 1. That in all cases of misdemeanors in violation of the ordinances of this city, the party accused shall be tried before the Mayor's or Recorder's court.

B. A. O. 26. § 1.

SEC. 2. That the proceedings in said court, when there is no specific provision in the act of incorporation, or by ordinance, in regard thereto, shall be governed by the laws of the State of Texas regulating proceedings in the justices' courts.

B. A. O. 26. § 2.

SEC. 3. That when an application is made for a jury in the Mayor's Court, the Mayor shall direct the Marshal to summon six disinterested qualified electors within the city to serve as a jury, unless the parties agree to a less number; and any person so summoned, who shall fail or refuse to attend, without showing good and sufficient cause for such failure or refusal, may be fined by the Mayor in any sum not exceeding twenty dollars, for the use of the city.

B. A.
O. 26.
§ 3.

SEC. 4. That either the prosecutor or defendant in all trials before the Mayor, may, without cause or reason assigned therefor, challenge two of the jurors summoned as aforesaid, when it shall be the duty of the Marshal to summon additional jurors to fill the vacancy.

B. A.
O. 26.
§ 4.

SEC. 5. The Mayor shall have power to punish all persons guilty of a contempt of his court by a fine not exceeding fifty dollars, and by imprisonment not exceeding twenty-four hours in the calaboose of the city, or by both fine and imprisonment, and he may commit such person until the fine imposed is paid; provided, that no one shall be imprisoned for a greater time than ten days, and that all warrants of commitment for contempt, shall set forth specifically the facts constituting the contempt.

B. A.
O. 26.
§ 5.

SEC. 6 Any person arrested for a violation of an ordinance of this city may be admitted to bail by executing a bond payable to the City of Fort Worth, with good and sufficient security, to be approved by the Mayor or Marshal, in double the amount of the highest penalty provided by ordinance for the offence alleged, conditioned that he or she will appear upon a day and at an hour therein named, before the Mayor's Court, to answer for the offence of which he or she is accused and there to await his or her trial and to appear from time to time until the case is finally disposed of, and which said bond shall be returned to the Mayor and filed among the records of his office.

B. A.
O. 26.
§ 6.

SEC. 7. When a person has entered into a bond as mentioned in the preceeding section, and his or her name is called at the door of the court room, on the day and at the time designated in the bond, or at any time during the day after said designated time, whenever the case shall be reached on the docket, and he or she shall fail to appear, a forfeiture of said bond shall be taken.

B. A.
O. 26
§ 7.

SEC. 8. Bail bonds shall be forfeited in like manner as the same are forfeited in the District Court, except that the *sciere focias* shall be made returnable on the first Monday in the month following the rendition of the judgment *nisi* and said judgment shall be made final unless for cause shown as required by law in cases of forfeiture in the District Court.

SEC. 9. That any person who may be adjudged to pay any fine and costs for a violation of any penal ordinance of this city, and who shall fail or refuse to pay the same, shall be committed to work on the streets or other public works of the city, and it shall be the duty of the Marshal to put such person to work on the streets or public works until such fine and costs are fully paid, subject, however, to the provisions and restrictions contained in the act incorporating this city, and in case any person shall fail or refuse to work as aforesaid, it shall be the duty of the Marshal to commit said person to the calaboose of the city, where he or she shall be fed on bread and water until he or she shall consent to work; provided that every person so committed to work shall be required to work only at such labor as his or her health will permit, and not to exceed eight hours each day.

SEC. 10. In all cases where a defendant is acquitted, the informant or prosecutor may be adjudged to pay the costs if it appear to the Mayor that the prosecution was instituted vexatiously or without probable cause; provided the informant or prosecutor is not an officer of the city.

Approved April 12, 1873.

ORDINANCE NO. LXXXIX.

An Ordinance authorizing the Mayor to remit fines.

Be it ordained by the City Council of the City of Fort Worth:

SECTION 1. That the Mayor shall have the right, in his discretion, to remit all or any portion of any fine or penalty imposed by him.

SEC. 2. That this ordinance take effect and be in force from and after its passage.

Passed April 18, 1878.

ORDINANCE NO. XC.

An Ordinance establishing the office of Recorder in and for the City of Fort Worth.

Be it ordained by the City Council of the City of Fort Worth:

B. A.
O. 270.
§ 1.
SECTION 1. That the office of Recorder for the City of Fort Worth be and the same is hereby established.

SEC. 2. The Recorder appointed by the City Council, shall, before entering upon the discharge of the duties of his office, execute
B. A.
O. 270.
§ 2.
a bond payable to the City of Fort Worth, in the sum of five hundred dollars, with security, to be approved by the Mayor, conditioned that he will faithfully perform all the duties of said office.

SEC. 3. All ordinances regulating proceedings in the Mayor's Court shall apply to proceedings in the Recorder's Court when not in conflict with the laws of the State.

SEC. 4. That this ordinance shall take effect and be in force from and after its passage.

Approved May 2, 1882.

ORDINANCE NO. XCI.

An Ordinance granting the Right of Way to the Rosedale Street Railway Company over and upon South Main Street in the City of Fort Worth.

Be it ordained by the City Council of the City of Fort Worth:

B. B.
O. 323.
§ 1.
SECTION 1. That in consideration of the stipulations and agreements, hereinafter contained, to be kept and performed by the Rosedale Street Railway Company, a corporation existing under and by virtue of the laws of the State of Texas, said Rosedale Street Railway Company is hereby granted the right of way over, along, and upon the streets hereinafter disignated, for the purpose of laying the track of a street railway and operating the same thereon.

B. B.
O. 323.
§ 2.
SEC. 2. Said street railway shall run over and upon the following streets in the following manner, beginning at Front Street on Main Street, and thence running southward on South Main Street to the city limits.

Sec. 3. Said corporation shall have the right to lay, erect, construct and put down their track in the center of said street, together with such a number of switches, spurs, turning tables and side tracks as may be necessary for the proper and advantageous conduct of the said Street Railway Line.

B. B. O. 323. § 3.

Sec. 4. Said right of way and privileges are granted upon the following conditions, viz. :—

B. B. O. 323. § 4

First.—That said corporation shall construct and have in operation and in good running order all of said line within six months from the passage of this ordinance.

Second.—That said corporation shall keep in good repair all street crossings along the line of their track, and that the track of said railway shall be laid in such manner as not to obstruct travel.

Third.—That said corporation shall keep level with the grade of the streets as adopted by the City Council, the space between their tracks, and for eighteen inches on each side thereof with similar material to that with which the balance of the street over which it passes may be constructed, and shall have the top of their rails on a level with the surface of said streets.

Fourth.—That said corporation shall at all times be subject to the police ordinances and regulations now existing or which may be adopted by the City Council under and by virtue of their power and authority to pass ordinances for the regulation and government of streets and railways.

Sec. 5. That this ordinance shall take effect and be in force from and after its passage.

Passed April 4, 1884.

ORDINANCE NO. XCII.

An Ordinance amendatory of an ordinance granting the Right of Way to the Rosedale Street Railway Company over and upon South Main Street in the City of Fort Worth.

Be it ordained by the City Council of the City of Fort Worth:

Section 1. That an ordinance entitled An Ordinance granting the Right of Way to the Rosedale Street Railway Company

B. B. O. 326. § 1.

over and upon South Main Street in the City of Fort Worth, and approved on the —— day of —— 1884, be, and the same is hereby amended in so far that § 2, of said ordinance shall be read as follows :

Said railway shall run over and upon the following streets, in the following manner, beginning at the south end of South Main Street running thence along South Main Street to Anne Street, thence along Anne Street to Galveston Avenue, thence along Galveston Avenue to Broadway, thence along Broadway to Jennings Avenue, thence along Jennings Avenue to Throckmorton Street, thence along Throckmorton Street to Fourth Street, thence along Fourth Street to Houston Street, thence along Houston Street to Weatherford Street, thence along Weatherford Street to Pecan Street, thence along Pecan Street to Bluff Street, thence along Bluff Street to Elm Street, thence along Elm Street to Samuel Street, thence along Samuel Street to the terminus of said street.

And that sub-section first of § 4 of said ordinance shall read as follows :—

That said corporation shall construct and shall have in good running order, all that portion of said line extending from the south end of Main Street to the Public Square, within six months from and after the passage of this ordinance, and the remaining portion of said line within one year from and after the passage of this ordinance.

SEC. 2. Said corporation shall lay down, maintain, and build from Fourth Street on Houston Street to Weatherford Street, a tram rail.

SEC. 3. Said Company shall keep and maintain said track in safe and proper condition so as not to obstruct travel, and shall leave all streets that said track may traverse in as good condition as said streets were before said tracks were put down on said streets.

SEC. 4. This ordinance shall take effect and be in force from and after its passage.

Passed May 8, 1884.

ORDINANCE XCIII.

An Ordinance amendatory of an ordinance granting the right of way to the Rosedale Street Railway Company over and upon South Main Street in the City of Fort Worth.

Be it ordained by the City Council of the City of Fort Worth :

SECTION 1. That an ordinance entitled An Ordinance granting the right of way to the Rosedale Street Railway Company over and upon South Main street in the City of Fort Worth and approved —— day of ————, 1884, be and the same is hereby amended in so far that said company shall be granted the right to construct their line of street railway over and upon Houston street, from Fourth street to Ninth street, thence along Ninth street and Hyde Park to Jenning's avenue, and that that portion of said ordinance granting right of way over and upon Throckmorton street be and the same is hereby repealed, provided that all of said railway track shall be with tram or Johnson rail from Pecan street on Weatherford street to Houston street, and on Houston street from Weatherford street to Ninth street, the road bed and eighteen inches on either side of the rail shall be paved with Telford-McAdam, and good and substantial crossings shall be made on all cross streets not less than thirty feet wide, and at a grade of one to ten ; no side track shall be constructed longer than one hundred and seventy-five feet, and shall cross no street.

B. B. O. 332. § 1.

SEC. 2 This ordinance shall take effect and be in force from and after its passage.

Passed June 20, 1884.

B. B. O. 332. § 2.

ORDINANCE NO. XCIV.

An Ordinance granting the right of way to the Rosedale Street Railway Company over and upon certain streets in the City of Fort Worth.

Be it ordained by the City Council of the City of Fort Worth:

SECTION 1. That in consideration of the stipulations and

ORDINANCES OF THE CITY OF FORT WORTH.

B. B.
O. 333.
§ 1

agreements hereinafter contained, to be kept and performed by the Rosedale Street Railway Company, a corporation existing under and by virtue of the laws of the State of Texas, the said Rosedale Street Railway Company is hereby granted the right of way over and upon the streets hereinafter designated for the purpose of constructing a street railway and operating the same thereon.

B. B.
O. 333.
§ 2.

SEC. 2. That said street railway shall run over and upon the following streets and in the following manner, to-wit: Beginning at Houston street, at the intersection of said street with Ninth street, thence running along Houston street to Fifteenth street, thence along Fifteenth street to the Gulf, Colorado and Santa Fe Railway.

B. B.
O. 333
§ 3

SEC. 3. Said corporation shall have the right to lay, erect, construct and put down their track in the center of said streets, together with such a number of switches, spurs, turntables and sidetracks as may be necessary for the proper and advantageous conduct of said street railway.

B. B.
O. 333.
§ 4.

SEC. 4. Said right of way and privileges are granted upon the following conditions, to-wit:

First.—That said corporation shall construct and have in operation all that portion of said line extending from the intersection of Houston and Ninth streets to the Gulf, Colorado and Santa Fe Railway within six months from and after the passage of this ordinance.

Second.—That said corporation shall keep in good repair all street crossings along the line of their track, and that the track of said railway shall be laid in such manner as not to obstruct travel.

Third.—That said corporation shall keep level with the grade, as adopted by the City Council, of the streets over which their rail passes, the space between their tracks and for eighteen inches on each side thereof shall be paved with the Telford-McAdam and shall have the top of their rails on a level with the surface of said streets.

Fourth.—That said corporation shall at all times be subject to the police ordinances and regulations now existing and which may be adopted by the City Council under and by virtue of their power and authority to pass ordinances for the regulation and government of street railways.

B. B.
O. 333.
§ 5

SEC. 5. That all of said railway track shall be laid with the tram or Johnson rail from Ninth, on Houston, street to Fifteenth street and on Fifteenth street to the Gulf, Colorado and Santa Fe Railway.

SEC. 6. That good and substantial crossings shall be made on all cross streets not less than thirty feet wide and at a grade of one to ten. No side track shall be constructed longer than one hundred and seventy-five feet, and shall not cross any street.

B. B.
O. 333
§ 6

SEC. 7. That the report of the committee on streets, alleys and side-walks, filed June the 20th, 1884, be made a part of this ordinance.

B. B.
O. 333
§ 7.

SEC. 8. That this ordinance shall take effect from and after its passage.

B. B.
O. 333.
§ 8

Passed June 20, 1884.

ORDINANCE NO. XCV.

An Ordinance relating to the gathering up and burning of combustible material near buildings.

Be it ordained by the City Council of the City of Fort Worth:

SECTION 1. That all persons owning or occupying houses within this city, either already built or in process of erection, are hereby required to remove or take to a safe distance and burn, all shavings, rags, paper or other combustible matter in and around such house.

B. A.
O. 28.
§ 1

SEC. 2. Any person failing to comply with the provisions of this ordinance, after notification by the City Marshal to remove or burn said combustible matter as above specified, shall, upon conviction, be fined not less than one nor more than ten dollars, and shall be subject to a like fine for each and every day he permits said combustible matter to remain after notification as above specified.

B. A.
O. 28.
§. 2.

SEC. 3. That this ordinance shall be in force and take effect from and after its publication as required by law.

B. A.
O. 28
§ 3

Approved April 12, 1873.

ORDINANCE NO. XCVI.

An Ordinance compelling persons to keep filth, rubbish, etc., from the streets, gutters and sidewalks.

Be it ordained by the City Council of the City of Fort Worth:

B. A.
O. 327
§ 1.
SECTION 1. It shall be unlawful for any person to allow any weeds, filth or any kind of rubbish to remain on the sidewalks, in the gutters and in the streets, to the center of the same, in front of the premises occupied by them, and any person who fails to comply with this ordinance, shall be deemed guilty of a misdemeanor and fined in any sum not less than five nor more than twenty-five dollars.

B. A.
O. 327
§ 2.
SEC. 2. That this ordinance take effect from and after its publication.

Passed May 20, 1884.

ORDINANCE NO. XCVII.

An Ordinance relating to the closing of all Saloons, Drinking Houses, Bar-rooms, Beer Saloons, and all places or establishments where intoxicating or fermented liquors are sold on Sundays, and prescribing the hours of closing them.

Be it ordained by the City Council of the City of Fort Worth:

B. A.
O. 197.
§ 1.
SECTION 1. That it shall be unlawful for any keeper of any drinking house, saloon, beer room or beer saloon and all places or establishments where intoxicating or fermented liquors are sold or kept within the corporate limits of the City of Fort Worth, to open such establishment, or permit the same to be opened on Sunday between the hours of twelve o'clock Saturday night and twelve o'clock on Sunday night or to exhibit the same to public view.

B. A.
O. 197.
§ 2.
SEC. 2. It shall be unlawful for the keepers or proprietors of any establishment mentioned in the first section of this ordinance to allow any billiard playing and games of any kind within their establishment or any disturbance of any kind, either of music, loud talking, or any disturbance whatever on Sunday between the hours of twelve o'clock Saturday night and twelve o'clock Sunday night.

Sec. 3. Any person violating the first and second sections of this ordinance, upon conviction thereof, shall be deemed guilty of a misdemeanor, and fined in any sum not less than five dollars nor more than twenty-five dollars.
B. A.
O. 197
§ 3

Sec. 4. That this ordinance shall take effect and be in force from and after its publication as required by law.
B. A.
O. 197.
§ 4

Approved July 2, 1879.

ORDINANCE NO. XCVIII.

An Ordinance establishing the office of City Scavenger, and defining the duties of the same.

Be it ordained by the City Council of the City of Fort Worth:

Section 1. That the office of City Scavenger be and the same is hereby established, which said office shall be filled by appointment by the City Council.
B. A.
O. 231.
§ 1

Sec. 2. The City Scavenger shall before entering upon the duties of his office, file in the office of the City Secretary a good and sufficient bond, subject to the approval of the Mayor, in the sum of two hundred and fifty dollars, payable to the City of Fort Worth, conditioned for the faithful performance of the duties of said office.
B. A.
O. 231
§ 2.

Sec. 3. It shall be the duty of the City Scavenger to haul off all filth, garbage, dead animals, rubbish and offensive matter when so directed by the City Marshal, Deputy Marshal, policeman and members of the Board of Health from any street, alley, public ground or private premises, where the city under the ordinance defining nuisance would be required to remove the same, and that the City Scavenger shall carry said matter to some place designated by the City Council for the depositing of said matter, and then so bury or inter the same that it shall not be offensive to persons passing the said burial grounds. It shall also be the duty of the City Scavenger to keep the privy of the calaboose in a clean condition.
B. A.
O. 231.
§ 3.

Sec. 4. That should the City Scavenger fail or neglect to perform any of the duties set forth in § 3 of this ordinance

B. A.
O. 231
§ 4
he shall be deemed guilty of a misdemeanor, and upon conviction thereof, shall be fined in any sum not less than five nor more than one hundred dollars.

B. A.
O. 231.
§ 5.
SEC. 5. The office of City Scavenger shall be filled and the salary of the same fixed by resolution of the City Council in whatever manner they may determine.

B. A
O. 231.
§ 6.
SEC. 6. This ordinance shall take effect from and after its publication as required by law.

Approved April 26. 1880.

ORDINANCE NO. XCIX.

An Ordinance regulating and requiring a Light on vehicles of Scavengers.

Be it ordained by the City Council of the City of Fort Worth:

B. B.
O. 324
§ 1.
SECTION 1. If any person engaged in the business of hauling privy filth and substances of like offensive character, dead animals, fish or fowls, shall fail to keep and carry on his vehicle in a conspicuous place a light at all hours during the night while engaged in said business and using said vehicle, he shall be deemed guilty of a misdemeanor, and upon conviction, shall be fined in any sum not less than ten nor more than fifty dollars.

B. B.
O. 324.
§ 2
SEC. 2. This ordinance shall not be so construed as to repeal any other ordinance or part thereof defining the duties of Scavenger, and not in conflict with this ordinance.

B. B.
O. 324
§ 3.
SEC. 3. That this ordinance shall take effect from and after its publication.

Passed April 17, 1884.

ORDINANCE NO. C.

An Ordinance authorizing and requiring the Mayor of the city of Fort Worth to order an election in reference to taxation for Public School purposes.

Be it ordained by the City Council of the city of Fort Worth:

SECTION 1. That the Mayor of said city be, and he is hereby authorized and required, as soon after the passage of this Ordinance as practicable, to order an election in accordance with the laws of the State of Texas and submit to the vote of the property tax payers of said city the question, "Whether a tax for Public School purposes shall be levied and collected from the inhabitants of said city."

B. A.
O.192.
§ 1.

SEC. 2. That this ordinance take effect and be in force from and after its passage.

B. A.
O.192.
§ 2.

Approved May 8, 1879.

ORDINANCE NO. CI.

An Ordinance to establish and provide for the support and maintainance of an efficient system of Graded City Free Schools in the city of Fort Worth.

Be it ordained by the City Council of the city of Fort Worth:

SECTION 1. That a system of Municipal Public Free Schools consisting of Primary Schools in each ward, with a Grammar and High School near the center of the city, shall be established.

B. A.
O.237.
§ 1.

SEC. 2. It shall be the duty of the Board of Trustees, elsewhere provided for, to frame such rules and regulations in conjunction with the public school laws of the State as will be suitable for carrying into operation the most efficient system of Public Graded Schools, and the board shall have the whole under their direct control and supervision.

B. A.
O.237.
§ 2.

SEC. 3. The superintendent, hereinafter provided for, shall permit no pupil under the grade of primary schools to be admitted into the Grammar and High Schools. He shall report from time to time to the Board of Trustees, as they may direct, and

B. A.
O.237.
§ 4.

make an annual written report to the Board, at the close of the free school term, of the condition of the public free schools throughout the city for the inspection of the city council.

B. A.
O.237.
§ 6.
SEC. 4. All children, within the ages of seven to eighteen years, shall be entitled to the benefit of the available free school fund.

SEC. 5. Pupils of scholastic age, and from other counties, may attend the city free schools upon payment of such tuition fees as may be agreed upon between the teacher and parents or guardian of such children. Pupils of scholastic age residing out

B. A.
O.237.
§ 13.
of the city limits, attending the city free schools, shall be entitled to tuition free as long as the State fund will pay the tuition. Pupils of Grammar and High Schools desirous of studying any of the sciences not embraced in article ——— the dead and modern languages, music and ornamental branches, shall pay such tuition as may be agreed upon between parents and guardians and teachers, but the Board of Trustees shall not enter into any contract, or permit any contract, whereby the interest of pupils may be subordinated to the interest of private pupils.

SEC. 6. The Primary Ward Schools shall be graded to admit only pupils studying orthography, reading, writing, elementary

B. A.
O.237.
§ 15.
English grammar, elementary geography, written arithmetic for beginners and mental arithmetic. Pupils passing a satisfactory examination on the above branches shall attend the Grammar and High Schools.

Approved July 7, 1880.

ORDINANCE NO. CII.

An Ordinance providing for the maintainance and regulation of the system of Public Free Schools in the city of Fort Worth.

Be it ordained by the City Council of the city of Fort Worth:

SECTION 1. That all money which may come to the city treasury from the State school fund, or from any other source for school purposes, shall be and the same is hereby specially set apart as a separate fund for the use and benefit of the public free schools of the city of Fort Worth.

B. A.
O.244.
§ 1.

SEC. 2. The public free schools of the city of Fort Worth shall be a system of graded schools comprising primary schools and grammar schools and higher English studies if thought expedient by the Municipal Board of Trustees.

B. A.
O.244.
§ 2.

SEC. 3. The primary schools shall be divided into three grades, known as the first, second and third grades, and each shall occupy a period of one scholastic year.

B. A.
O.244.
§ 3.

SEC. 4. The grammar schools shall be divided into two grades, known as the fourth and fifth grades, and shall each occupy a period of one scholastic year.

B. A.
O.244.
§ 4.

SEC. 5. Separate schools shall be established for the white and colored children.

B. A.
O.244.
§ 5.

SEC. 6. The public schools of the city of Fort Worth shall consist of a primary and grammar school in each ward.

B. A.
O.244.
§ 6.

SEC. 7. Any pupil not of scholastic age, who will persue branches included in the instructions, may be admitted upon the payment of one dollar and a half per month. Said sum to be paid to the treasurer in advance, who shall give his receipt for the same and credit it to the school fund. Provided, that no such pupil shall be received into any public free school to the detriment of the free school pupils.

B. A.
O.244.
§ 8.

Sec. 8. Any pupil who will persue branches beyond those included in the course of instruction may be admitted upon the payment of such an amount as may be agreed upon between teacher and patron; one dollar and a half per month of said sum to be paid into the city treasury in advance and to go to the city school fund, the surplus to be paid to the teacher of the grade.

B. A. O.244. § 9.

Sec. 9. Scholastic pupils will be permitted to enter any of the ward schools of the city of their grade but will not be permitted to change to another ward school for that scholastic year without the consent of the superintendent.

B. A. O.244. § 10.

Sec. 10. Scholastic pupils residing beyond the corporate limits may, according to the laws of the State of Texas, obtain a transfer from the county judge, and may attend any of the city ward schools for such a length of time as their pro rata will pay for tuition in the same, after which they may attend upon the conditions prescribed in Section 7.

B. A. O.244. § 11.

Sec. 11. Pupils beyond the scholastic age, residing beyond the corporate limits, may be admitted upon the conditions stated in Sections 7 and 8.

B. A. O.244. § 12.

Sec. 12. The superintendent shall see that no one is admitted in the schools except those qualified as above.

B. A. O.244. § 13.

Sec. 13. The public schools of the city of Fort Worth shall commence on the first Monday in September each year, and shall continue forty weeks. Provided, that if the school fund is not sufficient to continue the same for such length of time, then said schools shall continue as long as there may be funds to sustain the same. The scholastic year shall be divided into two terms of twenty weeks each.

B. A. O.244. § 14.

Sec. 14. The public schools of the city shall be closed on every Saturday and Sunday, Christmas week and New Year's day, on National and State thanks giving days and on every national and State holiday.

B. A. O.244. § 15.

Sec. 15. The Board of Trustees shall elect, subject to the approval of the city council, a superintendent, who shall supervise all the public schools of the city of Fort Worth, who shall also act as principal of one of the ward schools and whose terms of office shall commence on the first of September and continue for one year.

B. A. O.244. § 17.

Sec. 16. It shall be the duty of the Board of Trustees, in conjunction with the superintendent of the public free schools, to examine applicants for appointments as teachers under such regulations as they themselves may establish, and they shall report the names of those selected as teachers to the city council for approval.   B. A. O.244. § 18.

Sec. 17. All pupils residing within the corporate limits of the city, within the scholastic age, shall be entitled to tuition free in the following branches, to-wit: Orthography, reading, writing, English grammar, composition, geography, arithmetic and such other English branches as the Board of Trustees may direct.   B. A. O.244. § 19.

Sec. 18. That the Board of Trustees shall prescribe the grade of the public free schools and the text books to be used, and submit the same to the city council for approval.   B. A. O.244. § 20.

Sec. 19. The superintendent shall devote himself exclusively to teaching and supervision. He shall visit all the schools every two weeks and as much oftener as his duties will permit, and shall pay particular attention to the classification and grading of the pupils in the several schools and to the apportionment among the several classes of the prescribed studies. In passing from school to school he shall endeavor to transfer improvements and remedy defects. He shall carefully observe the teaching and discipline of the teachers employed in the public schools, and shall report to the Board of Trustees whenever he shall find any teacher deficient or incompetent in the discharge of his or her duties. The superintendent shall also hold a teachers institute at least once a month, and as much oftener as practicable.   B. A. O.244. § 21.

Sec. 20. The salaries of the superintendent and teachers of public schools shall be fixed by the Board of Trustees, subject to approval by the city council. Provided, that for the teachers the same shall not exceed that fixed by the laws of the State.   B. A. O.244. § 22.

Sec. 21. The teachers' salary roll shall be made out every four weeks by the superintendent, and the account, after approval by the Board of Trustees, shall be paid by the city treasurer out of the school fund upon the draft of the Board of Trustees, signed by the chairman and countersigned by the secretary of said school board.   B. A. O.244. § 23.

SEC. 22. The Board of Trustees may discharge the superintendent or any public-free school teacher by resolution declaring their want of confidence in such superintendent or teacher, or whenever they may be satisfied that a necessity does not exist for the further employment of such teacher.

A. B.
O.244.
§ 24.

SED. 23. That there shall be one teacher appointed by the Board of Trustees in each public school building who shall be principal of all the grades taught in said building and shall hold said office for one year, and shall have charge and control of all the grades taught in said building, subject, however, to the instruction of the superintendent. The said principal shall report to the superintendent the conduct and discipline of the teachers and pupils in said school, and said principal shall see that the instructions and regulations of the superintendent shall be conformed to. But said principal shall receive no additional pay for said service.

B. A.
O.244.
§ 25.

SEC. 24. That this ordinance take effect and be in force from and after its passage.

Approved December 14, 1880.

B. A.
O.244.
§ 26.

ORDINANCE NO. CIII.

An Ordinance to authorize the City Council of the City of Fort Worth to appoint a Board of School Trustees and fixing their duties.

Be it ordained by the City Council of the city of Fort Worth:

SECTION 1. That the City Council of the city of Fort Worth shall appoint six persons, of good moral character and qualified voters of such city, as a Board of Trustees to act for the Public Free Schools of said city, of which board the mayor shall be ex-officio chairman.

B. B.
O.307.
§ 1.

SED. 2. Said Board of Trustees shall adopt such rules, regulations and by-laws for their own government as they may deem proper.

B. B.
O.307.
§ 2.

SEC. 3. Said Board of Trustees shall elect a superintendent of Public Free Schools, whose duties are prescribed in Ordinance No. ——. Said election to take place any time within two months prior to the first of September of each year, and his or her term of office shall be for one year beginning with the first of September of each year and continuing until his or her successor shall be qualified; and the election of said superintendent shall always, before he begins his duties, be subject to the approval of the city council.

B. B.
O.307.
§ 3.

SEC. 4. The teachers shall be selected by the Board of Trustees, subject, however, to the approval of the City Council, and their salaries shall be fixed by said trustees, subject to the approval of the City Council.

B. B.
O.307.
§ 4.

SEC. 5. That a necessity existing for this ordinance the same shall take effect from and after its passage.

B. B.
O.307.
§ 5.

Passed July 21, 1883.

ORDINANCE NO. CIV.

An Ordinance prescribing the powers, duties and qualifications, etc., of the Board of Trustees.

Be it ordained by the City Council of the city of Fort Worth:

B. B.
O.308.
§ 2.
SECTION 1. That the trustees appointed for the public schools of the city shall serve without compensation, and shall hold office for the term of three years, or until their successors are qualified; and an appointment to fill a vacancy shall be for the unexpired term only. But the term of two of the trustees first appointed, under this and the foregoing ordinance, shall expire on the first Tuesday in April. A. D. 1884, and two on the first Tuesday in April of each succeeding year. and the term for which each shall hold his office shall be determined at the first regular meeting of said board by lot.

B. B.
O.308.
§ 3.
SEC. 2. Before any trustee enters upon the discharge of the duties of his office he shall swear that he will faithfully and impartially discharge the duties of such office, and that he, before his election to the office of trustee, was not pledged to vote for any particular person for superintendent of schools.

B. B.
O.308.
§ 5.
SEC. 3. The Public Free Schools of this city shall be under the control and supervision of the Board of Trustees, and said board shall have power to control, manage and govern the same.

B. B.
O.408.
§ 7.
SEC. 4. That this ordinance take effect and be in force from and after its passage.

Approved July 31, 1883.

ORDINANCE NO. CV.

An Ordinance entitled An Ordinance to provide for the disbursement of the School Fund of the City of Fort Worth.

Be it ordained by the City Council of the city of Fort Worth:

SECTION 1. That the city treasurer shall place to the credit of the Board of School Trustees all school funds now in his hands or hereafter paid over to him, and that he shall pay out and disburse the same on the order of the Board of School Trustees, signed by the chairman and countersigned by the secretary of said school board. Provided, the said Board of Trustees shall draw no warrant except on accounts as they become due.

B. B. O.311. § 1.

B. B. O.311.

SEC. 2. That this ordinance take effect and be in force from and after its passage.

§ 2.

Passed October 2, 1883.

ORDINANCE NO. CVI.

An Ordinance authorizing the issuance of City Scrip and regulating the same.

Be it ordained by the City Council of the city of Fort Worth:

SECTION 1. That hereafter when an account shall be allowed by the City Council said account shall be numbered, filed and the date of the allowance endorsed thereon by the secretary, and entries of the same, together with the amount thereof, made in a book to be kept by the secretary for that purpose.

B. A. O. 37. § 1.

SEC. 2. That in all scrip hereafter issued by the city secretary, by order of the City Council, the said scrip shall state on the face of the same for what purpose and to satisfy what claim

B. A. O. 68. § 1.

against the city the same is issued, and at what meeting of the council the said scrip was authorized to be issued.

B. A.
O. 37.
§ 2.
SEC. 3. That the secretary shall, on the request of the owner of any account, issue warrants upon the city treasurer to the full amount of such account, numbering said warrants in the order that they issue in sums of not less than One Dollar. unless the whole account be a less sum than one dollar.

B. A.
O. 37.
§ 3.
SEC. 4. That said warrants shall be signed by the mayor and shall be countersigned by the secretary. and shall issue under the corporate seal, and shall be payable in the order in which they are numbered by the City Treasurer upon presentation thereof, except as is provided in Section 5.

B. A.
O. 58.
§ 1.
SEC. 5. That it shall be the duty of the treasurer of said city to pay off and discharge the city warrants first due, and when he has sufficient to pay off and discharge the number so first due, he shall post notice in three public places in said city to that effect, and after ten days notice from such posting if said number shall not be presented, then he shall in like manner publish the next number due, and continue in like manner until a payment be made of a seriatim number, and then shall go back and take up the first number which shall then recover its precedence. Provided, that this section shall not apply to the payment of officers' salaries out of the special fund for that purpose.

B. A.
O. 37.
§ 5.
SEC. 6. This ordinance shall take effect and be in force from and after its passage.

Approved May 27, 1873.

ORDINANCE NO. CVII.

An Ordinance authorizing the Mayor and City Secretary to give notes of the city for the purpose of funding the floating debt incurred for improvements done on the streets and alleys prior to April 1st, A. D. 1884.

WHEREAS, Many parties have done work for the city of Fort Worth upon the streets and alleys of said city prior to the 1st day of April, A. D. 1884, which said work was to be paid for in cash out of a fund created for that purpose, and which payments would have been made to said parties if it had not been that money was borrowed from said fund for other purposes. Therefore,

Be it ordained by the City Council of the city of Fort Worth:

SECTION 1. The mayor and city Treasurer of said city are hereby authorized and empowered to issue evidences of indebtedness to said parties in writing; said instruments of writing shall be delivered to the parties who hold the claims above mentioned, and shall be made to read in substance as follows: On or by the 15th day of March. A. D. 1885, the City of Fort Worth promises to pay to —— or bearer the sum of —— dollars, for work done on the streets and alleys of the City of Fort Worth with interest at the rate of seven (7) per cent. per annum from date thereof. Said city here reserves the right to, at any time, prior to the first day of January, pay off said amount with interest accrued to the time of payment either in lawful currency of the United States or in bonds of the city of Fort Worth. at the option of said city.

SEC. 2. That this ordinance take effect from and after its passage.

Passed August 11, 1884.

ORDINANCE NO. CVIII.

An Ordinance relating to the duties of the office of Secretary of the City of Fort Worth.

Be it ordained by the City Council of the city of Fort Worth:

B. A.
O. 54.
§ 1.
SECTION 1. That it shall be the duty of the secretary of said city that whenever any funds of the city shall come into his hands, as an officer of said city, that he shall pay over to the treasurer thereof in kind received.

B. A.
O. 54.
§ 2.
SEC. 2. That this ordinance take effect and be in force from and after its passage

Passed May 12, 1874.

ORDINANCE NO. CIX.

An Ordinance creating the office of City Assistant Secretary.

Be it ordained by the City Council of the city of Fort Worth:

B. A.
O. 67.
§ 1.
SECTION 1. That the office of Assistant Secretary of this city is hereby created and established.

B. A.
O. 67.
§ 2.
SEC. 2. That said office shall be filled by a majority vote of all the aldermen. They selecting said assistant secretara from suitable persons, citizens of said city.

B. A.
O 67.
§ 3.
SEC. 3. That the powers, duties, salary and fees of said assistant secretary shall be the same as is now prescribed and authorized by law and by the charter of this city for the office of secretary. Provided, that said assistant secretary shall only receive salary, and fees during the absence of the secretary, or the office of secretary from any cause vacant, and then in both cases in lieu of the secretary.

B. A.
O. 67.
§ 4.
SEC. 4. That this ordinance shall take effect and be in force from and after its passage.

Approved January 20, 1875.

ORDINANCE NO. CX.

An Ordinance to prevent the encumbering, filling up or injuring in any manner of Drains or Sewers in the City of Fort Worth.

Be it Ordained by the City Council of the City of Fort Worth:

SECTION 1. That it shall be unlawful for any person or persons to encumber. fill up or injure in any manner any drain or sewer upon any street. alley or public thoroughfare in the city of Fort Worth with any substance or material whatever. B. A. O.203. § 1.

SEC. 2. That any person or persons violating the provisions of this ordinance shall be deemed guilty of a misdemeanor, and upon conviction thereof shall be fined in any sum not more than fifty dollars. B. A. O.203. § 2.

SEC. 3. That this ordinance take effect and be in force from and after its publication as required by law. B. A. O.203. § 3.

Approved August 6, 1879.

ORDINANCE NO. CXI.

An Ordinance to provide for sewerage and surveying of the City of Fort Worth.

Be it Ordained by the City Council of the City of Fort Worth:

WHEREAS, It is necessary to commence a system of internal improvements in the City of Fort Worth and inaugurate a system of sewerage and street improvements, etc., in order to police the city and protect the inhabitants, and for other purposes, and it, therefore, becomes necessary that proper measures be now taken by the City Council of Fort Worth to carry out such measures as may be deemed most advantageous and beneficial to said city. Therefore,

Be it ordained by the City Council of the city of Fort Worth:

B. A.
O.275.
§ 1.

SECTION 1. That the mayor of the city of Fort Worth be and he is hereby authorized to have a typographical survey and map made of this city for the purpose of adopting a system of drainage and sewerage for the city.

B. A.
O.275.
§ 2.

SEC. 2. That in order to provide for the necessary means, and to astertain the limit of expense that may be incurred in making such improvements, the mayor of the city of Fort Worth is hereby authorized to make the necessary arrangements and appoint suitable persons for taking a complete census of all the inhabitants of this city.

B. A.
O.275.
§ 3.

SEC. 3. This ordinance to take effect and be in force from and after its passage.

Passed June 8, 1882.

ORDINANCE NO. CXII.

An Ordinance relating to the protection of the Public Sewers and the making of connections with the same.

Be it ordained by the City Council of the city of Fort Worth:

B. B.
O.306.
§ 1.

SECTION 1. It shall be a misdemeanor to do, or cause to be done any of the following acts except as herein provided, and any and all persons guilty thereof shall be fined not more than fifty dollars.

B. B.
O.306.
Sub §
1.

Sub-Sec. 1. To uncover the public sewers for any purpose or make connections therewith or uncover the public connections or branches thereof, unless and except by the consent and under the supervision of the city engineer or his duly authorized agent, or agents, whose duty it shall be to insure full compliance with this ordinance in relation to connections; and failure of duty in this respect shall subject such engineer or agents to all the penalties of this ordinance.

Sub-Sec. 2. To make, or cause to be made, any such connection, except as above provided, and by a competent and skillful mechanic or mechanics, acting as the agents and employes of individuals or firms who have been duly appointed by the city council after making a satisfactory bond ot $1500; such bond being held as indemnity against damages to the public sewers which may result from the carelessness or incompetency of such agents or employes, and as security for fines and costs which may be imposed for careless or wilful violation of any of the requiremeuts of this ordinance or for making connections with the sewers in any other manner as follow, etc.: [B. B. O.342. § 1.]

A. Every pipe connecting the sewer, whether of cast iron or earthenware, must be sound and impervious in all its parts. [B. B. O.306. Sub § 2.]
B. Gaskets must be used in all cases. No other metal than cast iron will be allowed, and joints in iron pipe must be of well caulked lead.
C. Cement pipes is not be used, but earthenware pipes of the best quality, jointed with fresh, strong cement mortar.
D. No traps or any manner of obstruction to the free flow of air through the whole course of the drain and soil pipe to be allowed, and any bonded firm or individual who shall directly or indirectly place, make, or cause or allow to be placed or made, any trap, coutraction or other obstacle anywhere in the course of such pipe, in addition to the penalty herein prescribed, shall forfeit his appointment and shall not be elligible to reappointment for one year, and any other person offending as above shall be subject to the penalties of the ordinance, and shall in addition pay the costs of rectifying the wrong done. [B. B. O.242. § 2.]
E. Every connection at a water closet, sink, basin or other vessel connected with the pipe, must be separated from it by a trap offering an obstacle to the passage of air equal to not less than three-eights of an inch debth of water.
F. All details of plumbing work, such as water closets, sinks, etc., must be in accordance with the plans and descriptions in the office of the city engineer, such plans always bearing the approval of the City Council.

Sub-Sec. 3. For the owner or occupant of any building, or any portion of any building, any portion of which is used for any purpose during any portion of the day, to fail to have at least one water closet connect with the public sewer fifteen [B. B. O.306. S. § 3.]

days after notification from the city engineer, by order of the City Council or Board of Health, and to fail to have such water closets suitably arranged for use as a urinal unless a separate urinal is provided.

B. B. O.306. Sub § 4.
Sub-Sec. 4. For the owner or occupant of any building in which food is cooked or clothes are washed, to fail to have suitable sinks, slop stone or hopper for the reception of waste water.

B. B. O.306. S. § 5.
Sub Sec. 5. To allow any surface water or rain water from the ground or roof of houses to enter any sewer, or drain, or vessel, or slop stone connected with any sewer or drain, or to admit of any drainage water from any cellar to a sewer, provided, however, that drainage for cellars may be provided in accordance with the regulations, plans and descriptions in the city engineer's office, and subject also to the restrictions of sub-section one of this ordinance.

B. B. O.306. S. § 6.
Sub-Sec. 6. To use, or cause to be used, any house drains for any other purpose or purposes than those specified in this ordinance.

B. B. O.306 S. § 7.
Sub-Sec. 7. To throw or deposit, or cause or permit to be thrown or deposited in any vessel or receptacle connected with a public sewer, any garbage, hair, ashes, fruit or vegetables, peelings or refused rags, cotton, cinders or any other matter or thing whatsoever, except forces, urine, the necessary closet paper and liquid house slops, and it is hereby made the duty of all citizens to aid the police in bringing offenses against the ordinance to punishment, and also to prevent branches of the same.

B. B. O.306. S. § 8.
Sub-Sec. 8. To use, or allow to be used, any soil pipe or extension of the sewer connection whatever use it may serve which does not extend at least six inches above the eaves or parapet or dividing walls of the house or building in which the same is constructed, and all ventilating pipes for sewer connections or water closets are hereby required to be extended at least six inches above the eaves, parapet or dividing walls of every house or building in or near which there is a sewer connection.

B. B. O.306. S § 9.
Sub-Sec. 9. To use, or allow to be used, any bell-trap or any other trap, depending for its seal on an easily movable part. or to construct or use, or cause or allow to be constructed or used, any water closet which has an unventilated space of more than one hundred cubic inches capacity between two

water seals, or which has such unventilated space of any capacity in which any part of the uncleanliness moves or the walls of which are not flushed at all points at each use of the closet.

Sub-Sec. 10. To fail or refuse to connect all wash stands or slop stands in the house or yard with the sewer, or to allow any slop, wash or waste water of any kind to flow over the pavement or under the pavement, on or into the street.

_{B. B. O.306. Sub § 10.}

Sec. 2. That any person who shall, knowingly, omit or refuse to comply with, or who resists or wilfully violates any of the provisions of this article, or any of the rules, orders or sanitary regulations or ordinances establishing or declared by the Board of Health in carrying out the provisions of this article or the execution of any order or special regulation of the Board of Health, made for that purpose, is hereby declared to be guilty of a misdemeanor and on arrest and conviction, he or she shall be fined for each offense in any sum not exceeding fifty dollars. It is hereby provided that this ordinance shall apply to owners or occupants of property in blocks through which the sewer pipes pass.

_{B. B. O.306. § 2.}

Sec. 3. That this ordinance take effect and be in force from and after its publication as required by law.

_{B. B. O.306. S. § 3.}

Approved July 19, 1883.

ORDINANCE NO. CXIII.

An Ordinance for the protection of Shade and Ornamental Trees within the city.

Be it ordained by the City Council of the city of Fort Worth:

B. A.
O. 19.
§ 1.
SECTION 1. No person shall cut, deface nor in any way injure any tree or sapling used for shade or ornamental purposes standing or growing in any of te streets or alleys or along the side-walks or within any of the public places belonging to or within the city of Fort worth; nor shall any person hitch or cause to be hitched any horse, mule, ox or other animal to any such tree or sapling standing or growing as aforesaid or to any boxing which may be placed around said trees or saplings for their protection. Nor shall any person, not not being the owner or agent thereof, commit any of the offenses aforesaid upon such trees as may be standing upon any lot within the city.

B. A.
O. 19.
§ 2.
SEC. 2. An person violating this ordinance, upon conviction thereof, shall be fined not exceeding ten dollars; one half thereof to go to the informer and the remainder to the city.

B. A.
O. 19.
§ 3.
SEC. 3. This ordinance to take effect and be in force from and after its publication as required by law.

Approved April 10, 1873.

ORDINANCE NO. CXIV.

An Ordinance regulating the setting out of Shade Trees, etc.

Be it ordained by the City Council of the city of Fort Worth:

SECTION 1. All shade trees hereafter set out on the streets of Fort Worth shall be placed on the curbing of the sidewalks. and shall be twelve inches from the curbing so as to make all trees on any given straight street in a straight line; said trees shall be set out so as to be not nearer than three feet of each other.

SEC. 2. Any person violating any of the provisions of Section one of this ordinance, shall be deemed guilty of a misdemeanor, and fined in any sum not less than five nor more than fifty dollars for each one set out.

SEC. 3. That this ordinance take effect from and after its publication.

Approved February 20, 1884.

ORDINANCE NO. CXV.

An Ordinance regulating Shooting Galleries.

Be it ordained by the City Council of the city of Fort Worth:

B. A.
O. 7.
§ 1.

SECTION 1. That it may and shall be lawful for any person to set up, keep and maintain a shooting gallery within the corporate limits of the city of Fort Worth after complying with the following rules and regulations.

B. A.
O. 7
& 119.
§ 2 & 1.

SEC. 2. That he or she shall pay to the Assessor and Collector the sum of two dollars and fifty cents per month, taking his receipt for the same and obtaining license as in other cases provided.

B. A.
O. 7.
§ 3.

SEC. 3. That any person setting up or keeping such shooting gallery shall first enclose the place or places where the same shall be situated, and shall secure the same in such a safe manner that no accident may arise therefrom; provided, that they shall keep an orderly house or place where the same shall be situated; and provided further, that they shall close and keep closed upon the Sabbath day, commonly called Sunday.

B. A.
O. 7.
§ 4.

SEC. 4. This ordinance to take effect and be in force from and after ten days publication as required by law.

Approved April 9, 1873.

ORDINANCE NO. CXVI.

An Ordinance relating to and regulating and enforcing the construction and repairing of sidewalk.

Be it ordained by the City Council of the city of Fort Worth:

SECTION 1. All sidewalks within this city which may be hereafter ordered by resolution of the City Council, shall be constructed under the superintendence and to the satisfaction of the committee on streets, alleys and sidewalks and all sidewalks hereafter constructed on any street. the grade of which has been established by the city council shall be built in strict conformity to said grade.

B. A.
O.243.
§ 1.

SEC. 2. All sidewalks shall be made by the owners or occupants of the premises fronting thereon, and shall be built within fifteen days after publication of notice in the official newspaper of the city, as herein after provided.

B. A.
O.243.
§ 2.

SEC. 3. Unless a different width be specified in the resolution ordering their construction, all sidewalks hereafter constructed shall be of the following width: 1st. On all streets eighty feet in width the sidewalks shall be twelve feet wide, and on all other streets the sidewalks shall be ten feet wide.

B. B.
O.301.
§ 1.

SEC. 4. All sidewalks hereafter constructed shall have a uniform slope of one inch in six feet from the building on front line of the lot or lots in front of which the same are built to the outside edge thereof.

B. A.
O 243.
§ 4.

SEC. 5. All sidewalks in the city of Fort Worth hereafter constructed sball be built only of iron, stone, brick. gravel or other suitable and durable material, and no sidewalk shall be made or constructed of wood. When built of gravel, then said sidewalk shall be laid in gravel to a depth of not less than six inches and shall be protected by a substantial curbing of stone or plank not less than two by eight inches in width and thickness well tied in and placed along the outer edge of the sidewalk.

B. A.
O.282.
§ 1.

SEC. 6. The city council, by resolution, may at any time order the building of sidewalks on any square, street or alley of the city; such resolution shall prescribe the street or place along which the same shall be built and the material of which it is to be constructed, and may be in the following form: "Be it re-

B. A.
O.243.
§ 6.

solved by the City Council of the city of Fort Worth, that the owners or occupants of all property fronting on the (north, south, east or west) side of ―――― street, from ―――― (place of beginning) to ―――― (place of ending), in said city be and the same are hereby ordered to construct a sidewalk of ―――― (kind of material) in front of said property, in conformity with the ordinance relative to sidewalks."

B. A.
O.243.
§ 7.

Sec. 7. On the passage of an order for the building of any sidewalk the city secretary shall cause notice thereof to be published for five days in the official newspaper of the city which shall be dated and signed by the secretary, and shall specify the day on or before which such sidewalk shall be constructed by the owner or occupant, and may be in the following form: "Notice is hereby given that the City Council have ordered a sidewalk to be constructed as follows: "On etc., ―――― (giving the description as contained in the resolution ordering the same). Now unless the same shall be constructed in the manner required by the ordinance relative to sidewalks on or before the ―――― day of ―――― next the same will be built by the city and the expenses assessed on the premises fronting thereon.

B. A.
O.243.
§ 8.

Sec. 8. The city secretary shall likewise make out and cause to be served upon the owner or occupant of such real estate, when known and can be found, a written or printed notice thereof, dated and signed by himself and in form substantially as follows: "Mr. ―――― (name of party). Sir: You are hereby notified that the City Council of the city of Fort Worth has ordered a sidewalk to be constructed of ――――(kind of material) in front of lot No. ―――― block No. ―――― on ―――― street, in the original town (or in any addition thereto, specifying what addition, if any. Now unless you shall construct the same to the satisfaction of the committee on streets, alleys and sidewalks, in the manner required by ordinance on or before the ―――― day of ―――― (day and month mentioned in the published notice), the same will be built by the city and the expenses assessed upon the premises."

B. A.
O.243.
§ 9.

Sec. 9. The notice required by the preceeding section shall be served by delivering a copy thereof to such owner or occupant in person or by leaving the same at the residence or place of business of such owner or occupant; such notice may be also served upon any known agent of the parties aforesaid. The person serving such notice shall endorse thereon his return showing when, how and upon whom the same has been served, and return the same to the office of the city secretary, who shall file and preserve the same.

SEC. 10. Should the owner or occupant of any real estate in front of which any sidewalk has been ordered to be built, fail or refuse to construct the same within the time mentioned in the notice aforesaid, or to the satisfaction of the committee on streets, alleys and sidewalks, it shall be the duty of said committee to report the same to the city council; said report shall be in writing, and shall give a description of the lot or other premises, also the name of the owner or occupant on whom notice has been served and the manner of service, or, if any owner be unknown, or cannot be found as the case may be, the said committee shall procure and file with such report a copy of the sidewalk notice published in the newspaper doing the city printing with an affidavit by the publisher of its due publication.

B. A. O.243. § 10.

SEC. 11. On receiving said report the city council may order the committee on streets, alleys and sidewalks to construct the sidewalk mentioned therein, which order may be in the following form: "Whereas, The owner of the following described real estate, to-wit: Lot number ——, block number ——, original town (or any addition as the case may be), has failed, after due notice to construct a sidewalk thereon in pursuance of an order passed on —— day of —— (giving date of resolution ordering the same.) It is, therefore, ordered that the committee on streets, alleys and sidewalks construct the same forthwith, in conformity with the original order, and report the expenses for assessment."

B. A. O.243. § 11.

SEC. 12. An accurate account shall be kept by the committee on streets, alleys and sidewalks of the cost of every sidewalk constructed by order of the city council, and they shall report the same in writing as soon as practicable in substance in the following form: "Your committee on streets, alleys and sidewalks beg leave to report that in compliance with an order of the city council, passed on the —— day of —— (giving date of order), they have constructed a sidewalk on the premises hereinafter described at an expense set opposite thereto, to-wit: Lot number ——, block number, —— original town or —— $——." To be signed by the chairman or other member of the committee and addressed to the city council.

B. A. O.243. § 12.

SEC. 13. The city council shall, on receiving the report report required by the preceding section, by a resolution passed by a vote of two-thirds of all the members, assess the expenses on the real estate described therein; which resolution may be substantially in the following form: Be it resolved by the City Council of the City of Fort Worth, that the sums of money set opposite the following lot, to-wit: "Lot number —, block number —, original town or addition (as the case may be), —, $— be and the same is hereby assessed thereon to defray the expenses of a sidewalk constructed by the city in pursuance of an order passed on the —— day of —, 18—.

<small>B. A. O.243. § 13.</small>

Sec. 14. It shall be the duty of the city secretary, as soon as practicable, after the passage thereof, to furnish the assessor and collector a certified copy of the resolution provided for in the preceeding section, signed by the mayor and attested by himself, with the seal of the corporation attached thereto; which certified copy, as aforesaid, shall be full and sufficient authority for the assessor and collector to receive and collect the assessment therein specified.

<small>B. A. O.243. § 14.</small>

Sec. 15. Upon receiving such certified copy of said resolution as set forth above, it shall be the duty of the assessor and collector to cause to be published for ten days in the official newspaper of the city a notice of such assessment as ordered by the city council and demanding payment of the same within thirty days after the date thereof; said notice shall be dated and signed by the assessor and collector, and may be in the following form: "Notice is hereby given that the sum of money set opposite to the following lot to-wit: Lot number —— block number, original town (or addition as the case may be), ——$—, has been assessed thereon by the city council for the cost of a sidewalk constructed by the city and payment of said amount is hereby demanded within thirty days from the date hereof.

<small>B A. O.243. § 15.</small>

Sec. 16. Should the owner of any real estate so assessed fail or refuse to pay the amount of such assessment, or any portion thereof within thirty days after the date of the first publication of the notice prescribed in the preceeding section, the assessor and collector shall, by virtue of his certified copy of the resolution of assessment, signed by the mayor and countersigned by the city secretary under the seal of the corporation as provided in section fourteen of this ordinance, seize, levy upon and sell such delinquent premises or real estate, or so much thereof as may be necessary, whether belonging to residents or non-res-

<small>B. A. O.243. § 16.</small>

idents, for the payment of the assessment due thereon together with the costs of sale accruing thereon.

SEC. 17. The assessor and collector shall advertise such delinquent premises or real estate for sale in the official newspaper of the city for three successive weeks, giving in said advertisement such a description as is given to the same on the certified copy of the resolution of assessment in his hands, giving the name of the owner, if known, and if unknown say "unknown," together with the time, place and terms of sale; said sale to be for cash to the highest bidder at public outcry at the courthouse door of this county, and shall be between the legal hours on the first Tuesday of the month.

B. A.
O.243.
§ 17.

SEC. 18. The assessor and collector, in making sales for assessments due upon real estate for the construction of sidewalks shall sell at public outcry, at the time and place appointed so much of said real estate as may be necessary to pay the assessment and all costs accruing thereon, and shall offer said real estate to the bidder who will pay the assessment due and costs of sale and execution of deed for the least amount of said real estate, who shall be deemed the highest bidder. Should a less amount of said real estate than the whole tract, or parcel levied upon, be sold for the assessment due and costs of sale and execution of the deed, the assessor and collector shall, in making his deed to the purchaser, begin at some corner of said tract or lot, and designate the same in a square as near as practicable.

B. A.
O.243.
§ 18.

SEC. 19. The assessor and collector shall execute to the purchaser upon the payment of the amount for which the real estate was sold, and costs, a deed for the real estate sold; giving in said deed such description of the land as is given on the certified copy of the resolution of assessment in his hands and such other description as may be necessary to the better identification of the same; which deed shall vest a good and absolute fee in said land in the purchaser if not redeemed in two years as hereinafter provided; said deed shall state the cause of sale, the amount sold, the name of the person, firm, company or corporation on whom the demand for such assessment for sidewalk was made, provided the name is known, and if unknown, say "unknown," and when such real estate has been sold he shall convey, subject to the right of redemption provided for in the following section, all right and interest which the former owner had therein at the time the assessment was made.

B. A.
O.243.
§ 19.

B. A.
O.243.
§ 20.

Sec. 20. The owner of real estate sold for the payment of any assessment for the construction of sidewalks, or his heirs or assigns, or legal representatives may, within two years from the date of sale, redeem the estate sold by paying or tendering to the purchaser, his heirs or legal representatives, or when the purchaser or his representative cannot be found, by depositing with the assessor and collector double the full amount of his bid for said land and all costs of sale.

B. A.
O.243.
§ 21.

Sec. 21. Should the assessor and collector fail to make sale of any real estate for want of a purchaser, he shall bid the same off to the city for the amount of the assessment due and costs accruing thereon, and execute and deliver to the city a deed to the same in the same manner as provided for to individuals for real estate sale. Said deed shall be recorded in the county clerk's office and shall vest a good and absolute title to the city in said land if not redeemed as herein provided. The owner of such real estate bid in by the assessor and collector may redeem the same at any time within two years from the date the assessor and collector bid in said property by paying to the assessor and collector the full amount of money for which said property was bid in and costs, with interest thereon at the rate of twelve per cent. per annum from the day of sale; and upon such payment being made by the owner or his agent, the assessor and collector shall procure from the city secretary and deliver to such party a quit claim deed to such property, which deed shall be signed by the mayor and attested by the city secretary and delivered under seal of the city.

B. A.
O.243.
§ 22.

Sec. 22. Whenever the assessor and collector shall have made sale of any real estate under this ordinance, it shall be his duty to make return of said sale to the city council, stating in said return the land sold, the name of the owner, if known, and if unknown state the fact, the time of the sale, the amount for which said sale was made together with the name of the purchaser, which return shall be entered of record on the minutes of the proceedings of the city council.

B. A.
O.243.
§ 23.

Sec. 23. The assessor and collector on final settlement of his accounts with the city council shall be entitled to a credit for the amount of all assessments for the construction of sidewalks due the city for which the lands or lots were bid off to the city; and in all cases where property is levied on and sold for assessments for sidewalks, he shall receive the same compensation as is allowed by law for making a levy and sale for taxes.

SEC. 24. Nothing contained in this ordinance shall be construed to deprive the city of any right, power or authority which it may have to collect said assessments for the construction of sidewalks or the value of work and labor done and material furnished in constructing sidewalks by instituting suit in the corporate name in any court having jurisdiction thereof. B. A. O.243. § 24.

SEC. 25. No assessments for the construction of sidewalks as herein contemplated shall be deemed to be invalid in any case where the same shall be made in conformity with law, although the same shall not be made in strict conformity with the proceedings and forms herein prescribed. B. A. O.243. § 25.

SEC. 26. That in all cases when sidewalks have been built in conformity with any order of the city council, it shall be the duty of the city to build and construct crossings to meet and connect the same. B. A. O.243. § 26.

SEC. 27. Whenever any sidewalk shall become broken or otherwise out of repair, it shall be the duty of the committee on streets, alleys and sidewalks, the city marshal, or any member of the police force to cause a written or printed notice, dated and signed by the mayor or any member of the committee on streets, alleys and sidewalks to be served upon the owner or his known agent, or the occupant of the premises fronting thereon, requiring the same to be repaired within a reasonable time to be mentioned therein; which notice may be in form as follows: Mr. —— (name of party), Sir: You are hereby notified to repair the sidewalk in front of lot number —— block number —— on the —— side of —— street, in the original town of Fort Worth (or in any addition thereto), in conformity with the ordinance relative to sidewalks of said city within —— hours or (—— days) after service of this notice. B. A. O.243. § 27.

SEC. 28. In all cases where any owner or agent or occupant cannot be found, or fails or refuses to repair any sidewalk, in pursuance of notice as prescribed in section twenty-seven of this ordinance, it shall be the duty of the committee on streets, alleys and sidewalks, within a reasonable time after the expiration of the time specified in said notice to repair the same and report the expenses thereof to the city council for assessment against the premises fronting thereon; such report may be made in the same form, and the assessment for the repairs made and B. A. O.243. § 28.

collected in the same manner as provided in this ordinance in relation to the building of sidewalks.

SEC. 29. The notices required by sections eight and twenty-seven of this ordinance may be served and returns thereof made by the city marshal or any policeman or by any member of the committee on streets, alleys and sidewalks.

B. A. O.243. § 29.

SEC. 30. Any person being the owner, agent or occupant of any premises in front of which any sidewalk may be broken or otherwise out of repair, who shall fail or refuse to repair such sidewalk within the time required by the notice prescribed in section twenty-seven of this ordinance shall be deemed guilty of a misdemean, and on conviction shall be fined not less than five nor more than one hundred dollars, and each day that such person shall fail or refuse shall be deemed a separate offense.

B. A. O.243. § 30.

SEC. 31. Any person who shall construct, aid or assist in the construction, or cause to be constructed any sidewalk contrary to the grade established by the city council, where any grade has been so established or contrary to the provisions of this ordinance, shall be deemed guilty of a misdemeanor, and upon conviction shall be fined not less than five nor more than one hundred dollars.

B. A. O.243. § 31.

SEC. 32. That, whereas, a public necessity exists for the immediate passage and enforcement of this ordinance; therefore, that this ordinance shall take effect and be in force from and after its passage.

B. A. O.243. § 32.

Approved October 13, 1880.

ORDINANCE NO. CXVII.

An Ordinance prohobiting the obstruction of the Sidewalks and streets of said city, and the throwing of dirt, straw and rubbish into or upon said streets.

Be it ordained by the City Council of the city of Fort Worth:

SECTION 1. It shall be unlawful for any one to obstruct any sidewalk in this city by selling or offering for sale by auction or otherwise any goods wares or merchandise on such sidewalk. B. A. O.263. § 1.

SEC. 2. It shall be unlawful for any one to place any barrel or barrels, box or boxes, or wood or other substance on any sidewalk in this city so as to obstruct the passage along such sidewalk or any part thereof. B. A. O.263. § 2.

SEC. 3. It shall be unlawful for any person or persons to obstruct any sidewalk in front of any church, theatre or other public place, or place of business, or in any other way obstruct the passage in or out of any such church, theatre or other public place. B. A. O.263. § 3.

SEC. 4. Nothing in this ordinance shall be so construed as to prevent any merchant from occupying not to exceed one-half of any sidewalk in receiving or forwarding goods, wares or merchandise. Provided, they shall not occupy said sidewalk for a longer space of time than twelve hours. Every merchant or owner of a building fronting on any street shall be allowed not to exceed thirty-six inches on the inside of the walk for show windows or the display of goods, but nothing on the outer edge of said sidewalk, except as to butchers, and they shall be allowed twenty-four inches on the outer edge of said sidewalk. B. A. O.263. § 4.

SEC. 5. Every day that any obstruction shall remain upon any sidewalk, in this city shall be considered a violation of the police regulations herein contained, and shall constitute a separate offense and be punished as such. B. A. O.263. § 6.

SEC. 6. It shall be unlawful for any person to place upon any sidewalk, street or alley or gutter of any street within said city any straw, dirt, filth, ashes, chips, shells, paper, glass or other rubbish or trash, and it shall be unlawful for anyone to B. A. O.263. § 7.

throw, place or sweep any paper, dirt, trash or rubbish from any store into the streets or gutters of said streets.

B. A.
O.263.
§ 8.
Sec. 7, It shall be unlawful for any mechanic, laborer or builder to place or deposit upon the sidewalks of said city any lumber or material for building.

B. A.
O.263.
§ 9.
Sec. 8. It shall be unlawful for any mechanic, laborer or builder to stop up the gutters of any street in said city.

B. A.
O.263.
§ 10.
Sec. 9. Anyone violating any section of this ordinance shall be deemed guilty of a misdemeanor, and upon conviction thereof shall be fined in any sum not exceeding twenty-five dollars.

B. A.
O.263.
§ 11.
Sec 10. That this ordinance shall be in force and take effect from and after its publication as required by law.

Passed December 20, 1881.

ORDINANCE NO. CXVIII.

An Ordinance regulating Slaughter Pens.

Be it ordained by the City Council of the city of Fort Worth:

B. A.
O. 10.
§ 1.
Section 1. That any person or persons who shall kill or slaughter any beef cattle, sheep or hogs for market within the corporate limits of this city otherwise than at the regular slaughter pens established by the city shall be deemed guilty of a misdemeanor, and upon conviction thereof shall be fined a sum not less than five nor more than fifty dollars for each and every offense.

B. A.
O. 10.
§ 2.
Sec. 2. This ordinance to take effect and be in force from and after ten days publication as required by las.

Approved April 9, 1873.

ORDINANCE NO. CXIX.

An Ordinance granting to M, B. Loyd and C. H. Higby and their assigns the privilege to use for stairway purposes three feet of the north side of Second street, between Houston and Main streets, and adjoining the lot on which the proposed National Bank is being erected.

Be it ordained by the City Council of the city of Fort Worth:

SECTION 1. That M. B. Loyd and C. H. Higby and their assigns be and the same are hereby granted the privilege to use for stairway purposes three feet of the north side of Second street. between Houston and Main street, and adjoining the lot on which the proposed National Bank building is being erected.

B. A.
O. 90.
§ 1.

SEC. 2. That this ordinance take effect and be in force from and after its passage.

B. A.
O. 90.
§ 2.

Approved December 18, 1876.

ORDINANCE NO. CXX.

An Ordinance concerning Books and Stationery for the different officers.

Be it ordained by the City Council of the city of Fort Worth:

SECTION 1. That the following named officers, viz: Mayor, Tax Assessor and Collector, Treasurer, City Attorney and Secretary be authorized to procure all books and stationery necessary to the conduct of their respective offices, and that the same be paid for out of any monies that may be in the city treasury upon the presentation of the accounts for the same by the respective officers with their affidavit attached as to the justness of the same.

B. A.
O. 4.
§ 1.

B. A.
O. 4.
§ 2.

SEC. 2. That this ordinance shall take effect and be in force from and after its passage.

Approved April 5, 1873.

ORDINANCE NO. CXXI.

To open and extend the following streets, to-wit: To open and extend Bluff street through Block 123 to Elm street, sixty feet wide. Also to open a street, sixty feet wide, from the river bluff through Block 123 to Belknap street, so as to leave four blocks in block 123, 200 feet square.

Be it ordained by the City Council of the city of Fort Worth:

B. A.
O. 61.
§ 1.

SECTION 1. That Bluff street be extended through block No. 123 (said extension being sixty feet wide) to Elm street.

B. A.
O. 61.
§ 2.

SEC. 2. That a street sixty feet wide wide from river bluff be extended through block No. 123 to Belknap street so as to leave four blocks in Block 123 two hundred feet square.

B. A.
O. 61.
§ 3.

SEC. 3. That the mayor immediately appoint three disinterested appraisers, whose duty it shall be to enter upon the premises, and, together with the city engineer, after having been duly sworn to faithfully perform their duties as such appraisers, and with fidelity and impartiality to, to view and estimate the value of all property within the limits of the streets so opened as aforesaid and estimate and ascertain all damages sustained by the citizens of the city as owners of property within said limits by reason of the opening or extending of said streets, and faithfully report the same to the city council at their regular meeting in September next, the same being the 8th day of the month.

B. A.
O. 61.
§ 4.

SEC. 4. That the publication of this ordinance in one of the city papers for four consecutive weeks shall be a sufficient notice to all parties concerned, and final action will be had on the same at a regular meeting to be held on the 22d day of September, A. D. 1884.

Approved August. 14, 1874.

ORDINANCE NO. CXXII.

An Ordinance to open and extend the following street, to-wit: Bluff street from Houston street turought Block 4, 224 feet. Said street to be sixty feet wide.

Be it ordained by the City Council of the city of Fort Worth:

Ss.CTION 1. That Bluff street be extended through block No. 4 to Mrs. Gamble's east line, a distance of 224 feet from Houston street.

SEC. 2. That this ordinance take effect and be in force from and after its passage.

Passed March 28, 1876.

B. A.
O. 73.
§ 1.

B. A.
O. 73.
§ 2.

ORDINANCE NO. CXXIII.

An Ordinance regulating the opening, establishing, widening, straightening, extending and laying off of streets and alleys.

Be it ordained by the City Council of the city of Fort Worth:

SECTION 1. That whenever it shall be deemed imperatively necessary to open, establish, widen, straighten, extend or lay off any street or alley within the corporate limits of the city of Fort Worth, the city council shall order the city engineer to make a correct survey and plat of the street or alley to be opened, established, widened, straightened, extended or laid off and of the lot or lots of land that it may be necessary to appropriate for that purpose, which survey and plot shall be kept on file in his office for public inspection.

SEC. 2. That after an examination of the said survey and plot, should it appear necessary to take private property for such purpose, the mayor shall appoint three disinterested citizens, who shall be free holders within the said city and shall

B. A.
O. 80.
§ 1.

B. A.
O. 80.
§ 2.

have been residents thereof for at least one year next preceeding said appointment, whose duty it shall be to enter upon the said premises and appraise the property to be so appropriated and estimate the value thereof, which said valuation shall be returned under oath by the said commissioners to the council and filed in the office of the city secretary.

SEC. 3. That should the council then consider that the public interest requires the payment of said valuation and the appropriation of the said property, they shall cause notice in writing to be issued by the city secretary and served by the city marshal, or his deputy, on the owner or owners of the said land that the said valuation will be presented to the council at its next regular meeting for action thereon, which notice shall be served not less than ten days before said council meeting. The said notice shall be served by delivering a copy thereof to the owner or leaving it at his place of business or residence. If the owner be a non-resident the notice shall be published three weeks in a newspaper published in Fort Worth. Said notice shall state the time when the council will meet and contain a discription of the property.

SEC. 4. That at said meeting the said valuation shall be examined with any objections that may be made thereto by the owner or owners of the property and the council may, if it sees proper, order another valuation by the commissioners or confirm the same.

SEC. 5. That when said valuation shall have been confirmed the council shall order the amount so found due the owner to be paid to him in money, or deposited in the city treasury subject to his order.

SEC. 6. That when the amount found due each owner has been paid him, or deposited in the treasury, as provided for in the proceeding section, it shall be the duty of the city marshal to notify the owners of said property to remove, within ten days, any obstructions that may be on the land so appropriated, and if not so removed the city marshal shall proceed to remove the same.

SEC. 7. That any person aggrieved by the said valuation shall have the right to appeal in the county court, provided, that the city shall not be required to suspend work on said street or alley pending said appeal.

SEC. 8. That the expense of opening, establishing, widening, straightening, extending and laying off said street or alley, surveying the same and plotting the said property shall be paid by the city.

B. A.
O. 80.
§ 8.

SEC. 9. That this ordinance shall take effect and be in force from and after its passage.

B. A.
O. 80.
§ 9.

Approved August 11, 1876.

ORDINANCE NO. CXXIV.

An Ordinance validating and establishing the survey of the city engineer and the public square and the streets of the city of Fort Worth.

Be it ordained by the City Council of the city of Fort Worth:

SECTION 1. That the map and plot of the city of Fort Worth returned to the council by I. C. Terry, city surveyor and engineer, upon the 11th day of November, 1873, together with the field notes thereof, be and it is hereby ratified, validated and declared to be the official map and plot of this city and the streets, alleys and public squares of said city as therein laid out are hereby declared to be the proper and public streets, alleys and squares of this city, and the names of said streets as given upon said map and plot are hereby declared to be the proper and official names of said streets.

B. A.
O. 49.
§ 1.

SEC. 2. That the secretary endorse upon said map his certificate, to which he shall affix the seal of the city to the effect that said map was, upon said 11th day of November, 1873, produced to the city council of this city by Isaac O. Terry. city surveyor and engineer, and by them ratified, validated and confirmed and ordered to be recorded as the official map and plot of the city of Fort Worth.

B. A.
O. 49.
§ 2.

Approved November 11, 1873.

ORDINANCE NO. CXXV.

An Ordinance validating and establishing the Map and Plot of Daniel O'Flaherty and and public square, streets, alleys, blocks and lots of the city of Fort Worth.

Be it ordained by the City Council of the city of Fort Worth:

B. A.
O.121.
§ 1.

SECTION 1. That the map and plot of the city of Fort Worth presented to the city council by Daniel O'Flaherty, a citizen of this city, upon the 26th day of June, A. D. 1877, together with the field notes thereof, be and the same is hereby ratified, validated and declared to be the official map and plot of this city and the streets, alleys, blocks and lots and public square of said city, as therein laid out, are hereby declared to be the proper and public streets, alleys and squares of this city; and the names of said streets and the numbers of said blocks and lots as given upon said map and plot are hereby declared to be the proper and official names of said streets and the number of said blocks and lots. Provided, that should any conflict occur between this map and plot of the city and the map and plot of the city heretofore adopted on, to-wit: the 11th day of November, A. D. 1873, that the map and plot heretofore adopted shall control.

B. A.
O.121.
§ 2.

SEC. 2. That the secretary endorse upon said map his certificate, to which he shall affix the seal of the city to the effect that said map was upon said 17th day of July, 1877, produced to the city council of this city by Daniel O'Flaherty and by them ratified, validated and confirmed and endorsed to be recorded as the official map and plot of the city of Fort Worth.

B. A.
O.121.
§ 3.

SEC. 3. That this ordinance take effect and be in force from and after its passage.

Approved September 13, 1877.

ORDINANCE NO. CXXVI.

An Ordinance to regulate work on streets and sidewalks within the city limits, and erection and repairing of any buildings within the fire limits, and to prohibit the interruption or breaking of streets and sidewalks.

Be it ordained by the City Council of the city of Fort Worth:

SECTION 1. That all contracts for public improvements on the streets and sidewalks within the city limits shall be subject to the approval of the city engineer and the contractors shall construct the same in accordance with and subject to his orders.
B. A. O.133. § 1.

SEC. 2. That all persons desirous of erecting or repairing any building of any material whatsoever, within the fire limits, shall, before commencing the same, first obtain from the city engineer a permit therefor.
B. A. O.133. § 2.

SEC. 3. That any person desiring to remove or interrupt any sidewalk or excavate any part of the public street shall so notify the city engineer and obtain from him a permit which shall distinctly state the time during which such obstruction will be allowed.
B. A. O.133. § 3.

SEC. 4. That any person violating any of the provisions of this of this ordinance shall be deemed guilty of a misdemeanor, and upon conviction thereof, shall be fined in any sum not less than ten nor more than fifty dollars.
B. A. O.133. § 4.

SEC. 5. That this ordinance take effect and be in force from and after its publication as required by law.
B. A. O.133. § 5.]

Approved December 21, 1877.

ORDINANCE NO. CXXVII.

An Ordinance opening and establishing a street sixty feet wide, running from a point on the west line of the S. G. Jennings survey and adjoining the northwest corner of block 39 to the east bank of the Clear Fork of Trinity river. Said street to be called Weatherford Road.

Be it ordained by the City Council of the city of Fort Worth:

SECTION 1. That a street sixty feet wide be opened and established from the west line of the S. G. Jennings survey to the east bank of the Clear Fork of Trinity River. The center line of said street to run as follows, to-wit: Beginning on the west line of the S. G. Jennings survey at a point thirty feet north of the northwest corner of block 39; thence due west one hundred and fifty feet, thence due south three hundred and sixty-two and one-half feet to the continuation of the south line of said block 39, thence in a southerly direction with the meanderings of the bluff to the north line of the Texas and Pacific railroad donation, thence west with the north line of said railroad donation to the east bank of the Clear Fork of Trinity river, thence up the bank of said stream to the old VanZandt crossing of Clear Fork river.

SEC. 2. That this ordinance take effect and be in force from and after its passage.

Approved January 16, 1878.

ORDINANCE NO. CXXVIII.

An Ordinance entitled An Ordinance assessing and regulating the taxes for grading, paving and guttering and curbing on Main, Houston, Weatherford and cross streets.

Be it ordained by the City Council of the city of Fort Worth:

SECTION 1. Main street, Houston street, Weatherford street, and all the cross streets between Rush and Throckmorton streets inclusive, to fifteenth street, having been by contract with and by order of the city council of said city, graded, paved and guttered and curbed, and an estimate of the costs having been filed with the city secretary by the city engineer as well as the sizes and ownerships of property fronting and being on said streets. Therefore, a tax of one-third the estimated costs of the grading and paving of said streets in front of the property on said streets is hereby assessed against the property fronting and adjacent to said streets so graded and paved.

B. B.
O.313.
§ 1.

SEC. 2. Said tax shall be collected one-fifth annually, and shall be paid on or by the first day of March, of each year after the levy of this tax.

B. B.
O.313.
§ 2.

SEC. 3. The lists of the lots so placed on file in the office of the city secretary, which said list embraces all the lots on Main, Houston and Weatherford, and cross streets between Throckmorton and Rusk streets, all of which front on and are adjacent to said work so constructed by the city council of the city of Fort Worth is hereby referred to and made a part of this ordinance.

B. B.
O.313.
§ 3.

SEC. 4. It shall be the duty of the officer collecting the tax herein levied to notify the owner of said property by postal card of this levy and the amount of tax due on his or her property by reason of this levy, and where payable.

B. B.
O.313.
§ 4.

SEC. 5. A tax of one-third the cost of the work done in front of the property respectively is assessed against said property as follows as per list hereto attached marked Exhibit A, and considered a part hereof.

B. B.
O.313.
§ 5.

Passed November 22, 1883.

ORDINANCE NO. CXXIX.

An Ordinance for the Protection of paved streets.

Be it Ordained by the City Council of the City of Fort Worth:

B. B.
O.313.
§ 1.
SECTION 1. That it shall be a misdemeanor to do or cause to be done any of the following acts, except as herein provided, and any and all persons guilty thereof, upon arrest and conviction, shall be fined in any sum from five to twenty-five dollars.

B. B.
O.313.
§ 2.
SEK. 2. That any plumber, or other person, desiring to cut or open any street in the city of Fort Worth, which has been paved or graded, for the purpose of laying in gas, water or sewer pipe, or for any other purpose whatever, shall first obtain a permit from the city engineer to open the street.

B. B.
O.313.
§ 3.
SEC. 3. That when any street has been cut or opened, as aforesaid, for the purpose of laying in gas, water or sewer pipes or for other purposes, the party or parties doing the same shall puddle and ram the back filling so as to prevent the street settling at the place cut, and stone or gravel pavements taken up shall be restored with similar workmanship and material to that existing in the pavements before they were torn up; all the work to be replaced to the satisfaction of the city engineer, whose duty it shall be to inspect the same after it is done, and to be completed and replaced within the time specified in the permit.

B. B.
O.313.
§ 4.
SEC. 4. In all cases where the surface of the street is disturbed, whether paved or unpaved, the party or parties so cutting or opening the street shall place lights at night and maintain suitable barracades to protect persons from danger, and leave the street in as good condition as before it was disturbed.

B. B.
O.313.
§ 5.
SEC. 5. That this ordinance take effect and be in force from and after its paublication.

Passed December 18, 1883.

ORDINANCE NO. CXXX.

An Ordinance entitled An Ordinance assessing and regulating the taxes for grading, guttering graveling and curbing Fifteenth street, from Rusk street to the Gulf, Colorado and Santa Fee Railway depot.

Be it ordained by the City Council of the city of Fort Worth:

SECTION 1. Fifteenth street from Rusk street to the Gulf. Colorado and Santa Fe depot having been by contract with and by order of said city, graded, graeled and guttered and curbed, and an estimate of the cost having been filed with the city secretary, by the engineer, as well as the sizes and ownerships of the property fronting and being on said streets. Therefore, a tax of one-third of the estimated cost of grading and graveling of said streets in front of property on said streets is hereby assessed against the property fronting and adjacent to said streets so graded and graveled.

SEC. 2. Said tax shall be collected one-fifth annually, and shall be paid on or by the first day of March each year after the levy of this tax.

SEC. 3. The list of the lots so placed on file in the office of the city secretary, which said list embraces all the lots on Fifteenth street from Rusk street to the Gulf, Colorado and Santa Fe railway depot, all of which front on or adjacent to said work so constructed by the city council of the city of Fort Worth is hereby referred to and made a part of this ordinance.

SEC. 4. It shall be the duty of the officer collecting the tax herein levied to notify the owners of said property by postal card of this levy and the amount of tax due on his or her property by reason of this levy, and when payable.

SEC. 5. A tax of one third the cost of the work done in front of property respectively is assessed against said property as per list hereto attached and marked Exhibit A, and considered a part hereof:

| \multicolumn{4}{c|}{EXHIBIT A.} | \multicolumn{3}{c}{TOTAL COST IMPROVEMENTS.} |

Block.	No. Lot.	Front.	Total Front	Fifteenth Street.	Dollars.	Tax.
D 1	1	100		$250 43	$83	43
D 1	40	100		250 43	93	43
D 2	189	200		500 86	166	86
E 1	8	100		238 34	79	45
E 1	10	100		239 24	79	45
E 2	1	100		235 34	79	45
E 2	9	100	800	239 34	79	45

Passed January 7, 1884.

ORDINANCE NO. CXXXI.

An Ordinance entitled An Ordinance assessing and regulating the tax for grading, graveling, guttering and curbing on Twelfth street.

Be it ordained by the City Council of the city of Fort Worth:

SECTION 1. Twelfth street from Rusk street to the Gulf, Colorado and Santa Fe railway having been by contract with and by order of the city council of said city, graded, graveled, guttered and curbed, and an estimate of the cost having been filed with the city secretary by the city engineer as well as the sizes and ownerships of the property fronting and being on said street. Therefore, a tax of one-third the estimated cost of the grading and graveling of said street in front of the property on said street is hereby assessed against the property fronting and adjacent to said street so graded and graveled.

SEC. 2. Said tax shall be collected one-fifth annually, and shall be paid on or by the first day of March of each year after the levy of this tax.

SEC. 3. The list of the lots so placed on file in the office of the city secretary, which said list embraces all the lots on twelfth street from Rusk street to the Gulf, Colorado and Santa Fe railway, all of which front on and are adjacent to said work so constructed by the city council of the city of Fort Worth is hereby referred to and made a part of this ordinance.

Sec. 4. It shall be the duty of the officer collecting the tax herein levied to notify the owners of said property by postal card of this levy and the amount of tax due on his or her property by reason of this levy and when payable.

B. B.
O.335.
§ 4.

Sec. 5. A tax of one third the cost of the work done in front of the property respectively is assessed against said property as follows, as per list hereto attached, marked Exhibit A, and considered a part hereof.

B. B.
O.335.
§ 5.

Passed July 15, 1884.

ORDINANCE NO. CXXXII.

An Ordinance entitled An Ordinance assessing and regulating the taxes for grading, graveling, guttering and curbing on Jones street.

Be it ordained by the City Council of the city of Fort Worth:

Section 1. Jones street from the Texas and Pacific donation to Fifteenth street, having been by contract with and by order of the city council of said city graded, graveled, guttered and curbed, and an estimate of the cost having been filed with the city secretary by the city engineer as well as the sizes and ownerships of the property fronting and being on said street. Therefore, a tax of one-third the estimated cost of grading and graveling of said street in front of the property on said street is hereby assessed against the property fronting and adjacent to said street so graded and graveled.

B. B.
O.336.
§ 1.

Sec. 2. Said tax shall be collected one-fifth annually and shall be paid on or before the first day of March of each year after the levy of this tax.

B. B.
O.336.
§ 2.

Sec. 3. The lists of lots so placed on file in the office of the city secretary, which said list embraces all the lots on Jones street from the Texas and Pacific donation to Fiteenth street, all of which front on and are adjacent to said work so constructed

B. B.
O.336.
§ 3.

by the city council of the city of Fort Worth is hereby referred to and made a part of this ordinance.

B. B. O.136. § 4.
SEC. 4. It shall be the duty of the officer collecting the tax herein levied to notify the owners of said property by postal card of this levy and the amount of tax due on his or her property by reason of this levy and when payable.

B. B. O.136. § 5.
SEC. 5. A tax of one-third the cost of the work done in front of the property respectively is assessed against said property as follows as per list hereto attached, marked Exhibit A, and considered a part hereof.

Passed July 15, 1884.

ORDINANCE NO. CXXXIII.

An Ordinance entitled An Ordinance assessing and regulating the taxes for grading and graveling the alley between Weatherford and First streets.

Be it ordained by the City Council of the city of Fort Worth:

B. B. O.337. § 1.
SECTION 1. That the alley between Weatherford and First streets having been by contract with and by order of the city council of said city, graded and graveled and an estimate of the cost having been filed with the city secretary by the city engineer as well as the sizes and ownerships of the property fronting and being on said street. Therefore, a tax of one-third the estimated costs of the grading and graveling of said street in front of the property on said street is hereby assessed against the property fronting and adjacent to said street so graded and graveled.

B. B. O.337. § 2.
SEC. 2. Said tax shall be collected one-fifth annually and shall be paid on or by the first day of March of each year after the levy of this tax.

B. B. O.337. § 3.
SEC. 3. The list of the lots so placed on file in the office of the city secretary, which said list embraces all the lots on the alley as aforesaid, all of which front on are adjacent to said work so constructed by the city council of the city of Fort Worth is hereby referred to and made a part of this ordinance.

SEC. 4. It shall be the duty of the officer collecting the tax herein levied to notify the owners of said property by postal card of this levy and the amount of tax due on his or her property by reason of this levy and when payable. B. It.
O.337.
§ 4.

Sec. 5. A tax of one-third the cost of the work done in front of the property respectively is assessed against said property as follows as per list hereto attached marked Exhibit A, and considered a part hereof. B. R.
O.337.
§ 5.

Passed July 15, 1884.

ORDINANCE NO. CXXXIV.

An Ordinance to enforce the observance of the Sabbath.

Be it ordained by the City Council of the city of Fort Worth:

Sektion 1. That any person who shall hereafter labor or compel, force or oblige his employes, workmen or apprentices to labor on Sunday in this city shall be deemed guilty of a misdemeanor, and on conviction shall be fined not less than ten nor more than fifty dollars. B. A.
O.215.
§ 1.

Sec. 2. The preceeding section shall not apply to household duties, works of necessity or charity, nor to necessary work on farms or gardens in order to prevent the loss of any crop; nor to the running of railroad or street cars, wagon trains, common carriers; nor to the delivery of goods by, or the receiving or storing of said goods by the parties os their agents to whom said goods are delivered; nor to stages carrying the United States mail or passengers, nor to persons traveling; nor to keepers of hotels, boarding houses and restaurants and their servants, nor to any person who conscientiously believes that the seventh or any other day of the week ought to be observed as the Sabbath, and who actually refrains from business or labor on that day for such reason. B. A.
O.215.
§ 2.

Sec. 3. Any person who shall run or be engaged in running any horse race, or who shall permit or allow the use of any nine or ten-pin alley, or who shall be engaged in match shooting or B. A.
O.215.
§ 3.

any species of gaming for money or other consideration within the limits of this city on Sunday, shall be deemed guilty of a misdemeanor, and on conviction shall be fined not less than twenty nor more than fifty dollars.

B. A.
O.215.
§ 4.
SEC. 4. Any merchant, grocer or dealer in wares or merchandise, or trader in any lawful business whatsoever who shall barter or sell on Sunday, shall be fined not less than twenty nor more than fifty dollars. Provided, that this section shall not apply to markets or dealers in provisions as to sales made by them before nine o'clock a. m.

B. A.
O.215.
§ 5.
SEC. 5. The preceeding section shall not apply to the sale of drugs and medicines on Sunday, nor to the sale of milk, ice and newspapers.

B. A.
O.215.
§ 6.
SEC. 6. That this ordinance take effect and be in force from and after its publication as required by law.

Approved December 4, 1879.

ORDINANCE NO. CXXXV.

An Ordinance to regulate the sale of spirituous, vinous or malt liquors or medicated bitters, and to fix the rate of occupation tax upon persons engaged in the sale of said liquors.

Be it ordained by the City Council of the city of Fort Worth:

SECTION 1. That hereafter there shall be levied upon and collected from any person, firm or association of persons, engaged or engaging in the business of selling spirituous, vinous or malt liquor or medicated bitters an annual tax upon every such occupation or separate establishment as follows, to-wit:

B. A.
O.252.
§ 1.
For selling spirituous, vinous or malt liquors or medicated bitters in quantities less than one quart, - $150.00

For selling such liquors or medicated bitters in quantities of one quart and less than five gallons, - - - 100.00

For selling such liquors or medicated bitters in quantities of five gallons or more, - - - - ‧ - 150.00

For selling malt liquors exclusively, an annual tax of - 25.00

Provided, that nothing in this section shall be construed as to prevent wholesale liquor dealers or merchants who pay occupation tax as such from selling unbroken packages containing less than five gallons without being required to pay an additional tax as quart dealers.

SEC. 2. There being an emergency, this ordinance shall take effect and be in force from and after its passage.

Approved June 10, 1881.

B. P.
O.252.
§ 2.

ORDINANCE NO. CXXXVI.

An Ordinance in regard to the levying of the occupation tax.

Be it ordained by the City Council of the city of Fort Worth:

SECTION 1. That there shall be and is hereby levied an annual occupation tax on and to be collected from every person, firm, company, corporation or association of persons pursuing any of the following named occupations in the city of Fort Worth an annual tax. except where herein otherwise provided on every such occupation or separate establishment as follows: From every merchant whose purchases amount to one hundred thousand dollars annually, $62.50; from every merchant whose purchases amount to fifty thousand dollars, $30; from every merchant whose annual purchases amount to twenty-five thousand dollars, $12.50, from every merchant whose annual purchases amount to fifteen thousand dollars, $10; from every merchant whose annual purchases amount to ten thousand dollars, $6; from every merchant whose annual purchases amount to five thousand dollars, $3; from every merchant whose annual purchases amount to two thousand dollars or less, $1.50.

A merchant, within the meaning of this ordinance, is any person, firm or association of persons or corporation engaged in

B. B.
O.315.
§ 1.

buying and selling goods, wares and merchandise of any kind whatever.

From every traveling person selling patent or other medicines, $87.50; and no traveling person shall sell until said tax is paid; provided, that this tax shall not apply to commercial travelers, drummers or salesmen making sales or soliciting trade for merchants engaged in selling drugs or medicines who shall be taxed as other drummers. From every fortune-teller, $87.50; from every clairvoyant or mesmerist, who plies his or her vocation for money. an annual tax of $50; from every person, firm or association of persons engaged in discounting and shaving paper or engaged in business as money brokers or bankers or in buying and selling bonds, state or county, warrants or other claims against the state. an annual tax of $40; from every operator or owner of any daguerrian, photograph or other such like gallery, by whatever name called, an annual tax of $7; and from every person soliciting work for and daguerrian, photograph or other such like gallery or for persons engaged in the business of copying or enlarging pictures or photographs of any character, where such gallery is not situated in or such business is not in the county in which he solicits such work $3.50; from every auctioneer, an annual tax of $22.50; from every keeper of a toll bridge, an annual tax of $3.50; from every person, firm or association of persons selling upon cammission, an annual tax of $3.50; from land agents there shall be levied and collected an collected an annual tax of $2.50; the term land agent shall be construed to mean any person, firm or association of persons performing for compensation any of the following services: Purchasing or selling real estate for others; purchasing or selling land certificates for others. But this term, land agent, shall not be so construed as to levy any tax upon attorneys in addition to the one hereinafter levied. From every person practicing law, $2.50; provided, said person lives in said city of Fort Worth. From every physician, surgeon, occulist or medical specialist of any kind, traveling from place to place in the practice of his profession, an annual tax of $40, from every dentist an annual tax of $2.50, provided, he resides in said city of Fort Worth. From every other person, or firm or association of persons, pursuing the occupation of posting up advertising bills or notices, tacking up advertising cards or notices of tin, wood or other material, printing or lettering words or pictures on fences or other places as a means of advertising, the sum of $4; provided, that this clause shall not be so constructed as to tax persons advertising their own business; from every person or firm keeping a shooting gallery at which a fee is paid or demanded, an annual tax of $16.

For every billiard table, bagatelle, pigeon hole, devil among the tailors, or Jenny Lind table, or anything of the kind used for profit, an annual tax of $10; and any such table used in connection with any drinking saloon or other places of business where intoxicating liquors are sold or given away, or upon which any money or other thing of value is paid, shall be regarded as used for profit.

For every person, firm or association of persons selling, or offering for sale illustrated Police News, Police Gazettes or other illustrated publications of like character, the sum of $500 annual tax. For every person or persons who shall sell pools on horse races $2 50 for each and every day they may so sell said pools; for every nine or ten-pin alley, or any other alley used for profit, by whatever name called, constructed or operated upon the principal of bouling alley and upon which balls are rolled, without regard to the number of pins used, or whether pins are used or not, or whether the balls are rolled by hand or with a cue, an annual tax of $500; any such alley used in connection with any drinking saloon or any drug store, where intoxicating liquors are sold or given away, or upon which any money or thing of value is paid, shall be regarded as used for profit; from all persons keeping or using for profit any Hobby Horse or Flying Jennie, or device of that character, with or without name, an annual tax of $16; from every foot peddler, $5; from every peddler with one horse or one yoke of oxen, $15; from every peddler with two horses or two yokes of oxen, $30. Provided, nothing herein contained shall be so construed as to include traveling vendors of tin or earthen ware. Provided, that nothing herein contained shall be so construed as to include traveling vendors of literature exclusively religious in character, or traveling vendors of fruit trees exclusively. For every theatre or dramatic representation from which pay for admission is demanded or received, one dollar for each day they may perform, or $25 per quarter. Provided that theatrical or dramatic representations given by performers for instruction only or entirely for charitable purposes, shall not be herein included.

For every circus where equestrian or acrobatic feats and

performances are exhibited, for which pay for admission is received or demanded for each performance thereof, $25, notwithstanding more than one performance may take place daily; for every exhibition where acrobatic feats are performed for profit, not connected with the circus, $5 for each performance, for every slight-of-hand performance or exhibition of legerdemain, $5, for every fight between men and bulls, or between dogs and bulls, or between bears and dogs, or between bulls and any other animals, $250 for each performance per year; for every cock pit, when kept for profit or upon which money or thing of value is bet or paid, $12.50, for every menagerie, wax-work or exhibition of any kind, where a separate fee for admission is demanded or received, $5 for every day on which fees for such admission are received. Provided, that exhibitions by associations, organized for promotion of art, science, charity or benevolence, shall be exempt from taxation. For every concert, where a fee for admission is demanded or received, $1. Provided, that entertainments when given by the citizens for charitable purposes or for the support or aid of library or associations, are excepted.

For every livery or feed stable, fifteen cents for each hack, buggy or other vihicle let for hire not connected with a livery stable, $1; for every wagon yard not connected with a livery or feed or sale stable, $2.50.

For every life insurance company doing business in said city, $7 annual tax; for every fire or marine or guarantee insurance company, an annual tax of $7.

From every person, firm or association of persons dealing in lightning rods, an annual tax of $18; from every person or persons, firm or association of persons following the occupation of cotton broker, cotton factor and commission merchant, an annual tax of $17.50. Provided that a merchant who pays an occupation tax as herein prescribed, shall not be considered as a cotton buyer. From every person, firm or association of persons dealing in sewing machines, an annual tax of $7; from every person canvassing for the sale of sewing machines, an annual tax of $7. Provided, a merchant who pays an occupation taxes required by this section, shall not be required to pay this special tax for selling sewing machines.

From each telephone company doing business in the city, $10; from each gas company manufacturing gas, an annual tax of $17.50. Provieed, that the fact that a tax is levied by this ordinance upon Bagatelle, Pigeon Hole, Devil Among the Tailors, Jenny Lind tables, or anything of the kind used for profit and upon any nine or ten-pin alley or other alley used for profit, shall not be construed to exempt from the punishment prescribed by law any person who may violate any of the provisions of chapter three of the Penal Code. Provided, further, that this ordinance shall not be construed to prevent persons or firms of persons who pay an occupation tax for persuing the occupation of a merchant in said city of Fort Worth from soliciting trade within the corporate limits of said city.

SEC. 6. That this ordinance take effect and be in force from and after its publication as required by law.

Approved October 18, 1882.

ORDINANCE NO. CXXXVII.

To provide for the levy and collection of an advalorem and poll tax for the year A. D, 188

Be it ordained by the City Council of the city of Fort Worth:

B. B.
O.341.
§ 1.
SECTION 1. There shall be collected an annual direct advalorem municipal tax of two-fifths of one per cent. of the cash value thereof estimated, in lawful currency of the United States, on real property situated in and on all moveable property owned in this city on the first day of January, A. D. 1884, except so much thereof as may be exempted by the constitution and laws of the State of Texas, which cash value shall be estimated in lawful currency of the United States.

B. B.
O.341.
§ 2
SEC. 2. There shall be levied and collected an annual direct special advalorem tax of one-half of one per cent. of the cash value thereof, in lawful currency of the United States, on all real property situated, and movable property owned in this city on the first day of January, A. D. 1884, except so much thereof as may be exempted by the constitution and laws of the State of Texas; said tax being as a public building fund.

P. P.
O.341.
§ 3.
SEC. 3. There shall be levied and collected an annual direct special advalorem tax of two-fifths of one per cent of the cash value thereof in lawful currency of the United States, on all real property situated, and all movable property owned, in this city on the first day of January, A. D. 1884, except so much thereof as may be exempted by the constitution and laws of the State of Texas; said special tax being for the support and maintainance of public Free schools in said city.

B. B.
O.341.
§ 4.
SEC. 4. There shall be levied and collected an annual direct special advalorem tax of two-fifths of one per cent. of the cash value thereof in lawful currency of the United States on all real property situated in and all movable property owned in this city on the first day of January, A. D. 1884, except so much thereof as may be exempted by the constitution and laws of the State of

Texas. Said special tax being for the purpose of paying the interest on the out standing bonded indeptedness to-wit: The one hundred and ninety thousand dollars in bonds of the city of Fort Worth, which said bonds were issued on the ...... day of ...... A. D. 1883, for street improvement and sewerage; also for the creating of a sinking fund of two per cent. on said amount as provided in Ordinance No. 293.

SEC. 5. There shall be levied and collected from every mail person between the age of twenty-one and sixty years of age, resident in this city on the first day of January, A. D. 1884, an annual poll tax of one dollar each. Provided, the following persons are exempt from poll tax, to-wit: Insane, blind, deaf and dumb persons, and those who have only one hand or one foot. B. B.
O.341.
§ 5.

SEC. 6. That this ordinance take effect and be in force from and after its passage.

Passed August 5, 1884.

ORDINANCE NO. CXXXVIII.

An Ordinance regulating job wagons and street hacks, and establishing a license on the same.

Be it ordained by the City Council of the city of Fort Worth:

SECTION 1. Hereafter there shall be collected an occupation tax of fifteen dollars per annum from each party who run a job wagon or float, which said amounts shall be collected on each job or express wagon or float so run by any person. B. B.
O.317.
§ 1.

SEC. 2. There shall be collected from each party or person who runs a carriage or street hack for hire in said city, an annual occupation tax of thirty dollars for each carriage or hack so run by said person. B. B.
O.317.
§ 2.

SEC. 3. It shall be the duty of the tax assessor and collector to give, without charge, to each party who pays an occupation tax on such job or express wagon a number for him to place on his said wagon, and it shall be the duty of said assessor and collector to keep a record of the numbers so made out and delivered to the party paying said tax. B. B.
O.317.
§ 3.

SEC. 4. The assessor and collector shall also deliver, with-

B. B.
O. 317.
§ 4

out charge, to each party paying a tax, as indicated in Section 2, a number to be placed on his said hack or carriage, and like record keep as is mentioned in Section 3.

B. B.
O. 317.
§ 5.

SEC. 5. Any and all persons running a hack, carriage or express or job wagon in said city for hire without having on said vehicle the number selected for him by the assessor and collector, shall be deemed guilty of a misdemeanor, and fined in any sum not exceeding twenty-five nor less that five dollars.

B. B.
O. 317.
§ 6.

SEC. 6. Any person violating section one or two of this ordinance, or failing to pay the tax therein named, while engaged in the business therein indicated, is guilty of a misdemeanor, and shall be fined in any sum not exceeding the tax, which said amount shall be remitted upon the payment of the said tax and costs therein incurred.

SEC. 7. That the tax above be collected semi-annually in advance.

SEC. 8. That this ordinance take effect and be in force from and after its puublication as require by law.

Passed January 15, 1884.

ORDINANCE NO. CXXXIX.

An Ordinance punishing the keeper of variety shows, theatres and such like places.

Be it ordained by the City Council of the city of Fort Worth:

B. A.
O. 111.
§ 1.

SECTION I. That any person who shall keep a house where leud, indecent or immodest theatrical representations or plays are exhibited, or theatrical representations or plays in which leud women or prostitutes, or women of ill fame or bad repute take part or aid, or where singing or dancing by characters is therein permitted, shall, on conviction thereof, be fined in any sum not less than ten nor more than fifty dollars.

B. A.
O. 111.
§ 2.

SEC. 2. That any person who shall exercise control over such a house, or who shall be in any wise concerned or interested in the keeping of such house, or shall aid persons so offending, shalled be regarded as the keeper thereof, within the meaning of this ordinance, and shall be punished as such.

SEC. 3. Any person who shall rent a house, room or premises to another to be used for the purpose mentioned in the first section of this ordinance, shall be considered as an aider in the commission of the offense defined in this ordinance. B. A. O.215. § 3.

SEC. 4. That this ordinance take effect and be in force from and after its publication as required by law.

Approved May 31, 1877.

ORDINANCE NO. CXL.

An Ordinance prohibiting variety shows, theatres, concerts, or shows of any kind from being given on Sunday.

Be it ordained by the City Council of the city of Fort Worth:

SECTION 1. That it shall be unlawful for any person or persons to give, have or exhibit any variety show, theatre, concert, or show of any kind on Sunday within the corporate limits of this city. B. A. O.124. § 1.

SEC. 2. That any person violating the provision of this ordinance, shall de declared guilty of a misdemeanor, and upon conviction thereof, shall be fined in any sum not less than fifty nor more than one hundred dollars. B. A. O.124. § 2.

SEC. 3. That this ordinance take effect and be in force from and after its publication as required by law.

Approved September 13, 1877.

ORDINANCE NO. CXLI.

An ordinance regulating the construction of theatres and public halls.

Be it ordained by the City Council of the city of Fort Worth:

SECTION 1. That all theatres or public halls in this city open or used for dramatic or other entertainments, shall be provided with one doorway of at least twelve feet in width, or with two doorwas of at least eight feet in width, each.

SEC. 2. That all doors to such theatres or halls shall be so arranged as to open outward in all cases.

SEC. 3 That all stairways leading to the doorway of any theatre or public hall in this city shall be the same width of the doorway, and shall be built firm and strong, capable of bearing a weight equal to thirty thousand pounds. All stairways shall be provided with good railings on all sides.

SEC. 4. That all approaches to any stairway leading to any theatre or public or public hall in this city shall be at least twelve feet in width and shall extend unobstructed from the foot of the stairway to the street.

SEK. 5. That it shall be the duty of the city marshal to notify all owners or agents of any theatres or public hall in this city of the requirements of this ordinance, and to inspect all such doorways, stairways and approaches and report any refusal or neglect of any owner or agent of such theatre or public hall to the city attorney.

SEC. 6. Any owner or agent of any theatre or public hall, without complying with the requirements of this ordinance, shall be deemed guilty of a misdemeanor, and upon convition, shall be fined in any sum from fity to one hundred dollars for each offense, and each entertainment or exhibition shall constitute an offense.

SEC. 7. That this crdinance take effect and be in force from and after its publication according to law.

Passed December 20, 1879.

ORDINANCE NO. CXLII.

An Ordinance prohibiting certain conduct in theatres and opera houses during performances.

Be it ordained by the City Council of the city of Fort Worth:

SECTION 1. That any person or persons who shall be guilty of wilful loud talking, laughing, hissing, whistling, cat calling, smoking, throwing paper or other missiles from one place to another, or any other act or conduct tending to harrass, annoy or disturb any of the spectators, or actors or performers in any theatre or opera house while any performance is going on, or while persons are assembled for the purpose of witnessing any performance, shall be deemed guilty of a misdemeanor, and upon conviction thereof shall be fined in some sum not less than ten dollars nor more than one hundred dollars.

SEC. 2. That this ordinance shall take effect and be in force from and after its publication as require by law.

Passed April 4, 1884.

ORDINANCE NO. CXLIII.

An Ordinance regulating theatres and variety shows where intoxicating liquors are sold or drank.

Be it ordained by the City Council of the city of Fort Worth:

B. A.
O.227.
§ 1.

SECTION 1. That it shall be unlawful for any person or persons to give, carry on or maintain in this city any theatre or variety show in any house or place where intoxicating liquors are sold or drank without first having obtained from the city council a permit to give, carry on or maintain said theatre or variety show. Provided, that no permit shall be valid for more than three months, and any person or persons violating the provisions of this ordinance shall be deemed guilty of a misdemeanor, and upon conviction thereof, shall be fined in any sum not less than twenty-five nor more than one hundred dollars.

B. A.
O.227.
§ 2.

SEC. 2. That in no case shall the city council give the permit required in the foregoing section until the party desiring the same shall file a written application therefor, accompanied with the receipt of the assessor and collector for the sum of sixty-two dollars and fifty cents, the amount of city tax for theatres for three months, and the written consent of two-thirds of the citizens living within one block of the house or place where such theatre or show may be given, and shall file a bond, payable to the city of Fort Worth in the sum of two hundred and fifty dollars, conditioned that he or they will pay a salary of forty dollars per month to a policeman, to be appointed by the city council, whose duty it shall be to be and remain in and around said house or place where such theatre or shows are being given and preserve order, and arrest all offenders against the ordinances of the city and laws of the State.

B. A.
O.227.
§ 4.

SEC. 3. That this ordinance take effect and be in force from and after its publication as required by law.

Approved April 21, 1880.

ORDINANCE NO. CXLIV.

An Ordinance regulating railway trains.

Be it ordained by the City Council of the city of Fort Worth:

SECTION 1. That any person or company who shall, in this city, run or cause to be run any locomotive. engine or car at a greater rate of speed than six miles an hour, shall be deemed guilty of a misdemeanor. and on conviction thereof, be fined not less than one nor more than twenty-five dollars. B. A. O.256. § 1.

SEC. 2. No person or railroad company shall obstruct any street, alley, sidewalk crossing or other thoroughfare of said city by leaving thereon any car or rolling stock for a longer time than five minutes; or to stop, or cause to be stopped, any railway engine or car across any street, alley, road, highway or other passway so as to obstruct or interfere with free passage thereon for a longer time than five minutes under a penalty of not less than one nor more than twenty-five dollars. B. A. O.256. § 2.

SEC. 3. Whoever, not being an employe or passenger on any railroad car, engine or tender shall jump on or off, cling to or hang on to the same while in motion, shall, on conviction thereof, be fined not less than one nor more than twenty-five dollars. B. A. O.256. § 3.

SEC. 4. Any person or corporation who shall conduct, run or cause to be run, any railway locomotive or engine without ringing a bell attached thereto before starting, and all the time such locomotive or engine shall be in motion, within the corporate limits of this city, shall be deemed guilty of a misdemeanor, and on conviction shall be fined not less than one dollar nor more than twenty-five dollars. B. A. O.256. § 4.

SEC. 5. All railroad companies whose tracks now or may hereafter enter or pass through the corporate limits of the city of Fort Worth, shall respectively construct, repair, keep and maintain good, safe and sufficient culverts, crossings and bridges, with good, safe and easy approaches taereto on all public alleys. streets and highways where the respective tracks pass under, across or over any alley, street or highway within said city. B. A. O.256. § 5.

SEC. 6. Whenever any crossing, culvert or bridge shall be needed upon the line of any railroad within this city, or the same shall be deemed insufficient or unsafe, or shall need repairing, it shall be the duty of the street commissioners or the mayor to give to such company five days notice of the work to be done and the place where required, and any railroad company neglecting or refusing to construct or repair any crossing, culvert or bridge after having received five days notice to do so, shall be fined not less than one nor more than one hundred dollars.

SEC. 7. This ordinance shall take effect and be in force from and after its publication by law.

Approved August 17, 1881.

ORDINANCE NO. CXLV.

An Ordinance granting the right of way to the Texas and Pacific Railway Company over and upon the streets therein named.

Be it ordained by the City Council of the city of Fort Worth:

SECTION 1. That the Texas and Pacific Railway Company is hereby fully authorized and empowered with the right to construct, equip, operate, maintain, own and control a steam railway, together with all necessary switches, turnouts, sidings and depots on either or all of the following named streets and their extensions in said city of Fort Worth, to-wit: Belknap, Weatherford, Hayes, First, Second, Third, Fourth, Hampton, Eighth, Ninth, Tenth, Eleventh, Morgan, Luella Avenue, Fourteenth, Elm, Fifteenth, Sixteenth, Brewer, Seventeenth, Pecan, Nineteenth and Grove streets, and the streets connecting and intersecting therewith as long as said Texas and Pacific Railway Company may operate the said railway.

SEC. 2. That this ordinance take effect and be in force from and after its passage.

Passed January 19, 1831.

ORDINANCE NO. CXLVI.

An Ordinance prohibiting the unlawful entering or intruding upon the premises of another person without his consent.

Be it ordained by the City Council of the city of Fort Worth:

SECTION I. It shall be unlawful for any person or persons to enter or intrude upon the premises of another without his consent, and that any person or persons violating the provisions of this ordinance shall be deemed guilty of a misdemeanor, and upon conviction thereof, shall be fined in any sum not more than ten dollars.

SEC. 2. That this ordinance take effect and be in force from and after its publication as required by law.

Approved May 7, 1880.

B. A.
O.232.
§ 1.

B. A.
O.232.
§ 2.

ORDINANCE NO. CXLVII.

An Ordinance regulating the erection or the placing of telegraph poles or telephone poles, and the height from the ground which wire may be placed on the same on the streets of the city of Fort Worth.

Be it ordained by the City Council of the city of Fort Worth:

SECTION 1. No telegraph or telephone company shall hereafter erect any telegraph or telephone pole or poles on the streets of the city of Fort Worth except as hereinafter stated.

SEC. 2. Every telegraph or telephone pole or poles to be erected on the streets or sidewalks of the city of Fort Worth shall be placed on the outside of the sidewalk and put within the curb line.

SEC. 3. No telegraph or telephone company shall hereafter place any telegraph or telephone wire or any telegraph or telephone pole or poles in any other way than hereinafter mentioned on any street in the said city of Fort Worth.

SEC. 4. No telegraph or telephone wire shall hereafter be placed nearer than twenty-five feet from the sidewalk; that is, said wires shall be at least twenty-five feet in the clear above the sidewalk on Main and Houston streets.

B. B.
O.316.
§ 1.

B. B.
O.316.
§ 2.

B. B.
O.316.
§ 3.

B. B.
O.321.
§ 1.

B. B.
O.321.
§ 2

Sec. 5. No telegraph or telephone wire shall hereafter be placed at a height of less than twenty-two feet from the sidewalk on Throckmorton and Rusk streets.

B. B.
O.321.
§ 3.

Sec. 6. No telephone or telegraph wire shall be placed at a height less than twenty feet from the sidewalk on all streets not specially enumerated in this ordinance.

B. B.
O.316.
§ 7.

Sec. 7. All telegraph and telephone wire shall cross the said streets of the said city of Fort Worth at right angles, or as near to right angles as possible.

B. B.
O.316.
§ 8.

Sec. 8. All telegraph or telephone poles which are on the street of said city of Fort Worth shall be placed in the same manner as indicated in Section two of this ordinadce.

B. B.
O.316.
§ 9.

Sec. 9. All telegraph and telephone wire now in operation and across the streets, or on the streets of said city shall be placed as indicated in Sections 4, 5, 6 and 7 of this ordinance.

B. B.
O.321.
§ 4.

Sec. 10. All telegraph and telephone poles not placed as required by this ordinance (Sec. 2), and all telegraph and telephone wires which are not placed as indicated in Sections 4, 5 and 6 of this ordinance, are hereby declared a public nuisance.

B. B.
O.321.
§ 5.

Sec. 11. That the managers and parties having control of any telegraph and telephone companies in said city who shall allow any poles or wires belonging to respective companies to remain or be placed in any other manner than as required by this ordinance, shall be deemed guilty of a misdemeanor, and upon conviction, shall be fined in any sum not less than five dollars nor more than fifty dollars, each day being a separate offense.

P. B.
O.316.
§ 12.

Sec. 12. No telegraph or telephone company shall hereafter have the right to erect any telegraph or telephone pole or poles on any street or sidewalks of the city of Fort Worth without having an agent or some person legally authorized to sign a contract on behalf of said company, or guaranteeing to the said city of Fort Worth the right to use the top arm or top cross or center of every such pole so erected for municipal purposes, the use of the same to be free of charge to the said city of Fort Worth.

B. B.
O.316.
§ 13.

Sec. 13. That this ordinance take effect and be in force from and after its publication as required by law.

Sections 1, 2, 3, 7, 8, 9 and 12, passed Jan. 7, 1884.
Sections 4, 5, 6, 10, 11 and 13 passed March 18, 1884.

ORDINANCE NO. CXLVIII.

An Ordinance defining nuisances in the erection and maintaining of telephone and telegraph wires and polls, and to punish the violation thereof and provide for the abatement of such nuisance..

Be it ordained by the City Council of the city of Fort Worth:

SECTION 1. That it shall not be lawful for any telegraph or telephone company to erect or maintain on Houston or Main streets. in the city of Fort Worth, more than one line of poles and wires, and it shall be unlawful for any telephone or telegraph company to erect or maintain more than three posts or poles on any one side of any one block on any one street of this city unless by special permission from this council. That it shall be unlawful for any telephone or telegraph company to allow any of their telephone or telegraph wires to be or remain within twenty-five feet of the surface of the sidewalk on Houston or Main streets. That it shall be unlawful for any agent, manager or superintendent of any telephone or any telegraph company to manage, use, control or superintend any telephone or telegraph company wires or poles in this city erected or being contrary to this ordinance.

R. B. O.343. § 1.

SEC. 2. That any person found guilty of violating this ordinance shall be deemed guilty of a nuisance and punished by fine of not less than twenty nor more than one hundred dollars, and in addition thereto may be imprisoned in the city prison for a period of not more than five days.

B. B. O.343. § 2.

SEC. 3. That any telephone wire or poles, any telegraph wire or poles erected or maintained contrary to Section 1, of this ordinance, shall be and is declared a nuisance, and the owner or agent or manager or superintendent or operator of any such telephone wires or poles, or any agent, owner, manager, superintendent or operator of any such telegraph company wires or poles, shall, upon notice of the city marshal, within twenty-four hours after the receipt of any such notice, abate the said nuisance.

B. B. O.343. § 3.

SEC 4. If any person whose duty it is under Section 3 of

this ordinance, to abate the said nuisance, shall fail or refuse to abate the same upon notice, then the city marshal of the city of Fort Worth be and he is hereby instructed and authorized, after he has given the notice required by this ordinance, and after the expiration of the time allowed such person to abate the said nuisance, to remove and abate the said nuisance either by cutting the poles or wires or both as to him shall seem best.

B. B.
O.343.
§ 4.

SEC. 5. That this ordinance take effect and be in force from and after its publication as required by law.

B. B.
O.343.
§ 5.

Approved August 8, 1884.

ORDINANCE NO. CXLIX.

An Ordinance prohibiting washing, bathing or swimming, or washing, bathing or swimhorses or other animals in certain portions of the Trinity river or in either branch of the same.

Be it Ordained by the City Council of the City of Fort Worth:

SECTION 1. That it shall be unlawful for any person or persons to wash, bathe or swim their persons or articles of any kind, or to wash, bathe or swim horses or other animals in the Trinity river within six hundred yards of the forks of said river or in either branch of the same above said forks within the corporate limits of the city of Fort Worth. Provided, that it shall be lawful for any person to wash buggies, carriages or other vehicles or to wash or bathe horses in the Trinity river at any place below where the water-works are now situated and where the pumps from the same enter said river.

B. A.
O.230.
§ 1.

SEC. 2. That any person or persons violating the provisions of this ordinance shall be guilty of a misdemeanor, and upon conviction thereof, shall be fined in any sum not less than five dollars nor more that than fifty dollars.

B. A.
O.230.
§ 2.

SEC. 3. That this ordinance take effect and be in force from and after its publication as required by law.

B. A.
O.230.
§ 4.

Approved April 26, 1880.

ORDINANCE NO. CL.

An Ordinance to define and punish vagrancy.

Be it ordained by the City Council of the city of Fort Worth:

SECTION 1. That every vagrant in this city shall, upon conviction, be fined in any sum not exceeding ten dollars.

B. A.
O.213.
§ 1.

SEC. 2. The following persons are vagrants within the meaning of the preceeding section:

First—An idle person who lives without any means of support, and makes no exertions to obtain a livelihood by honest employment.

Second—Any person who strolls idly about the streets, having no local habitation, and no honest business or employment.

B. A.
O.213.
§ 2.

Third—A person who strolls about to tell fortunes or to exhibit tricks not licensed by law.

Fourth—A common prostitute.

Fifth—A professional Gambler.

Sixth—Any person who goes about to beg alms who is not afflicted or disabled by a physical malady or misfortune.

Seventh—A habitual drunkard who abandons, neglects or refuses to aid in the support of his family.

SEC. 3. That this ordinance take effect and be in force from and after its publication as required by law.

B. A.
O.213.
§ 3.

Approved November 19, 1879.

ORDINANCE NO. CLI.

An Ordinance relation to vehicles passing each other.

Be it ordained by the City Council of the city of Fort Worth:

B. A.
O. 21.
§ 1.

SECTION I. In case of persons meeting each other in any highway, street or thoroughfare in this city, each person so meeting shall turn off and go to the right side of the highway, street or thoroughfare so as to enable such vehicles to pass each other without accident. Whoever shall violate this ordinance shall be deemed guilty of a misdemeanor, and on conviction shall be fined not less than one nor more than ten dollars.

B. A.
O. 21.
§ 2.

SEC. 2. That this ordinance take effect and be in force from and after its publication as required by law.

Approved A 10, 1873.

ORDINANCE NO. CLII.

An Ordinance dividing the city into wards and defining the same.

Be it ordained by the City Council that the city of Fort Worth be and the same is hereby divided into four Wards:

SECTION 1. The First Ward shall embrace all the territory north of a line running with Ninth street and east of a line running with Main street in said corporation to the corporate limits of the same.

SEC. 2. The Second Ward shall embrace all the territory within the corporate limits west of the west line of the First Ward and north of Ninth street—the north line of S. G. Jennings' survey and J. M. C. Lynsh survey.

SEC. 3. The Third Ward shall embrace all the territory within the corporate limits south of a line running with Ninth street and east of Main street.

SEC. 4. The Fourth Ward shall enbrace all that territory in the corporate limits south and west of Ninth street of the north line of S. G. Jennings' survey, and the north line of the J. M. C. Lynch survey and west of the line of Main street.

SEC. 5. That this ordinance be in effect from and after its passage.

Approved July 5, 1883.

ORDINANCE NO. CLIII.

An Ordinance to provide for a system of Water Works for the city of Fort Worth for the extinguishment of fires, sanitary and other purposes.

This contract, made and entered into this the 26th day of May, A. D. 1882, by and between the Fort Worth Water Works Company, a corporation of the city of Fort Worth in the county of Tarrant and State of Texas, party of the first part, and the city of Fort Worth, a body corporate of the county of Tarrant and State of Texas, party of the second part, witnesseth: Whereas, the city council of the said city of Fort Worth deem it necessary to provide for a more efficient protection of the property of tax payers of the said city from fire, and also to secure to the citizens of said city a supply of water suitable for domestic purposes and for the further benefit to the city of Fort Worth hereinafter mentioned. Therefore,

Be it ordained by the City Council of the city of Fort Worth:

B. B.
O.273.
§ 1.
SECTION 1. That there is hereby given and granted to the "Fort Worth Water Works Company" the right and privilege for twenty-five years from the date of the execution of this contract of supplying the city of Fort Worth, and the citizens thereof, with good, healthful and wholesome water for domestic use, and for the extinguishment of fires and for manufacturing purposes.

B. B.
O.273.
§ 2.
SEC. 2. The said company is hereby authorized to establish, construct, maintain and operate said works in the said city of Fort Worth, to receive, take and store, conduct and distribute water through the city; to construct and extend acqueducts, mains and pipes through all the streets, alleys, lanes and public grounds, across any streams or bridges in said city; to erect and maintain all engines, machinery and all necessary appliances for the proper conducting of said works, and for supplying said city and the inhabitants thereof with good, healthful and wholesome water for domestic, manufacturing, fire and other purposes. The said Fort Worth Water Works Company shall have the

right to take up all pavements or sidewalks on streets, alleys, lanes, and public grounds, and make such excavations thereon as may be necessary to lay, repair and maintain acqueducts and pipes below the surface of the ground for conveying and distributing said water as aforesaid. Provided, said company shall, within a reasonable time and with all proper dispatch, replace, and repair all pavements and sidewalks and fill all such excavations and restore the streets in as good condition as they were before as nearly as practicable.

SEC. 3. Said company shall be liable for all damages occasioned by a failure to protect and guard persons and property from injury by reason of the removal of such pavements and sidewalks and the making of such excavations as aforesaid.
    B. A.
0.273.
§ 3.

SEC. 4. The said water works shall be constructed with not less capacity than two million gallons in twenty four hours, and also to produce the fire streams hereinafter mentioned, and there shall be an auxiliary reserve high pressure pump of the same capacity making an aggregate easy working capacity of four million gallons in twenty-four hours.
    B. A.
0.273.
§ 4.

SEC. 5. Said Fort Worth Water Works Company shall lay not less than nine miles of mains including hydrant connection as shown on the plat of said city marked "Exhibit A," and which is hereby made a part of this contract for the distribution of water within the corporate limits of said city so located as best to secure the fire protection of the city and for the supply of water for domestic purposes. Said mains to be located as the city council may direct. All mains shall be of standard weight and strength to insure the fire streams hereinafter mentioned, and tested so as to stand a pressure of three hundred pounds to the square inch, and all mains shall be of such size as to procure an easy flow of water through the entire system of pipes, and such mains shall be from six to sixteen inches in their inner diameter.
    B. A.
0.273.
§ 5.

SEC. 6. The said Fort Worth Water Works Company shall erect eighty double nozzles fire hydrants of the most approved pattern upon the mains and pipes as provided for in this ordinance; the said hydrants to be located by the city council before the said mains and pipes are first laid.
    B. A.
0.273.
§ 6.

SEC. 7. The said city of Fort Worth agree to pay said Fort Worth Water Works Company an annual rental of one hundred dollars for each of said hydrants for the purposes contemplated
    B. A.
0.273.
§ 7.

in this contract, which said rental shall be payable semi-annually on the first days of June and December of each year in a warrant drawn on the city treasarer—that is to say, at the end of each six months of each year during the full time specified in this contract; the first payment, or a pro rata proportion thereof for each of said hydrants to become due and payable on the first day of June and December, as the case may be, after said hydrant is placed in position and ready for use; and for the purpose of providing for the payment of all hydrant rental becoming due under the provisions of this contract, the said city shall annually make an appropriation sufficient to pay the same out of the first monies not otherwise appropriated arising from the general revenues of the city.

SEC. 8. For all extension of mains which the city may hereafter order for fire purposes in addition to the mains contemplated in the contract, the said company shall erect not less than ten fire hydrants to the mile, for which the said city shall pay the rental of one hundred dollars each per year until the whole number shall amount to one hundred hydrants, and for all further extensions ordered by the city council for fire purposes, the said Water Words Company shall erect not less than ten fire hydrants to the mile, for which the city shall pay an annual rental of fifty dollars for each hydrant payable as hereinbefore provided.

SEC. 9. The said Fort Worth Water Works Company shall permit any owner or occupant of any building to erect stand pipes and connect the same with the mains hereby authorized to be laid, or any main hereafter laid by order of the city council of said city of Fort Worth under the provisions of this contract, and they shall have the use of water through such stand pipes and connections for the prevention and extinguishment of fires, free of charge, upon giving the said Fort Worth Water Works Company a written agreement that they will not use the water from said pipes and connections for any other purpose whatever. The said city of Fort Worth shall have the right to erect and connect fire hydrants to the mains at any time under the provisions of this contract at the expenses of said city, and use the same for the prevention and extinguishment of fires free of charge. Provided, always, that the said city of Fort Worth hall first pay a resntal on the first eighty hydrants contemplated in this contract. The city of Fort Worth shall have by the city after first paying a rental for at least ten hydrants for every mile of the first ten miles. The owner or occupant of any property may also connect stand pipes or hydrants with the mains upon the city paying the rental hereinbefore mentioned as soon as the works are completed. The said Fort Worth Water Works Company shall cause the fire streams, hereinafter mentioned,, to be produced in the presence of the city council, or such committee as the council may appoint, which test shall take place within five days after the completion of said works, and at the first meeting of the council after the full and faithful performance of the test hereinafter specified the city council shall accept the works, and the date of such acceptance shall be the time at which the city shall commence to pay the rental for the hydrants at that time located.

SEC. 10. Said water works, when constructed, shall have the capacity of discharging eight fire streams through one-inch nozzles from any eight hydrants located upon pipes or mains not less than eight inches in their diameter, as shown on the plat submitted herewith, and four streams from hydrants located on pipes not less than six inches in diameter through fifty feet of two and one-half inch hose to a height of one hundred feet or maintain its equivalent in pressure at the nozzle of said hydrants so long as it may be necessary for the extinguishment of any fires, B. A. O.273. § 10.

SEC. 11. The said city shall have the right to use water free of charge from the hydrants for the purpose of flushing gutters and sewers whenever the council shall deem it necessary for the interest of the city on giving notice to the person in charge of the works; the city shall also have water free of charge for the department buildings, city hall and offices occupied for city purpose, for all public schools of the city, for six public watering places for man and beast, and also for six fountains in parks and grounds owned by the city the, jets of which shall not exceed one-sixteenth inch orifice and to run not to exceed six hours a a day for eight months in a year; said public watering places and fountains to be erected by said Fort Worth Water Works Company and kept in repair by said company at their own proper expense, and to be located at such points in the city as may be designated by the city council. B. A. O.273. § 11.

SEC. 12. The rates and charges of said company to private the same right to connect stand pipes to all mains ordered persons shall not exceed the following table of yearly water rates payable quarterly:

Alcohol, per each barrel made, ten cents, ale cellar from $10 to $50; bakery, each oven, $10 to $50; barber's shop, first chair, $8, each addition $3.50, bath, private, $4, bath, boarding house, $6; bath public, each tub $14; beer, each barrel brewed, five cents; beer house from $8 to $40; billiard saloon, each table, $3, boarding house, eabh room, $1 25. but no license less than $10; book binding, $10 to $75; brick work per M, eight cents; brick yard, meter rate; candle manufacturing, meter rate; candy manufacturing, $10 to 75; church, $5 to $10; baptestry, $5 to $10; cigar manufacturing, per hand, $1.50 no license less than $10; club room $20 to $100; coffee saloon $5 to $20; confectionery, $10 to $75; cow, $1.50; distillery. special rates,——; dram shop, $10 to $100; dyeing and scouring $15 to $100; forge, each, $3; fountain for six months, running not more than four hours per day, $10 to $150; hall $5 to $50; hat manufacturing, $20 to $100; horse $1.50; hose for private stable, $5; hose for livery stable, $20 to $75; washing pavements per foot front 20 cents, street and sidewalks, 25 cents; hotel, per room, $1.50; ice cream saloon, $10 to $50; labratory, special or meter, ——; laundry, special or meter, ——; livery stable, per stall, $2.50; malting, per bushel, 1 cent; Office, $5 to $25; oyster saloon, $10 to $45; packing house, or meter, ——; photograph gallery, $10 to $36; plastering, per square yard, ¾ cent; rectifying whisky, eer barrel, 3 cents; residence, by one family, one to four rooms, $3; residence, by one family, five to six rooms, $10; residence..one family, seven to eight rooms, $12; residence, one family, eight to ten rooms, $14; residence, one family, ten to twelve rooms, $16; over twelve rooms, each room, $1.50; restaurant, $10 to $125; sale stable, per stall, $2; school, free, it public; shop, $5 to $35; slaughter house. special or meter, ——; soap manufacturing, special or meter; soda manufacturing, special or meter; spirits gas, each barrel made, 8 cents; public garden sprinkling, $20 to $100; starch factory, special or meter, ——, steam boilers, special or meters; stock yards, special or meter; stone work, per perch. 4 cents; store, $5 to $40; tanning, per vat, $5; no license less than $25; tenement, per room, $1.25; tobacco factory per s. and hogshead, $2; urinal basin $3; urinal basin, public, $6 to $30; vault, residence. $5, ——; vehicle, $2.50; vinegar, each barrel manufactured, 5 cents; washing bottles, $5 to $30;

B. A.
O.273.
§ 1.

washing barrels, 5 cents; water clost, private, $5; water closet, public, $8.

Any person or corporation shall have the right and privilege to purchase and have supplied to them water from said company for consumption at their residence or place of business at the meter rates herein prescribed; the quantity to be ascertained by meters of accurate and approved pattern and action. It is further agreed by the Fort Worth Water Works Company, that when the population of said city shall reach fifteen thousand inhabitants, to be ascertained by the city council, then the rates or price for water for private purposes as above fixed shall be reduced twenty per cent.

SEC. 13. The city of Fort Worth shall have the right, at its option, to acquire, by purchase, and become the sole owner of said works, including all grounds, machinery, mains, pipes, buildings, franchisies and property thereto appertaining at the expiration of five years or any time thereafter from the date of the acceptance of the works, upon giving one year's notice of such intention, upon paying therefor, to the owners thereof, the value of said property, to be ascertained by appraisal as follows, viz: The said city shall select one competent person and the owner of the water works another, and the two selected shall select a third, or in case they cannot agree upon such third person, a third person shall be appointed by the district judge of Tarrant county, and the three men so determined upon shall appraise the value of said property, exclusive of franchise, at its then cash value, which appraisal shall be binding upon said Fort Worth Water Works Company as to the value thereof, but shall not be binding upon the city unless said appraisal shall be satisfied by the city council and the city shall have the right to become the owner of said works and property at the appraised value when said appraisement shall have been satisfied by the city council. In case the said city shall not purchase and become the owner of said works and property, as aforesaid, at the expiration of twenty-five years, then all the rights, franchises and privileges .... to the said Fort Worth Water Works Company shall be extended to said company for a ... er period of twenty-fiive years thereafter, subject to the right of said city to purchase, as aforesaid, and subject to all the duties, liabilities, obligations and penalties herein. Provided, however, if at the time of said purchase by the said city, said works and

B. A.
O.273.
§ 13.

franchises shall be unencumbered by mortgage, otherwise the city shall assume and pay such liability as part of the appraised value, as aforesaid, made and ascertained.

SEC. 14. It is hereby agreed by and between the said Fort Worth Water Works Company and the said city of Fort Worth, that so much of the hydrant rental to be paid by the city of Fort Worth, under the provisions of this contract, as will fully pay all the interest on all outstanding bonds of the said Fort Worth Water Works Company and all bonds that may hereafter be assessed by the said water works company shall be paid to the holder of said bonds through their trustee at the time specified in this contract for the payment of such hydrant rental to the said Water Works Company, so long and until all such bonds are fully paid and cancelled and the balance of the hydrant rental due, if any from the city, shall be paid to the said Water Works Company. It being understood that the hydrant rental which the said city of Fort Worth agrees to pay to the said Fort Worth Water Works Company for fire protection, or so much thereof as may be necessary to pay the interest on said bonds, shall be set aside and paid to the trustee of said bonds and by him used exclusively and only for the payment of interest upon said bonds when and so long as the same shall become due and payable; but in no event shall the city of Fort Worth pay the said trustee a greater sum for such interest than the amount agreed to be paid to said Fort Worth Water Works Company.

SEC 15. Said city of Fort Worth shall make all ordinances, appropriations, etc., necessary to secure the said Fort Worth Water Works Company in the rights and privileges granted in this agreement so long as the same may be in force that either or both the parties to this contract may be represented by agents, officers or assigns, or successors, who may be legally authorized to represent them severally and jointly as authorized.

SEC. 16. The works permitted to be constructed by this ordinance, shall be constructed so as not to interfere with the rights and property of others in said city, and any injury resulting from such interference shall be paid for by said Fort Worth Water Works Company. Said water pipes shall be laid at least two feet below the grade established by the city.

SEC. 17. If any person shall willfully or maliciously injure or destroy any portion of the water fixtures or other property appertaining to the Fort Worth Water Works Company, or shall wilfully interfere with or waste water from the fire hydrants, except for the purpose of extinguishing fires or for such other purposes as said hydrants, under this ordinance, may be used. Such person shall be guilty of a misdemeanor, and on conviction, shall be fined in any sum not less than five nor more than one hundred dollars.

    B. A.
    O.273.
    § 17.

SEC. 18. Said Fort Worth Water Works Company hereby agrees and binds itself during the continuance of the contract to furnish at all times good, healthful and wholesome water, and hereby agrees and binds itself to keep said fire hydrants and mains in good and efficient condition and service at all times except at instances of accident or other means beyond the control by the exercise of due dilligence and forethought. All mains supplying water to any fire hydrant shall be not less than six inches in inner diameter, except as the city council may order.

    B. A.
    O.273.
    § 18.

SEC. 19. The said Fort Worth Water Works Company agrees and binds itself to furnish at all times for all public and private uses of said city and its inhabitant a full and sufficient supply of good. healthful and wholesome water, well suited for domestic and manufacturing purposes.

    B. A.
    O.273.
    § 19.

SEC. 20. Said fire hydrant shall be under the control and supervision of the chief of the fire department of said city, who shall have the right, upon giving notice to the company. to provide for the opening and use of the hydrants for fire purposes for the testing of any fire aparatus and for the purpose of flushing and cleaning gutters whenever the city council shall deem it necessary, and the chief of the fire department shall leave said hydrants in good condition.

    B. A.
    O.273.
    § 20.

SEC. 21. The said Fort Worth Water Works Company agrees to commence erecting said water works in ninety days from the passage and approval of this ordinance, and agrees to complete said works by the first day of February, 1883, and a failure to comply with this section of this ordinance shall render said ordinance and contract null and void.

    B. A.
    O.273.
    § 21.

SEC. 22. It shall be unlawful for said Fort Worth Water Works Company to charge or tax any person for water more than the price fixed by the rate in Section 12 of this ordinance, and upon conviction thereof the said Fort Worth Water Works Company shall be fined in any sum not less than five nor more than fifty dollars.

    B. A.
    O 273.
    § 22.

B. A.
O.273.
§ 23

SEC. 23. This ordinance when adopted by the city council and approved by the mayor, and accepted within twenty days by the said Fort Worth Water Works Company in writing, which said acceptance shall be attached hereto, and made a part hereof, shall constitute the contract between the said city and the said Water Works Company. Approved May 27, 1882.

Passed May 23, 1882.

STATE OF TEXAS, TARRANT COUNTY.

To the Mayor and City Council of the city of Fort Worth:

GENTLEMEN—As directed by the stockholders of the Fort Worth Water Works Company, I hereby accept the terms and conditions and agreements contained in the ordinance passed by your honorable body on 23d of May, A. D. 1882, for and on behalf of the Fort Worth Water Works Csmpany, and as that the same be filed as by said ordihance provided.

MORGAN JONES,
President Fort Worth Water Works Company.

ORDINANCE NO. CLIV.

An Ordinance to provide for the acceptance of the Water Works by the city of Fort Worth, Texas.

WHEREAS, The Fort Worth Water Works Company have constructed, and in accordance with their contract, completed the water works in accordance with the franchise heretofore granted to said company by the council of the city, being Ordinance 273, passed may 23, 1882, and said works having been tested to the satisfaction of the city council of the city of Fort Worth. Therefore.

Be it ordained by the City Council of the city of Fort Worth:

SECTION 1. That the water works, as built and completed by the Fort Worth Water Works Company, be, and the same is hereby accepted by the city council of the city of Fort Worth, having been constructed in strict compliance with the franchise, and completed within the time specified in the original ordinance and the extension heretofore granted said company, and payment of hydrant rentals shall commence from this date.

SEC. 5. This ordinance shall take effect from and after its passage.

B. A.
O.303.
§ 1.

ORDINANCE NO. CLV.

An Ordinance instructing the mayor to purchase One Hundred Thousand Dollars worth of the Fort Worth Water Works Company stock.

Be it ordained by the City Council of the city of Fort Worth:

SECTION 1. That the mayor of said city be hereby authorized and instructed to purchase one hundred thousand dollars stock of the Fort Worth Water Works Company—that amount being one-half of the entire stock of said company—from J. S. Drake, at a price not exceeding thirty-two thousand five hundred dollars.

B. B.
O. —
§ 1.

SEC. 2. That the mayor be instructed to purchase the stock as stated in Section one of this ordinance, and make a contract with the said J. S. Drake to pay for the same in city bonds, which said bonds shall be payable in twenty years, and bear interest at the rate of seven per cent. per annum, payable semi-annually, and, further, to contract with said Drake to deliver said bonds within sixty days from the date hereof.

B. B.
O. —
§ 2.

SEC. 3. That this ordinance take effect and be in force from and after its passage.

Passed July 2, 1884.

ORDINANCE NO. CLVI.

An Ordinance in regard to carrying deadly weapons.

Be it ordained by the City Council of the city of Fort Worth:

SECTION 1. That it shall be unlawful for any person to carry about his person any pistol, Bowie knife or other deadly or unlawful weapon while within the corporate limits of this city.

B. A.
O. 13.
§ 1.

SEC. 2. Any person who shall be guilty of violating the provisions of this ordinance shall, upon conviction, be fined in a sum not less than ten nor more than fifty dollars.

B. A.
O. 5?.
§ 1.

SEC. 3. That this ordinance to be in force and take effect from and after its publication as required by law.

Approved April 10, 1873.

ORDINANCE NO. CLVII.

An Ordinance regulating the carrying of weapons and prohibiting the carrying of the same concealed.

Be it ordained by the City Council of the city of Fort Worth:

SECTION 1. Any person carrying concealed on or about his person any pistol, dirk, dagger, slung shot, sword cane, spear, brass knuckles, Bowie knife, or any other kind of knife manufactured or sold for the purpose of offense or defense, unless having or carrying the same on or about his person for the lawful defense of the State as a militiaman, in actual service, or as a peace officer or policeman, shall be guilty of a misdemeanor, and on conviction thereof, shall be punished by fine of not less than twenty-five nor more than one hundred dollars. Provided, that this section shall not be so construed as to prohibit any person from keeping or bearing arms on his or her own premises, or at his or her own place of business; nor to prohibit sheriffs or other revenue officer and other civil officer from keeping and bearing arms while engaged in the discharge of their official duties nor to prohibit persons traveling in this State from keeping or carrying arms with their baggage. Provided, further, that members of the legislature shall not be included under the term "civil officer, as used in this ordinance.

B. A. O.164. § 1.

B. A. O.181. § 1.

SEC. 2. That this ordinance take effect and be in force from and after its publication as required by law.

APPENDIX.

ORDINANCE NO. CLVIII.

An Ordinance repealing all of Ordinance No. 60, except so much thereof as applies to Main street in the city of Fort Worth, Texas.

Be it ordained by the City Council of the city of Fort Worth:

SECTION 1. That Ordinan No. 60, entitled "An Ordinance granting certain privileges to the Fort Worth Street Railway Company," be, and the same is hereby repealed, except in so far as the said ordinance gave said Fort Worth Street Railway Company the right to build, establish, equip and operate a line of railway and Main street.

B. B.
O.343.
§ 1.

SEC. 2. That this ordinance take effect and be in force from and after its passage.

B. B.
O.343.
§ 2.

Filed August 19, 1884. Passed August 19, 1884.

STUART HARRISON, City Secretary.

Recorded September 6. 1884.

STUART HARRISON. City Secretary.

Vetoed by his honor. Mayor, August 21, 1884, and vote passing same was reconsidered September 2, 1884, by the city council, and upon being placed before the council was adopted and passed September 2, 1884, notwithstanding the mayor's veto.

STUART HARRISON, City Secretary.

ORDINANCE NO. CLIX.

An Ordinance amending Ordinance No. ——, granting the Rosedale street Railway Company right-of-way over certain streets in the city of Fort Worth.

Be it ordained by the City Council of the city of Fort Worth:

SECTION 1 That the Rosedale Street Railway Company is hereby granted the right of-way to build, construct, maintain and operate a line of street railway over, along and through the middle of the following streets to wit: Beginning in the middle of Houston street, thence along —— Sixth street to Throckmorton street, thence along —— Throckmorton street to Hyde Park, thence over Hyde Park to any point on same, connecting with their line already built on Hyde Park.

B. B.
O.349.
§ 1.

SEC. 2. That said company may also construct such switches and side-tracts along said line, and turnouts, as may be necessary. Provided said company may lay on said line the Johnson or tram rail; but said track shall, in all other respects, conform to the conditions, plans and specifications mentioned and pre-

B. B.
O.349.
§ 2.

scribed in the ordinances heretofore passed granting said company the right-of-way over certain streets of said city.

B. B.
O.349.
§ 3.
SEC. 3. This ordinance is not intended to, nor shall it in any manner, affect or repeal any rights or privileges heretofore granted said company on Houston street.

B. B.
O.349.
§ 4.
SEC. 4. This ordinance shall take effect and be in force from and after its passage.

Filed September 2, 1884. Passed September 16, 1884.

STUART HARRISON, City Sec'y.

Recorded September 23, 1884.

STUART HARRISON, Ci'y Sec'y.

This ordinance not having been approved or disapproved within the three days, as prescribe by the Charter, takes effect the same as if approved. STUART HARRISON, City Sec'y.

ORDINANCE NO. CLX.

An Ordinance adopting the Revised Ordinances of the city of Fort Worth, Texas.

Be it ordained by the City Council of the city of Fort Worth:

B. B.
O.350.
§ 1.
SECTION 1. That these Revised Ordinances of the city of Fort Worth shall be known and cited as the "Revised Ordinances of Fort Worth."

B. B
O.350.
§ 2.
SEC. 2. That all ordinances in force when these Revised Ordinances take effect, and which are not included herein, or which are not hereby expressly continued in force, are hereby repealed.

B. B.
O.350.
§ 3.
SEC 3. That no ordinance relating to the city debt or to the city credit, or to taxation in the city of Fort Worth, shall be affected by the repealing clause hereof.

B. B.
O.350.
§ 4.
SEC. 4. That the "Revised Ordinances" of the city of Fort Worth shall take effect and be in force at twelve o'clock noon on October 1, A. D. 1884.

B. B.
O.350.
§ 5.
SEC. 5. That this ordinance take effect and be in force from and after its passage.

Filed September 17, 1884. Passed September 17, 1884.

Attest: STUART HARRISON, City Sec'y.

Approved September 18, 1884. J. B. ASKEW,
President pro tem. and acting Mayor.

Recorded September 20, 1884.

STUART HARRISON. City Secretary.

INDEX.

	PAGE.		PAGE.
Alleys — Opening of, through Peak's block	17	Bond of Secretary	16
		Bond of City Att'y	16
Assault and Battery—		Bond of Engineer	16
Definition of	14 to 15	Bonds, City—Bonds to	
What does not am't to	15	J. Kane	17
		Number, amount and	
Penalty for	15	conditions of	18
Assessor and Collector	16	When payable and	
Assistant Assessor and		how paid	18 to 19
Collector—Establishing office of	14	Bonds for Sewerage, etc.	19
Duties of	14	Number and amt's of	19 to 22
Salary of	14	Terms and conditions of	20 to 22
Attorney, city—Bond of	16	Where and when payable	21 to 24
Duties of	54	Funds for paym't of	20-21-23
Fees and Salary of	54	Buildings—When may	
Bail—Officers may take when	106	be pulled down	24 to 25
Forfeiture of	118 to 119	When may be blown up	63
Bonds, official—Bonds of Assessor and Collector	16	Butcher—May use sidewalk, how	157
Bond of Treasurer	16	Punishment of for	
Bond of Marshal	16	killing, except at	

	Page.		Page.
slaughter pen	158	cord of deaths, etc., and report to council	30
Calaboose—Talking to prisoners in	26	Fees of Sexton	31
Furnishing prisoners in, liquors, etc.	26	Conduct therein prohibited	30 to 31
Punishment for	26	Punishment for violation	30 to 31
Special Fund for expenses of prisoners	75	Chief Engineer Fire Department — (See Fire Department)	
Privy of, kept by whom	127		
Carriages—(See Hacks Vehickles.)		Chimneys— (See Fire Warden,) (Fire Limits)	
Cattle, Sheep, Goats, Horses and Mules— Running at large prohibited	26	Height of for Mills. etc.	32
Pound keeper for	108	Shall be repaired, when, and penalty for refusal	32
May be redeemed when	27	How and of what built in fire limits	33-34 35
Sold, when and how and where	27	How in the corporate limits	33
Proceeds of sale, how disposed of	27	Who shall inspect and when repaired	34
Punishment for allowing to run at large	27 to 28	Combustible Matter— Dealers in shall report to City sec'y	35-36-37
Punishment of persons for selling milk from diseased cows	65	Penalty for refusal	36
		Amount of oil, powder etc., that may be kept	36
Cemetery — Designation of	28		
Engineer shall survey	28	Penalty for violation	36
Lots, how, by whom and for what sold	28 to 29	Cotton Yard—Shall not be near place of fire	37
Strangers and parties not owning lots. where buried	29	Carrying fire, etc., into prohibited	37
Sexton shall keep, and duties of Sexton	29	Council City—Committees appointed by mayor	37 to 38
Sexton shall keep re-		Duties of committees	38

	PAGE.		PAGE.
Order of business of	38	with passengers	45 to 46
Rules of proceedure in	38 to 39	May be arrested, when	46
Time of meeting of	39	Drunkenness — (See Misdemeanors.)	
Dead Animals — Deposit for dead animals, filth, etc., place of	39 to 40	Election—For city officers, held when	47
		Officers of and fees of	48
How deposited	40	When, by whom held etc.	47
Penalty for depositing in ditch of another	40	Returns of	48
		Officers of Fire Department, election of	56 to 57
Owner of must remove, and penalty for refusal	41	Engineer—Bond of	16
		Duties of	49 to 51
Diseased Animals — Marshal may seize and kill when	41 to 42	Is ex-officio members of street committee	50
		Fees of	55
Must be removed by owner, when	41	Shall issue permits, etc.	51
Stables disinfected, when	42	Maps of city, made by	163 to 164
Penalty for refusal	42	Fast Riding and Driving—Penalty for	52 to 53
Disorderly Houses — (See Theatres.)		Penalty for running horse races	52
Dogs—Must be kept up, when	44 to 45	Penalty for leaving animals in streets unhitched	53
Must be killed, when	44 to 45		
May be impounded, when	43	Fees, Salaries, etc.—Of Mayor	53
Must be muzzled, when	44 to 45	Of Marshal	53 to 54
Penalty for violation of ordinance	44 to 45	Of Recorder	54
		Of Jurors	54
Drummers— Must wear badge, and penalty for violation	45	Of Policemen	54
		Of City Attorney	54
		Of City Secretary	54
Stopping people on streets, penalty for	45	Of Aldermen	54
		Of City Engineer	55
Penal for interfering		Of Treasurer	55

	PAGE.		PAGE.
Assessor and Collector	55	adulterated milk, etc	65 to 66
	55	Shall be inspected by city physician	66
Of Sexton	31	Fourth Street Railway Company—Right of way, etc.	67 to 68
Fences. Etc.—Penalty for hitching to court house fence	56	Ft. Worth and Denver City Railway Co.—Right of way to	68
Penalty for erecting tents, etc., and leaving wagons on public square	56	Ft. Worth Street Railway Co.—Right of way to	69 to 73
Fines (See Penalties)		Conditions of	69 to 75
Fire Warden (See Fire Department.)		On what streets	69 to 75
Fire Department—What shall consist of	56	Funds—Special for expenses of prison, etc.	75
Officers of	56	Public School Fund	180
Duties of officers	57 58-59	Gambling — Definition of gambling house	75
Officers, how elect	57		
Fire, police duties of	57 to 58		
Property of	58		
Hood and Ladder Co. may pull down and blow up houses when	63	Penalty for keeping	76
		What games prohibited	76
Fire Limits–What shall constitute	63 to 64	Penalty for allowing to play in house	76
Character of buildings allowed therein	64	Penalty for renting house for purposes of	76
Structures therein removed when	64	Penalty for betting at games	76
Fire-arms—Penalty for discharging	65	Card playing, punishment for	76
Food and Drink—Penalty for selling milk of diseased cow	65	Playing cards, at what house forbidden	76 to 77
Penalty for selling unwholesome meats, etc.	65	What evidence required for conviction	77
Penalty for selling unhealthy Ice, etc.	65	Permitting minors and intoxicated persons, punishment for	77
Penalty for selling		Gas Works-Exclusive privilege granted to Ft.	

Worth Gas Light Co.	77	of	87
Conditions, stipulations, etc.	78 to 79	May destroy furniture, when	88
City of Fort Worth may purchase, etc.	80	Hogs — (See Pound keeper, etc.)	
Goats—(See cattle, etc)		Horses—(See Cattle, etc)	
Grade, City-Of Throckmorton street	82	Hotel—(See Drummers) Houses—(See theatres)	
Of Main street	83	Penalty for keeping	
Of Houston street	82	brothel, bawdy house,	
Of Rusk street	83	etc.	88
Penalty for not building according to	83	Penalty for being inmate of	88
Gulf, Colorado & Santa Fe R. W. Co.—Right		Dance house, definition of	89
of way granted to	83 to 84	Penalty for keeping	89
Hacks (See Vehicles.)		May get license, terms	
License for	181 to 182	and conditions of	89
Driver of must carry		Must give bond	90
lights on of night	84	Disorderly house,	
Penalty for neglecting to	84	definitions of	90 to 91
		Penalty for keeping	90 to 91
Charges allowed for		Penalty for being in-	
carrying persons, etc	85	mate	90 to 91
Must have rates of		Penalty for prosti-	
tariff	85	tutes. etc., wandering	
Penalty for neglecting	85	on streets, etc.	90 to 91
		Penalty for prosti-	
Penalty for refusal to carry person	85	tutes, etc., plying her avocation by signs,	
Penalty for refusal to pay charges	85	etc.	91
		Indecency — Acts of	
Penalty for misrepresentation, etc.	85 to 86	prohibited, and punishment for	91 to 92
Hawkers—Where sales		Indecent plays, etc.,	
by, prohibited, etc.	86	prohibited and pun-	
Punishment for	86	ishment for	91 to 92
Health, Board of—Who		Job Wagons—(See	
shall compose	86 to 87	Hacks.)	
Duties of and powers		License — (See hacks,	

	PAGE.
occupation for, dance Houses), (Shooting gallery.)	
Limitations—Time in which prosecution may commence	92
Liquors—(See saloons and taxation.)	
Map of City—(See survey.)	
Market—Place of for stock	92
Penalty for selling elsewhere	93
Marshal—Bond of	16
Duties of	93-94-95-105-106
Powers of	93-94-95-105-106
Punishment for resistance of	96
Misdemeanors—Definition of and punishment for	96 to 97
Is to hinder marshal and in making arrest	96
Is to obstruct street railway	97
Is to use nigger shooters, etc	98
Is to be in an unlawful assembly	93 to 99
Mobs—Punishment of	98 to 99
Missouri, Kansas and Texas Railway Co.— Right of way to	99
Nuisances—Definition of	100 to 101
Punishment for keeping, etc.	101-102-103
Order for removal of	101
Place of removal to	102

	PAGE.
Vehicle for removal to	102 to 103
Penalties for not removing	102 to 103
Occupation—(See taxation.)	
Opium Smoking—Penalty for smoking	104
Penalty for keeping a house for smoking	104
Penalties, Fines—For assault and battery	15
For not removing dangerous buildings	25
For talking, etc., with prisoners in calaboose	26
For allowing cattle, etc., to run at large	27 to 28
For digging grave on lot of another, etc.	30
For shooting, etc., in cemetery	30
For being in cemetery before sun rise and after sunset	30 to 31
For certain persons walking in cemetery	31
For having unlawful chimneys to mills, etc	32
For erecting chimneys contrary to ordinance	33 to 35
For not repairing chimney when notified	35
For being drunk in public place	96 to 97
For not reporting combustible material to secretary	36

	PAGE.
For keeping more than 25 lbs. powder, etc.	36
For violating ordinance relating to cotton yards	37
For violating ordinance relating to depositing filth	40
For violating ordinance relating to diseased animals	41 to 42
For violating ordinance relating to dogs	43-44-45
For violating ordinance relating to hotel and street drummers	45 to 46
For violating ordinance relating to elections	48
For violating ordinance relating to fast riding, etc.	52 to 53
For violating ordinance relating to obstructing square, etc.	56
For violating ordinance relating to fire department, etc.	59 to 62
For violating ordinance relating to building in fire limits	64
For violating ordinance relating to shooting fire arms, etc	65
For violating ordinance relating to selling unwholesome food, etc.	65 to 66
For violating ordinance relating to gambling and keeping gambling house	76 to 77
For violating ordinance relating to gas works	81
For violating ordinance relating to grading of city	83
For violating ordinance relating to Hacks, etc.	84-85-86
For violating ordinance relating to Hawkers, etc	86
For violating ordinance relating to disorderly houses, etc.	88-89-90-91
For violating ordinance relating to indecency	91 to 92
For violation of ordinance relating to market for stock	92 to 93
For violation of ordinance relating to marshal's duties	94 to 95
For violation of ordinance relating to certain misdemeanors	96 to 97
For violation of ordinance relating to streets, alley, etc.	97
For violation of ordinance relating to mobs	98
For violation of ordinance relating to	

	Page.		Page.
nuisance, etc.	101-102-103	For violation of ordinance relating to slaughter pens	158
For violation of ordinance relating to opium smoking	104	For violation of ordinance relating to streets	165 to 168
For violation of ordinance relating to pigeons	105	For violation of ordinance relating to Sunday	173 to 174
For violation of ordinance relating to pound, etc.	110 to 111	For violation of ordinance relating to variety shows	182 to 183
For violation of ordinance relating to prostitutes	112 to 113	For violation of ordinance relating to running trains	187
For violation of ordinance relating to public peace	113 to 114	For violation of ordinance relating to trespass	189
For violation of ordinance relating to quarrantine	117	For violation of ordinance relating to telephone and telegraph wires	190 to 191
For violation of ordinance relating to combustible material	125		
For violation of ordinance relating to saloons on Sunday	127	For violation of ordinance relating to bathing in river	192
For violation of ordinance relating to duties of scavengers, etc	127 to 128	For violation of ordinance relating to vagrancy	193
For violation of ordinance relating to sewers, drains etc.	141 to 145	For violation of ordinance relating to vehicles passing	194
For violation of ordinance relating to shade trees	146 to 147	For violation of ordinance relating to water works.	
For violation of ordinance relating to shooting gallery	148	For violation of ordinance relating to weapons.	
For violation of ordinance relating to sidewalks	156 to 157	Pigeons—Raising, breeding, etc., prohibited	104

	PAGE.		PAGE.
Penalties	104 to 105	Penalties for violating regulations	117
Police—Police force shall consist of what	105	Quarantine Physician	115
Appointment and commission of	105	Duties of	115 to 116
Bonds of	105	Records—(See Recorder's Court, etc.)	
Duties of	105-106-107-108		
Rules for gov'ment of	108	Recorder's Court—Proceedings in	117-118-119
Poll Tax—(See taxation)		Trials in	117-118-119
Pounds—(See cattle)		Payment of fines	119 to 120
Keeper of	108	Office of recorder established	120
Bond of keeper	108		
Duties of keeper	109 to 110	Bonds, duties and salary of	120
Fees of keeper	110		
Sales of animals by keeper	109	Rosedale Street Rail'y Co—Right of way to	120-121-122-123-124
Penalty for breaking into pound	110	Conditions, etc., of rightofway	120-121-122-123-124
Penalty for hindering keeper	111	Rubbish-Shavings, etc, around houses must be burned	125
Poor and Dead—Support of poor	111	Penalty for refusal to burn	125
Burial of dead	111		
Privies—(See nuisances)		Salaries—(See fees, salaries, etc.)	
Prostitutes — Penalty for walking streets with	112	Saloons—Keeping open on Sunday prohibited	126
Penalty for riding and driving with	112	Permitting plays,etc, therein on Sunday prohibited	126
Penalty for employment of at saloons	112	Penalty for violation	127
Public Peace—Breaches of, and punishm't for	113 to 114	Scavenger—(See nuisances.) Office of established	127
Public Square — (See Fences.)		Bond and duties of	127
Quarantine—Establishment of	115-116-117	Penalty for neglect of duty	128
Rules and regulations of	115-116-117	Shall keep light on	

	PAGE.		PAGE.
his vehicle	84	Penalty for	141
Schools, Free — Election to determine if tax shall be levied for	129	Survey of city made for	142
Municipal public free school consist of what	129	Certain acts done to misdemeanors	142-143-144 145
		Penalty for violation	145
		Sexton—(See Cemetery.)	
Scholastic age	130	Shade Trees—Injuries to prohibited	146
Pupils not of scholastic age may attend, etc	131	Penalty for	146
Pupils out of city may attend, etc.	130	Shall be set out, where	147
Superintendent, election of	132 to 135	Penalty for violation	147
		Sheep—(See Cattle, etc.)	
Duties of and salary of	131-132-133	Shooting Gallery— Keeping allowed	148
Board of trustees, appointment and duties of	135	License for	148
		Keeper of, required to do what	148
Teachers, examination of	133	Sidewalks—Order for construction of	150
Teachers, salaries of	133	In what time to be constructed	150 to 151
School fund, provision for, how and by whom paid out	137	Width of and slope of	149
Separate schools for white and black	131	Of what material built	149
Branches taught	133	Form of, order for and raise of curbing for	150
Scrip, City—How and by whom issued	137		
How payable	138	Notice, served on whom	150
Secretary, City—Bond of	16	Where property owner fails to construct	151
Shall pay over funds in kind	140	When built by city	151
Fees of	54	Assessment against property	152
Assistant, Office of— Fees and duties of	140	Notice to pay assessment	152
Sewers—Encumbring, etc., prohibited	141	Property sold, where,	

	PAGE.
by whom, and proceeds	152 to 153
Deed to purchaser, form of	153
Owner may redeem, when, etc.	154
City shall build crossing to connect	155
How, when and by whom repaired	155
Penalty for not building in conformity with grade	156
Obstruction of, penalty for	157 to 158
Slaughter Pens—Penalty for kill except at	158
Stairway — Right to build on Second St. granted, etc.	159
Stationery—What officers may buy, how paid for	159
Streets—(See ——.)	
Bluff street, extensions of	160
When and how opened, straightened. etc.	161
Private property taken for, when and how, etc.	162
Map of, returned by Daniel W. Flaherty, adopted	164
Repairing, building, excavating, etd., under control of engineer	165
Construction of street from N. W. corner block 39 to Clear Fork	166
Assessment against property owners on Main	167
Houston, Weatherford and cross streets between Rusk	167
And Throckmorton to Fifteenth street	167
Officer collecting assessment shall notify owner	167
What acts to misdemeanors, penalty for	168
Assessment for grading 15th St. from Rusk to G. C. & S. F. depot	169
Collection of the assessment	169 to 170
Sunday — What acts prohibited on	173
Penalty for violation	174
Exceptions	174
Survey, City—(See streets.)	
Taxes—(See Taxation.)	
Taxation—Occupation tax on dealers in spirituous. vinous, etc., liquors	174
Occupation tax on what occupation and amounts of	175 to 176
Poll tax, who shall pay, and amount of etc.	181
Advalorem, what levied and for what purpose	180 to 181

	PAGE.		PAGE.
Occupation tax on job wagons and street hacks, etc.	181	Shall ring bell or blow whistle when	187
Numbers to be kept on job wagons, etc.	182	Penalty for failing to keep good crossings, etc., on tracks	187
Penalties for not paying occupation tax	182	Texas and Pacific Railway Co.—Right of way to	188
Theatres—Penalty for keeping of where lewd women, etc., take part	182	Trespass — Prohibited and penalty for	189
Penalty for renting house for keeping	183	Telephone—Posts, how constructed and penalty for neglect	189-190-191-192
Penalty for keeping, etc., on Sunday	183	Telegraph—(See telephone.)	
How theatres, public halls, etc., shall be constructed	184	Trinity River—Bathing, etc., in prohibited and penalty for	192
Penalty for keeping or constructing contrary to ordinance	184	Vagrancy—Definitions of and punishment for	193
		Vehicles—(See hacks.)	
Penalty for loud talking. etc., in theatres. etc.	185	Passing on streets, etc	194
License for keeping, etc., in house where intoxicating liquors are sold and drank, and penalty for violation	186	Wards—Number of and character of building in	195
		Water Works — Who may construct, priviliges of	196
		The Fort Worth Water Works Company	196
Bond of party obtaining license	186	Privileges of the Ft. Worth Water Works Company	196 197-198-199
Trains—Rate of speed allowed to run and Penalty for violation	187	Capacity of Ft. Worth Water Works Co.	197 to 198
Penalty for obstructing streets with, etc.	187	Compensation of	200
		Weapons—(See fire arms.)	
Penalty for jumping on, off, clinging to trains in motion	187	Carrying concealed prohibited, etc.	206
		Penalty for	207

www.ingramcontent.com/pod-product-compliance
Lightning Source LLC
Chambersburg PA
CBHW031817230426
43669CB00009B/1168